What Work Is

THE WORKING CLASS
IN AMERICAN HISTORY

Editorial Advisors
James R. Barrett, Thavolia Glymph,
Julie Greene, William P. Jones,
 and Nelson Lichtenstein

For a list of books in the series,
please see our website at www.press.uillinois.edu.

What Work Is

ROBERT BRUNO

UNIVERSITY OF
ILLINOIS PRESS
Urbana, Chicago, and Springfield

Cataloging data available from the Library of Congress
ISBN 978-0-252-04549-3 (hardcover)
ISBN 978-0-252-08760-8 (paperback)
ISBN 978-0-252-05511-9 (ebook)

Contents

Acknowledgments

I have been given a gift. For nearly thirty years, workers of all trades, occupations, genders, races, nationalities, and ages have allowed me on occasion to be their instructor. The worker-students have numbered in the thousands and the educational subject matter has touched nearly every aspect of working for a living. Although admittedly it's an unlimited domain of exploration; just as I end one class and type the last words on the page a unique perspective emerges to me. The moments have been precious opportunities for me to learn not only what work is but why individuals experience it as they do. Each labor studies class raises the fundamental question; does work have to be experienced this way? And what does it do to us as human beings to construct a society and an economy that treats workers as derivative of financial objectives instead of as individuals with moral value who create the world? My students can't uniformly speak for the experiences of millions of workers, but their experiences are raw, visceral, impactful, and enlightening. And I get the privilege of hearing their stories. I'm incredibly fortunate to be able to build relationships with workers so that we can trust one another enough to talk together about doing work. The indebtedness I feel for all the students who have taken my classes is beyond the language available to express my gratitude. So, until I find a more suitable vernacular, a deeply genuine thank you will have to suffice.

The opportunity to be an academic labor educator requires having a university program, like ours at the University of Illinois' School of Labor and Employment Relations that values lifting the voices of workers. Too many sister university labor studies programs have been wiped out or diminished across the country. My fellow labor educators do inspiring work with relatively shoestring budgets. I don't think it's coincidental that slashed labor studies programs have occurred while worker job quality has deteriorated over the last forty years. Not sure what is cause and what is effect but I'm confident they go together.

Getting students in my class requires having and building productive relationships with the state's labor movement. University labor studies programs owe their existence to organized labor's commitment to higher education and the value of training folks in labor relations. I am fortunate to teach in a state with a large and supportive labor movement. The individual unions who have sent their leaders and membership to our classes are too numerous to list. Trying to mention them by name risks unintentionally offending the one's left out. However, along with the Illinois AFL-CIO and Chicago Federation of Labor, over my career several unions have been regular anchors for our work and deserve to be noted: United Steelworkers District 7, International Union of Operating Engineers, Local 150, American Federation of State County and Municipal Employees, Council 31, International Brotherhood of Electrical Workers, Local 134 and IBEW 6th District, Chicago Laborers District Council, Service Employees International Union, Local 1, Mid-America Carpenters Regional Council, Illinois Federation of Teachers, Illinois Education Association, Illinois Postal Workers Union, and the Associated Firefighters of Illinois.

Books, like any other product of labor, don't just happen. Special thanks to University of Illinois Press Acquisition Editor Alison Syring Bassford. She was always encouraging, insightful, and enthusiastic about my project. I'm grateful she took my call when I came to her with a manuscript about "what work is." Every author should be as lucky as me to have such an editor to guide their ideas into print. Communicating the right ideas and using the correct grammatical sense was possible because of the patient, careful work of the UIP's Manuscript Editor Ellen A. Hurst. I'd rather do pretty much anything else than construct a book index, which is why I really appreciate people like Sheila Hill who did one for me. And several rounds of reading and correcting proofs were not a burden due to the press' Managing Editor Jennifer Argo's talents and good humor. In truth, there wouldn't be a book without the time the expert reviewers committed to conducting a rigorous and thoughtful reading of my manuscript. I'm grateful for their enthusiastic response and intellectually challenging comments. Additionally, a book shouldn't be judged by its cover but without one it would just be ink on a lot of white paper. It's not easy capturing in images "what work is" but Art Director Dustin Hubbart and his team nicely represented the book's themes in vibrant colors and expressive photos.

Despite the editorial work of the university press, nothing I write escapes the watchful trained eye of my wife Lynn. She has a Doctorate in Educational Leadership and taught reading and writing at the middle school level for years. Sometimes having an English teacher as a partner can be a blessing and a curse. Like when my ideas weren't so coherent, or commas were being overused and verb-noun alignment was spotty. But Lynn patiently read every page of my manuscript just as she did thousands of her students' papers. Her love, skills, and red pen are invaluable to me.

Lynn good naturedly constantly reminds me that I'm so incurably curious and protective about the working class because I'd rather not do the work millions of people faithfully do every day. Yes, and therefore I can't teach classes and write books without the workers who build the roads, manufacture the cars, wire homes and offices, drive busses and trains, construct buildings, take care of children, nurse the sick, teach everything, clean offices, deliver packages, keep track of records, brew the morning coffee, grow the food I eat, and pick up my garbage. My dependence on a massive chain of interdependent workers to simply breathe, let alone write a book, is mind blowing. Nobody flourishes without other workers. I'm thankful for all those I have taught and for those I will never know. This book is dedicated to their labors.

One last thing. I hope my daughter Sarah will read *What Work Is*. Work and what we make of it is always uncertain and contested. Except that most will have to live off their labor income to live decently, the future of work has never been harder to predict. Everyone, however, deserves to do work that will bring them happiness. I don't mean just a nice feeling that comes and goes with circumstances. I mean a life-long sense of personal affirmation. More like something they can be proud of doing. The Greek statesman, Solon, offered the dictum, "Call no man happy until he is dead." The point was to judge whether a person's life was well lived not on single incidences but on a life-long narrative. My daughter has a lot of work ahead of her. Perhaps the experiences of the voices on the following pages will show Sarah how meaningful her talents really are.

Introduction

WORK IS NOT GOING AWAY. More importantly, the people who will do it are like the people currently doing it and who have always done it—yet what work looks like in the future is anybody's guess. There are as many ideas about work as there are minds to speculate on it. Pandemic-forced changes and artificial intelligence have only accelerated and jumbled the possible transformations of skills, locations, jobs, and organizations of work. The seeds of social, technological, economic, environmental, and cultural development shaping how people will work tomorrow were already planted in the past. If you need to work for a living or depend on somebody who must work for a living, the most recent past is not a very comforting predictor of the future.

Over the past half century, bad jobs have proliferated, and once-good ones have been downgraded by government policies and employer practices. The 2020–2021 recession punished millions of hourly working-class workers. A post-recession boom produced a hot job market that put millions back to work, but a record number of millions also either chose to stay home, found a different boss to sign paychecks, or sought a free-form way to earn a living. Nothing about work seemed predictable, and questions proliferated. What is the future of work in America? Predicting what happens to productive work is a high-stakes parlor game about the most important of human activities. There's much that makes us human, but work—fully understood—is critical to our individual and social development. Society itself emanates from how we make, distribute, and use the products of our collective labor. Karl Marx stated it as an immutable law that "labor . . . is the condition of human existence which is independent of all forms of society." It is an "eternal and natural necessity which mediates . . . life itself."[1]

While the forms work takes—and importantly, how work is valorized in the future—are up for grabs, there are near certainties we can count on. Work will have an enormous contradictory impact on the workers and society they build. Anthropologist Herbert Applebaum draws on a biological metaphor to centralize the importance of work to the individual and society. Work, he notes, "is like the spine which structures the way people live, how they make contact with material and social reality, and how they achieve status and self-esteem."[2] Fortunately, we don't have to wait or guess about work's transformation in the future. I contend that, in order to develop policies and practices about work for the future, we should ask the workers right now what work is so that they can be the architects of their own destiny. As the United States struggles with an unchartered and unprecedented change in how people will work and think about work, this book recommends a "future of work" that listens to what workers say "work is."

At some point in their lives, most people in America will be employees. They largely self-identify as working or middle class. Many are working poor. Usually a few million always want to be someone's employee but can't find a job. Part of our secular religion is that work is character building and with enough sweat equity, anyone can convert honest labor into personal prosperity and fulfillment. We pay cultural homage to working class ethics, work-family ethnic esthetics, "blue collar" values, and hard-working "lunch pail" self-sacrificing men and women. From Aesop fables to annual reviews of retirement accounts, we are raised to prioritize the need to place work above leisure, contemplation, relationship building and prayer. Work is both how we earn a living and how we find dignity in our lives. Our labor contributes to the development of our moral character and enables us to live a life of purpose. Through our work we establish agency in the world. Because we work, we have a legitimate place in the social order and are entitled to the fruits of our labor. I work; therefore, I and we exist. A cornerstone of the American dream mythology is predicated on the faith-based belief that paid work pays off. It is so core to our belief system that we never ask, What is so good about work anyway? Now would be a good time to start asking. Despite our unexamined obsession with work, rapturous views of laboring for a living have not been universally held. Bertrand Russell sardonically expressed the opinion "that immense harm is caused by the belief that work is virtuous."[3] The question of work's goodness however isn't posed because the answer is typically treated as a given.

When I say I'm interested in understanding what work is, the "is" lies beyond the conventional concepts used to describe work. My assessment includes the physical, intellectual, and emotional mechanics of labor and all the attendant dynamics, but it goes deeper. I'm looking for the ways that a person's work manifests itself in the world and is then realized by the worker. The "is" I'm exploring in the pages that follow is how the worker perceives and understands his or her labor. Here work is not an object of thought but what the individual lives through.[4] In this sense I'm trying to uncover the phenomenology of work. My intention is to see work from the worker's point of view and explore why it matters.

To examine this question further, let me first define the kind of work I'm looking at.[5] The work I'm talking about involves the making, buying, or selling of goods or services, and most importantly it is paid labor. Household and family labor, volunteering, and community organizing are all essential life activities, and there is a growing opinion among economists and sociologists, which I agree with, that these nonmarket forms of work have real financial value and should be seen as contributing to the country's economy.[6] However, the questions raised in this book are about paid labor with workers employed in various occupations.

Worker-Students

In forming a perspective on this type of labor, I've sought out the opinions of the worker-students I've taught in labor education classes at the University of Illinois over the past quarter century. Two of the most popular classes I teach are labor history and labor studies. I've taught the subjects chronologically and thematically, and usually over multiple sessions. Students have taken classes on the university campus, at union halls, and in union apprenticeship schools. I have taught them in the morning, afternoon, at night, on weekdays, and on weekends. My classes have occurred all over the state of Illinois, across the Midwest, in Pennsylvania and as far as way as California, New York, Nevada, Louisiana, and Oklahoma. Across these places and times, my students have all been working adults enrolled in a nonmatriculating (i.e., they are not pursuing a college degree) noncredit class. While I have been teaching, there are in any given year approximately 20–24 percent female and 30–33 percent Black and Hispanic students. Their ages range from early twenties to late fifties. Student race and gender composition reflect national demographic labor force breakdowns. Women students, for example, account for a very small percentage of workers in the construction trades, while making up a very high majority of nurses, teachers, and employees in care and service occupations.[7] There is racial and gender diversity among students working in manufacturing, transportation, the postal service, and government agencies. Veterans are well represented in the building trades.

The majority of my students own homes and are raising children. They are Democrats, Republicans, Christians, and non-Christians, and most are non-college educated. The majority are rank-and-file members of a labor union. Most hold no senior elected or appointed union office.

Even more important than who they are demographically, though, is what my students represent. My students are part of the forgotten and abandoned working class—left behind in the last four decades as inequality raged and those at the top of the income distribution captured most of the gains. Yet because they are largely union members, they are not the most downtrodden or impoverished workers. Not yet anyway. Threatened by decades of political efforts to weaken or destroy labor unions, they have a tenuous hold on economic security. The workers I teach are the product of organized labor's monumental efforts and substantial achievements. They are neither the most marginalized nor the most elite Americans, but they have a great deal to say about work, and we would be wise to learn from their experiences.

"Work is" Assignment

As part of the classes, I ask my students to do an exercise where they complete the following sentence, using no more than six words: "Work is _____?" That's it. The words used don't even have to add up to a grammatically correct sentence. My favorite ungrammatical essay was "Work is sucks." But "work sucks" (which I have gotten a few times) or "work is sucky" (never heard this one) both communicate what the worker intends. Once the students have given their answers, we then discuss them as a class. I've gotten thousands of responses. Groups as large as two hundred workers and as small as a handful have taken the classes.

The discussions typically go on for one to two hours. Where possible I write out many of the responses on a white board. They add up to a beautiful and evocative collage of nouns, verbs, adjectives, adverbs, and intimate statements. Loss, pain, exhaustion, joy, strength, purpose, confusion, creation, destruction, happiness, anger, the first-person *I*, family, uncertainty, choice, money, integrity, life, death, time, and space are a small sample of what fills the board and our collective heads. Work is a lot—maybe too much. Or not enough. It could perhaps be everything. Sorting it all out comes next.

I use this writing and discussion exercise because workers are rarely given a chance to talk about work. I don't mean talk about their job but talk about work as a lived experience, as a heuristic. Subsequently, I mean work largely defined in all its dimensions by popular media, educational institutions, employers, and elected leaders. Schools are particularly problematic. The pedagogy used in secondary education typically ignores work all together. With few exceptions, university and college programs skip past a study of their students' future and inevitable work relationships. Any meaningful focus on the class-based system we live in is shoehorned into graduate level sociology courses for the relatively few fortunate enough to delay employment. The preponderance of my students, like most people working in hourly wage jobs, don't have college degrees. Therefore, writing a six-word essay is a small but impactful way for working-class men and women to begin thinking about and articulating what elements are essential to understanding their class relations. It is a step toward enabling workers to define themselves in terms relevant to their essential life activity. To know themselves as central to civil society and not as costs of production; objects of recruitment, observation, evaluation, and discipline; or according to productivity statistics. The essays are self-reflections designed to strengthen the ability of workers to be intentional and conscious actors in their working-class lives.

To faithfully convey what thousands of carpenters, laborers, electricians, steelworkers, autoworkers, journalists, government employees, operating engineers, teachers, nurses, retail and food workers, service workers, janitors, machinists, plumbers, pipe fitters, truck drivers, cabbies, bus drivers, painters, postal employees, firefighters, and workers from other occupations have said about work, I have categorized their responses into the following five themes: time, space, impact, purpose, and subject.

External Inspiration

My worker-student six-word essays (eight if you count the prompt "Work is") are also informed and inspired by two other sources. National Public Radio invited people to write six-word essays on race, called the "Race Card Project." Race in America is a powerful signifier of identity, and individuals experience it in ways that have profound effects on their sense of self.[8] After reading and listening to many of the essays on race, I realized that work could also be the catalyst for short, thoughtful, and emotional expressions. The subject of work has always inspired people and the catalogue of books, songs, plays, and movies dedicated to a working-class life is extensive.[9] Work has even been considered a form of prayer.[10] Unlike the way that philosophers, social scientists, economist, and popular commentators have spoken or thought of work, however, I endeavor in these pages to mostly describe how workers experience work.

The other inspiration for my class assignment was taken from an artistic form. The "What Work Is" exercise happens to be the title of an award-winning book of poetry published in 1992, *What Work Is* by former United States poet laureate Phillip Levine. Levine grew up in Detroit and worked in the city's auto factories. In working in and later writing about what he called "stupid jobs," he became "the laureate, if you like, of the industrial heartland."[11] Work is "stupid jobs." Powerfully said in only four words. Levine was more verbose when he added, "[Work at Cadillac and Chrysler was] so heavy and monotonous that after an hour or two I was sure each night that I would never last the shift."[12] In a tribute written after his death in 2015, the following excerpt describes the revelatory nature of Levine's poetry:

> We expect poets to describe the soul, the stars, the vitals from birth to death. We do not expect them to describe 'what work is.' But Philip Levine was America's pre-eminent poet of the working life. Like Whitman he 'heard America singing' but the song was on the graveyard shift, syncopated by the incredible clanging, the noise, the heat, the cold at your back, the fire in your face in the forge.[13]

After the workers and I were finished discussing their essays, I would read aloud the poem, "What Work Is." Full disclosure: I like reading and hearing poetry recited out loud. It is a type of performance art that I find very melodic and impactful. And to my pleasure, I discovered that workers liked hearing it also. Especially when I read Levine's seminal work.

They're curious as I begin. *"We stand in the rain in a long line waiting at Ford Highland Park. For work. You know what work is—if you're old enough to read this you know what work is, although you may not do it. Forget you."* Quickly their interest rises. *"This is about waiting, shifting from one foot to another. Feeling the light rain falling like mist into your hair, blurring your vision until you think you see your own brother ahead of you, maybe ten places."* The mention of a sibling triggers a closer listen.

"You rub your glasses with your fingers, and of course it's someone else's brother, narrower across the shoulders than yours but with the same sad slouch, the grin that does not hide the stubbornness, the sad refusal to give in to rain, to the hours of wasted waiting, to the knowledge that somewhere ahead a man is waiting who will say, 'No, we're not hiring today,' for any reason he wants." Hearing that *no* shakes up the room a bit.

"You love your brother, now suddenly you can hardly stand the love flooding you for your brother, who's not beside you or behind or ahead because he's home trying to sleep off a miserable night shift at Cadillac so he can get up before noon to study his German. Works eight hours a night so he can sing Wagner, the opera you hate most, the worst music ever invented." Nobody knows Wagner, but lots of folks have brothers and sisters they love.

"How long has it been since you told him you loved him, held his wide shoulders, opened your eyes wide and said those words, and maybe kissed his cheek? You've never done something so simple, so obvious, not because you're too young or too dumb, not because you're jealous or even mean or incapable of crying in the presence of another man." Mentioning tears leaves an emotional mark. I can hear a pin drop in the room. All eyes stay fixated on me. When I recite the last line—*"No, just because you don't know what work is"*—there's first silence, and then often applause.[14] I'm talking about applause from workers sitting in a classroom either before or after a long day's work, or more incredibly on a day off, for a poem.

Personal Inspiration

Nearly twenty years ago I spoke at great length and with the same level of emotional seriousness to my parents about working for a living. Our words didn't rhyme but in the prosaic, ordinary descriptions of their lives I realized how being working class mattered. Dad was a union steelworker for thirty-seven years and mom worked several jobs, including as a beautician and medical records manager in a mental health facility. I also had similar conversations with other steelworkers. I wrote about my discussions in *Steelworker Alley: How Class Works in Youngstown*, a book about being working class in communities in and near Youngstown, Ohio. Many of these folks are no longer alive. My mother, Lena, died in 2005. My dad, Robert, is a hearty ninety-four (at least as I write these words) and still playing tennis and pickle ball. Work was at the heart of their life stories. If not everything, work was pretty much the most important activity that influenced the people mom and dad had become.

Two decades after the hours I spent in neighbors' living rooms and kitchens and on their back porches, listening to workers, something I didn't fully explore at the time has nagged at me. I have been curious about one question I didn't ask anyone, particularly my dad: What was work to them? I don't mean the actual act of running a machine or picking up a tool. We spoke plenty of such things. Workers were mostly overjoyed to go into the minutia of their jobs. It took very little for folks to expound on the elements of every job task with precision. My dad was at first uncertain about talking, but once he got going stories streamed forward. I listened attentively to him and others, as would a student in a tutorial or an anthropologist hearing secrets being revealed. We talked about doing work, being paid for work, working with others, fighting with people who didn't work, living where other workers lived. But did we talk about what work is?

I went back to the boxes of interviews I did with everyone and listened to tape recordings with my father and mother that I never used. Nope. I didn't ask my parents what they thought work was. I asked a lot of other questions about work and family life of the men and women who once built Youngstown into an industrial powerhouse, but I never gave them a chance to describe what work is. We talked very easily about what they did for a living. Each person could elaborately and often prosaically dissect the mechanics of their work. They told me what they were paid for their labor and showed me pay-stubs. Many had artifacts from their jobs, and some made gifts of them to me. Folks colorfully described the workers they toiled next to and the bosses who really pissed them off. The sounds, smells, sights, and working conditions of the mill cascaded from our conversations. They showed me pictures of the people they loved and who motivated them to punch a mill clock.

I recall my father walking out of the back door of the house at night and wondering, Why in the world is he leaving now? And where is he going? I'd lay awake at night in my bed perplexed by the mystery of dad's back-door disappearance. Tucked safely under the covers, my confusion was later sur-passed by a sense of guilt when I found out what was going on. Mom said dad was just going to work. But why? And why at this hour? Because, my mother patiently explained, it's what he needed to do so that my brothers and I "would have a roof over our heads." That roof came with strong walls, a living room featuring a nice picture window, a few small upstairs bedrooms, and a yard big enough for a kid to play imaginary baseball. I knew my life was comfortable but had no clue as to the reason. Mom and dad both worked, and my three brothers and I enjoyed the pleasures of growing up in a safe, loving, tight-knit family. What I didn't know was what it took to have that childhood.

My parents never talked about the jobs they had. They just worked. Mom held jobs throughout most of my later childhood and teenage years, including in a factory and providing office support at a medical facility. Dad worked revolving eight-hour shifts, and his irregular and daily absences weighed heavily on my younger mind. To be honest, they triggered a contradictory sense of feelings, which was the source of my boyhood guilt. Before, during, and after writing *Steelworker Alley,* I spoke to my mother many times about her life and work. Most of the time the conversations included expressions of pride, fortitude, sacrifice, struggle, and happiness. Many, however, were laced with regret, loss, pain, and sadness. The sad ones were indelible. Mom admitted to me that she slept alone a lot of the time, though my parents never lived apart. Dad's rotating shift work had him leaving the house late at night in order to put in an 11:00 p.m. to 7:00 a.m. "good eight." Mom was guessing at the time her bed was half empty, but she felt the lost intimacy and emptiness caused by nearly four decades of shift work. By comparison, what I felt was of less impact, but on those occasions that dad ventured into the darkness doing God knows what while I rested secure in a warm bed, I felt guilty for not wanting to be where he was. Better him than me, I reasoned. My loving, protective, large, and extended working-class family bestowed a wonderful childhood on me, but I didn't understand how it was made possible. Yes, family and friends were essential, but work—the productive human activity that kept us together—provided only the aesthetic and arcana of a working-class life to a kid. Not the bone and sinew to a socially constructed material world. Guilt and growing up eventually inspired a burning curiosity about the God knows what.

Our home also came with a fruit cellar—a place where work and talk of labor was prominent. When he wasn't on strike or laid off, dad worked in the steel mill. On the days he wasn't at work, he didn't do traditional household chores. But he did put up a fence on one side of the driveway, paint the back side of the house, and put a bathroom in the basement. That last project paid off. You see, mom worked both away from and within the home. I don't mean just unpaid domestic labor, although there was a surplus of cleaning, cooking, doctoring, and educating. What I mean is that she worked in the basement near that fruit cellar getting paid to cut, style, and color women's hair. I know this well because as a boy I watched—or more exactly, listened. The voices of working women like mom, married to men who worked in manufacturing occupations like dad, filled my childhood memories. Their stories left such a strong impression that I was inspired to write a poem about the conversations. The poem brought me some very modest acclaim by winning honorable mention in a poetry contest. More about that later.

As mom twirled a scissor like a scalpel, her customers talked. And mom happily talked back. They spoke intimately, as if in a private refuge reserved just for women. Stories of kids, husbands, local news, sickness, family celebrations, and work were shared. I heard them talk while I was perched at the top of the stairs leading down into the beauty shop that dad built. He wasn't much of a craftsman—too willing to compromise on a corner or two—but he constructed the shop on his days off as a millwright. It had a lot of functional charm, and women came and went every day. The downstairs bathroom was crucial to production.

Mom's work was supercharged with human elements, some too subtle to appreciate. In retrospect this was true of every worker I spoke to in *Steelworker Alley*. I asked my mother about her jobs, just like I did workers in the three other books I wrote. That amounts to a lot of words. But I never asked her or any worker, What is work? Maybe it was just too obvious. What would people have said? Dad unintentionally gave me a clue. When we first sat down to chat about his job, he said very forthrightly and a bit dismissively, "Why in the heck does anyone care about my work?" He expressed legitimate surprise that I thought that what he and other steelworkers did to earn a buck would be something that people would want to read about. Dad never read Studs Terkel's *Working* or for that matter any book about people like himself and my mom.

Turns out, though, dad was wrong. Very wrong. People did read about him, mom, and thousands of working-class people like them who, through their labor, brought a world into existence and shaped personal identities. Work did all that. Not, of course, without other influences, but the job was a primary mover in the trajectory of the lives of working-class men and women. Over my career I have talked extensively with workers about their work. Yet in one critical sense we never said a word about their work. What did work mean? How was it experienced?

Reflecting on it now, my conversations were rich with evocative insights about what work was and how workers made meaning out of their work. I just never wrote about it. I was interested in class identity, and while doing work was essential to seeing those class relationships, I mostly elided over what was not in my line of sight. I missed the complex interpretations that workers gave to their labor and how work created meaning in their lives. What we didn't do was investigate work deeply. And it's tugged at my consciousness for years. This book is about wrestling with the question—What is work?—and offering what I've learned are plausible answers.

Student Responses

In chapter 1, work is measured and encapsulated in *time*. It is always done in the present and can be appreciated or scorned as it is being done. Hour to hour, day to day, shift to shift, assignment to assignment a person's labor is appropriated. Time and work are used and thereby used up. But the work can also and usually does endure. A person's labor can be thought of as a mere exchange for an immediate gain, but it is also an investment meant to be best realized at a later date—a down payment on the future. Workers' notions of time were conveyed in nearly every statement they made. In the context of work, ideas about the past, present, and future coexisted. Labor transcended time.

Work also always happens somewhere and is reflective everywhere. Chapter 2 examines the *space* that workers occupy, work on, bring into being, and transform. Workspaces are ubiquitous. We work everywhere. Not only does our labor appear in every nook and cranny of our lives but it also transforms the physical spaces we live in. No space is unworked. Every place is built up or at least touched by labor. The properties of earth, wind, water, and fire mixed with human labor produce the world that houses us. If all space is the product of work, then workers are creators. And yet who would know that? The names of workers don't appear on the buildings, clothing, schools, hospitals, computers, or automobiles that they construct or operate for owners, investors, and taxpayers. Every space bares their mark but leaves off their names.

Even without recognition, however, the *impact* of labor, or what it does to a person and society, is profound; this is the subject of chapter 3. Work hurts. Work disables and abuses. It exhausts, stresses, and ultimately kills. Work dictates life spans. It also invigorates, inspires, satisfies, and brings joy. Workers told me repeatedly how their labor gives birth, heals the sick, clothes the naked, feeds the poor, comforts the conflicted, and saves lives. Working for a living was a given. It was associated with not being able to live off profits, rents, dividends, or interest from borrowed money. But the physical, mental, and emotional effect of workers' labor on themselves and others was a conditional state of existence that workers had to constantly navigate.

While the impact is uncertain, workers do their jobs for a reason. Chapter 4 explores the reality that there always was *a purpose* for what they did. In fact, in nearly all cases there was more than one. People labored to afford medicine and pay a mortgage but also to feel good about themselves. Work had extrinsic rewards and intrinsic benefits. Workers did their jobs faithfully and seemingly without need for daily justification, but never without intent. Something motivated them to get out of bed in the morning or catch the late afternoon bus to arrive at work. Much of their labor felt compelled. If work was difficult, poorly paid, and disrespected—you know, a "shitty job"—then work was sacrifice. Or as one worker put it, "work ain't nothing but a job." But workers wanted more from their honest labors. If they painted a wall, they wanted to be respected as painters. When they dug a ditch, they expected to feel good about the use of a shovel. Workers knew that picking refuse up from the corner was as important to public health as administering a test to detect a deadly virus. They worked for bread and, yes, for roses too.

Finally, as presented in chapter 5, in the "What Work Is" responses, it was apparent that work always had a *subject*. Labor was always done for someone. Work—skilled, unskilled, or semi-skilled—was done for notions of the self as well as for people that were loved. And pounding a nail, delivering the mail, and administering a vaccine were all usually done for complete strangers. Who benefits when you work? No doubt the employer and the customer or end user. Certainly you benefit in a myriad of substantial and minimal ways. How about your son, spouse, partner, neighbor, or just the person driving down the highway? For whom does a firefighter climb a ladder? Work happens for selfish and altruistic reasons. But it always gets done because of and for people.

Why these concepts? Other ideas did reoccur, and there could be different ways to organize what these workers said. However, time, space, impact, purpose, and subject were the concepts that most animated discussion. They were resonant in every class, with every combination of workers, and in every setting. But reoccurrence alone is not the only reason for focusing on each idea. These ideas are also universal concepts that deepen our subjective understanding and appreciation for work's influence on our society and thus bare greater introspection.

Time is fleeting. Noting that things, like work, happen in time means in part that they happen according to a certain sequence. The cycle of life, from birth to old age and ultimately death, allows for only a window to do what we will. Nothing is permanent. And to do work in time means that work can be a measurement of time. One's life, therefore, goes by in units of time on the job. In the end, what we do with our lives depends on how we use our time. And a great deal of it, while awake, is consumed by working.

Space sets the limits of our lived experience. Our work has a spatial dimension and can be understood in relation to the work of others. We each act in and on the places we occupy. Whether in a coal mine, restaurant, school, or hospital, the space we work in is transformed by our labor. The space only exists because we or others before us first imagined it and then mixed blood and sweat with natural resources to bring the space into existence. Even when we're not working, the places we move through take form only because they are worked up. Simply put, work creates space. Without our collective labors, we would literally be nowhere.

The *impact* of our work is inevitable and ubiquitous. Good, bad, or indifferent, what we do leaves an impression everywhere. Through our work we imprint our lives on the landscape, and people imprint on us, others, and the world around us. The landscape is altered because of what we do to it. So is our body. The work we do triggers physical and emotional changes. It is simultaneously a creative and destructive act. Therefore, since no act of labor is without consequence, the impact of our work should be explored.

Purpose is why we act, why we choose, why we love, and why we work. A life without purpose holds no attraction. The hours of our labor are extensive and jam-packed with meanings, both unexceptional and awesome. We work for extrinsic and intrinsic reasons. Asking, What do you do? is equivalent to inquiring, What good do you do? and What are you good for? When we are really involved in our work, we feel an intimate connection to our labor. We become selfless. Obituaries mention loved ones left behind and occupations procured. Love and labor went together in life; they remain coupled in death.

The *subject* of our work reveals the individual agency and interdependency of our lives. Work is inspired by a desire for personal and social well-being. When we work, we form the self. The labor we do becomes a powerful contributor to our identity. But we are also the sum total of the labors of others. In the collective work we perform, our sense of self coexists with selflessness. Work is done for "me," but no worker failed to recognize the "we" behind a life of honest labor. We may work in isolation, but no one's labor is intended just for the person doing it. Every act that's a part of gainful employment will be for someone. Human beings may be innately social, but human community comes from hard work. Work in any fashion contributes to how we expand, discover, and produce knowledge about ourselves. Through our work we become a subject formed out of contingent historical possibility.

Let me note here that my insights are not drawn from worker surveys or interviews. What workers believe "work is" comes obviously from their perspective. Surveys and interviews are very useful information-gathering and analytical tools. There is however always a methodological concern about accuracy and bias when asking someone to self-report an answer to a question. The essay-writing prompt doesn't involve answering questions, but it may produce unreflective and illegitimate responses. Thankfully, I got very few of those.[15] Additionally, perhaps six words is insufficient to describe a person's experience with work. But in the same way that thinking about the relevance of race in our personal life stories invokes a powerful impression on consciousness, I believe work has the power to draw out an essential, unfiltered truth about our individual existence.

Along with sharing what workers have taught me about what work is, I will draw on occasion from other diverse academic and philosophical sources, including music and poetry—some of it my own—to help present workers' points of view and my understanding thereof. I also draw from my own experiences growing up in a working-class household to emphasize what the class exercise has revealed. Where helpful I will reference the insights of other theorists and writers. Selected works from Karl Marx, and particularly his analysis of capital and labor in *Capital* and the *1844 Philosophical Manuscripts*, proved to be particularly useful to presenting the five themes curated from my students' expressions. Adam Smith's *An Inquiry Into the Nature and Causes of the Wealth of Nations* will likewise make an appearance or two. Regarding work both men are invaluable sources and, surprisingly, have much in common. But this book is not meant as a comprehensive review of what has been written about work from an economical, sociological, psychological, philosophical, industrial relations, and ecclesiastical perspective. For readers interested in such books, I strongly suggest Professor John Budd's very well written and comprehensive *The Thought of Work*. Nor am I situating my perspective within or against any tradition or theoretical field of study. What has been written about the labors that people do stands as a testament to the subject's enduring quality. This is also not a statistical analysis of the words or concepts workers used to describe the reality of work. I will however cite numerous anonymous excerpts from my students' essays and comments. When I do, they will appear in quotation marks without attribution, as in the following excerpt that evoked an endless amount of speculation as to the writer's intention: "Work is what work was to never be." Additionally, while theories and philosophies of time, space, and identity are very informative, they aren't the focus here. My purpose is to share my understanding of how that most fundamental human activity—work—is actually realized. To provide some awareness about the applied and felt nature of our labor.

Defining Worker-Students (and Who They Are Not)

Let me, however, be clear about the folks I'm writing about. Like Philip Levine I'm writing about workers who depend on a form of labor to survive that is vulnerable to exploitation by those who own the products of that labor. It is *as workers* that my students create the wealth that the owners of capital come to possess, accumulate, and distribute. While the workers in my class fight for what they believe is a fair share of the wealth they produce, the relatively few people who own what gets made and sold in this country reap enormous financial returns. The disparities are neither justified by any fairness doctrine nor by natural differences in human assets. Marx wryly noted that "nature does not produce on the one hand owners of money or commodities, and on the other hand men possessing nothing but their own labour-power."[16] My students are, in other words, part of a working class that lives exclusively by its labor and not on the profit of any kind of capital. The workers could be considered as "productive workers," who are directly involved in producing goods or services. These pages are informed by the voices of largely hourly, waged workers that have sat in my classroom over the years. They made up part of the roughly 74 million people or 55 percent of all wage and salary employees paid an hourly rate.[17] Students largely worked in occupations within the retail, manufacturing, construction, health and education, transportation, and service industries. With rare exception, they were all union members. However, they also included workers not legally classified as employees, like taxi drivers and rideshare and delivery drivers.

Some workers, like K-12 teachers and nurses, were paid a salary. But if their total work hours were properly compensated, they weren't doing much better, on average, than minimum-wage employees. And each of these occupations, including those that required a college degree, historically have relied on unionization to raise the quality of the jobs. There is also an exceedingly small number of professional athletes, musicians, dancers, television and radio artists, and actors who make a living from their talents. Some of them have been in my class with laborers and health technicians. Of course, even athletes and performing artists, along with stage and studio hands, need and have a union because unless someone who owned a team, theater, studio, or concert hall hired them, they couldn't make a living hitting a baseball, dramatizing a character on stage or screen, or playing guitar. The same goes for institutions of higher learning. A few college professors, like me and many more without good paying and secure tenure positions (i.e., adjunct instructors) took my class, and they too either had a union or were trying to organize one.

My students are not largely drawn from app-platform, day-labor, minimum-wage, or nonunion employment. Few, to my knowledge, held multiple jobs at the same time. Few are noncitizens. I suspect, however, that if they had included the most vulnerable and oppressed workers, the idea of work would still hold out the promise of personal liberation, but work itself would be described (and experienced) more brutally. Nor did essay writers for the most part include workers who were middle management, administrators, administrative specialists, consultants, telemarketers, or corporate lawyers. Few considered themselves clerical. They were not, in other words, the kinds of workers that anthropology professor David Graeber of the London School of Economics described in *Bullshit Jobs: A Theory*.[18] Graeber argued that there are millions of people in "futile occupations that are professionally unsatisfying and spiritually empty."[19] With few exceptions, the workers in my class felt their jobs offered something genuinely useful to society. Work on any given day—depending on the situation—could be "shitty," but they benefited from a union and were far from the most vulnerable and exploited workers in our society. Collectively they weren't a "labor aristocracy" but did have enough political standing in their jobs to feel some ownership and investment in what they did for a living. Their relative job stability no doubt influenced how they responded in class.

These workers are the centerpiece of our capitalist economy. Duke University professor of women's studies Kathi Weeks nicely summarizes why waged employees should be at the center of conceptualizing work: "It is of course the way most people acquire access to the necessities of food, clothing, and shelter. It is not only the primary mechanism by which income is distributed, but also the basic means by which status is allocated and by which most people gain access to healthcare and retirement. After the family, waged work is often the most important, if not sole, source of sociality for millions."[20]

It likely doesn't need pointing out, but bankers, Wall Street traders, CEOs, private equity managers, technology moguls, sports franchise owners, and media executives did not take my class. One student's essay strongly insinuated who was a worker: "Work is for the working class." Importantly, the compulsion to work was not optional. "Work is mandatory when you're not wealthy." Nonetheless, I recognize that the economic elite and owners of massive amounts of capital do work. From their perspectives, they no doubt have valuable answers to "what work is." It's just that they don't depend on their own labors to survive. In fact, if they thought doing the work that made them wealthy was such an unconditional good, the rich would have a monopoly over productive labor, instead of over capital. The 1920s columnist and storyteller Don Marquis offered an appropriate skeptical quip to the claims of earned fortunes: "When a man tells you he got rich through hard work, ask him: 'Whose?'"[21] Take for example, Tony Xu, the CEO of DoorDash who was paid $414 million in 2020. The pandemic was terrific for his financial standing. I didn't have Mr. Xu in my class, but I did have some of his, as well as other, misclassified rideshare and delivery drivers. Perhaps some of Mr. Xu's takings grew out of the clever ways that the firm generated profits. In 2020 DoorDash agreed to pay $2.5 million to resolve a lawsuit that found them diverting customer tips intended for workers into company earnings to fund their operations.[22] A more essential and structural device to keep worker pay low and CEO pay extremely high is to insist that the drivers are not really employees at all but instead independent contractors. As a result, they are not even guaranteed a minimum wage. Perhaps that is why Maria Figueroa, director of labor and policy research for the Cornell University Worker Institute, referred to the food couriers as "the most vulnerable workers in digital labor."[23]

CEOs would likely have interesting things to share about how their work shapes their identity and influences their satisfaction with life. Research shows that once you've made enough money, additional increments of earnings don't add up to more happiness. However, the outsized questionable rewards bestowed on the occupants of C-suites—often weakly correlated to high performing companies—places them in the stratosphere of the capitalist class. A survey done by Equilar for the *New York Times* revealed that in 2020 the average CEO received 274 times the pay of the median employee at their companies. CEO pay in 2020 jumped 14.1 percent compared to the previous year. Worker median pay scratched out a measly 1.9 percent increase. In the first six months of 2022, labor shortages, supply-chain bottlenecks, and worker resistance pushed average wages up by 5 percent. Those were the biggest gains in years, and as inflation reached 8.5 percent the nation's bankers and employers blamed workers' earnings. Something they also did after prices spiked following World War I, World War II, and in the late 1970s. What they failed to note this time was that the average S&P 500 CEO pay had climbed by 17 percent.[24] That brought the median CEO compensation to $14.5 million. Earnings are different things depending on whether they're from labor income or asset appreciation.

The wealthiest in our society own or manage assets, like real estate, corporations, machines, and invested money that return financial shares well beyond the contributions of their own individual labor.[25] The greatest part of their wealth isn't even in earnings; it's in capital gains, and consequently they pay a lower tax rate than the childcare provider in my class.[26] Tom Wayman has found a wicked metaphor for this class-domination scheme in the children's game and poem "Paper, Scissors, Stone."

> An executive's salary for working with paper
> beats the wage in a metal shop operating shears
> which beats what a gardener earns arranging stone.
> But the pay for a surgeon's use of scissors
> Is larger than that of a heavy equipment driver removing stone
> which in turn beats a secretary's cheque for handling paper.[27]

CEOs do something for all that wealth, but it is not the kind of work the janitor, secretary, window washer, or waiter does. Instead, it's the kind of work that comes from controlling the right to exploit and profit from natural resources and the labors of others.[28]

My intention is to give workers, not employers, the opportunity to say "what work is" according to their experiences. That is to say, I aim to privilege a worker's meaning of work above the views of corporate owners, bosses, media heads, and politicians who use their power not only to exploit workers but to define them. More to the point, I want to shift what we think we know about work away from the self-serving narratives of those who most benefit from others' labor. My objective is to take seriously the most radical proclamation ever made about class relations in the American context. Sure, Marx's insightful and elaborate analysis of the interior workings of capitalism remains unparalleled. But when it comes to one powerful summative statement about the relationship between labor and capital, it was Abraham Lincoln who offered the most revolutionary understanding of whose vantage point should be privileged:

> Labor is prior to, and independent of, capital. Capital is only the fruit of labor and could never have existed if labor had not first existed. Labor is the superior of capital and deserves much the higher consideration.[29]

It was uncommon for my students to know of Lincoln's labor advocacy. I often shared the above quote after the six-word essays were written. But occasionally, without priming, a worker would offer that "work is something that precedes capital." Listening to the voices of workers will make clear that if left to its own devices capital doesn't just exploit a person's labor; it defines that labor in its own image. Our capital-centered understanding of work then gets embedded in laws, employment practices, education, popular representations, and cultural norms. Instead of abiding by Lincoln's assertion that we give "higher consideration" to the workers—the creators of wealth and the material and social communities we live in—our political-economic system defaults to the interests of capital to set the rules for employment.

Job Quality in American History

Protections for workers, creating high-quality employment and making investments in securing meaningful work, is always reactive. The history of American constitutional change and employment policy is a series of responses to worker abuse. From the Thirteenth Amendment's end of human bondage for profit-making through the Progressive Era's late nineteenth- and early twentieth-century workplace reforms, it has always been the owners of labor power that have established the rules for work. Only after muckraking exposés of the pernicious conditions caused by laboring in the "dark satanic mills" and disasters, like the 1911 Triangle Shirtwaist Fire did the political system see fit to institute reforms.[30] The New Deal provisions required a massive mobilization of workers and a forceful strike wave. Capitalism was teetering, and it needed to partner with the state to right itself. Labor's crowning achievement, the National Labor Relations Act (NLRA) was a dramatic systemic change to how power would be diffused within the employment relationship. Business chieftains and conservative political leaders were in a panic that the Communist revolution had begun. Workers knew better and swarmed into unions. The result was middle-class America. However, even "Labor's Magna Carta"—the NLRA—didn't embrace Lincoln's radicalism.

In fact, as seen in the law's preamble below, it further enshrined the opposite. The law's author, Senator Robert Wagner, had nobler intentions for the measure, but the fact that the law had to be framed as good for business to pass is itself revealing about labor's subordinate political status. I have added italics to highlight the true objective of labor's most protective public policy.

> The denial by employers of the right of employees to organize and the refusal by employers to accept the procedure of collective bargaining lead to strikes and other forms of industrial strife or unrest, which have the intent or the necessary effect of *burdening or obstructing commerce* by (a) impairing the efficiency, safety, or *operation of the instrumentalities of commerce*; (b) occurring in the current of *commerce*; (c) materially affecting, restraining, or controlling the flow of raw materials or manufactured or processed goods from or into *the channels of commerce,* or the prices of such materials or goods in *commerce*; or (d) causing diminution of employment and wages in such volume as substantially to impair or disrupt the market for goods flowing from or into the *channels of commerce.*[31]

Not only have the political-economic dimensions of American capitalism always defined the social relations of production in ways that disadvantage workers but history also reveals an enduring struggle over job satisfaction; job quality; and the relationship between work, self-actualization, and community welfare. Investigating what workers think about work in the United States through the prism of time, space, impact, purpose, and subject is necessary to determine the changing meaning society gives to its most precious and formidable wealth-creation social activity: selling labor power.

During the post–Civil War industrial revolution, factories and mines were dangerous and unforgiving places to work. The early age of American capitalism was characterized by twelve- to sixteen-hour workdays, low wages, dangerous conditions, and workplaces with little regard for worker rights. Men and women from every region of Europe came to the United States between 1880 and 1920, as part of the great "proletarian migration."[32] Ostensibly "free" citizens, a large portion of the 23.5 million immigrants were subjected to what critics of industrial labor have called "wage slavery." The country had abolished chattel slavery after the Civil War, but labor exploitation was so extreme that the metaphor proved potent. The *New York Times* described the emergent system of wage labor as "a system of slavery as absolute if not as degrading as that which lately prevailed at the South" and described workers' lack of legal protections with headlines like "WAGE SLAVERY OR SOCIAL SLAVERY?"[33] Historian Lawrence Glickman notes the term continued to be used well into the twentieth century. "References abounded in the labor press, and it is hard to find a speech by a labor leader without the phrase."[34]

In 1912 the plight of workers was so distressing that the US Congress created the Commission on Industrial Relations to scrutinize the nature of work and recommend new labor laws. Between 1913 and 1915 the commission studied industrial working conditions and heard testimony from workers and employers across the country. Its final report stated the shocking truth that in communities where employers ruled without limitation "democratic government as a rule [did] not exist." America had "within the body of the Republic, virtually principalities, oppressive to those dependent upon them for a livelihood and a dreadful menace to the peace and welfare of the Nation." On the topic of work's impact on income, the commission left no uncertainty as to their findings: "Have the workers received a fair share of the enormous increase in wealth which has taken place in this country during this period, as a result largely of their labors? The answer is emphatically, No!"[35] While work relations for undocumented immigrants and farmworkers can be oppressive, America no longer knowingly harbors feudal enclaves within its borders. But as to the perpetual and growing existence of wealth inequality? The commission's findings have not aged.

In the 1970s the country took another close look at how work was working out for workers. It wasn't a pretty sight. Based on the third Quality of Employment Survey conducted in the decade, analysts found that "the decline in job satisfaction has been pervasive, affecting virtually all demographic and occupational classes." The survey results revealed that between 1969 and 1977 American workers' job satisfaction was cratering and dragging down their "overall life satisfaction."[36] If it had been just a result of a chaotic and contentious economic time, perhaps there would be little reason to worry about working experiences. But it was instead a loud ringing fire alarm that work itself was degrading and workers were suffering. The human toll was so worrisome that in 1972 the US Senate Subcommittee on Employment, Manpower, and Poverty held hearings on "Worker Alienation." In opening remarks committee member Senator Edward Kennedy drew an ugly picture of work in the country: "Millions of Americans are alienated because they see their jobs as dead-ends, monotonous and depressing and without value." Concern over the spread of worker discontent led Kennedy to propose a bill that appropriated $10 million to provide research and technical assistance to address extreme worker job dissatisfaction. The legislation acknowledged the "alienation of American workers because the nature of their jobs is a problem of growing seriousness to the national economy and to individual workers."[37]

Inspired by a Labor Day message by President Nixon, a special task force was formed to explore worker unhappiness. Nixon, no friend to labor and unscrupulous in his desire to manipulate working-class voters, nonetheless expressed what was missing from the workday and was disillusioning an angry labor force: "In our quest for a better environment, we must always remember that the most important part, of the quality of life is the quality of work, and then new need for job satisfaction is the key to the quality of work." The task force found, "[Many] adults are generally dissatisfied with jobs that fail to keep pace with changes in worker attitudes, aspirations, and values."[38] A final report included chapters titled "Blue Collar Blues" and "White Collar Woes." Work didn't seem to be making anyone happy.[39]

For workers near the middle and below the median socioeconomic classification—kind of like the folks writing essays in my class—job quality kept falling throughout the 1980s and 1990s. Economist John Schmitt noted that over the two decades "wages . . . failed to rise as fast as the general price level; access to employer-provided health care . . . declined; and employees [were] shifted in large numbers out of defined benefit pension plans toward less desirable defined contribution plans, where workers bear a much greater share of the risk surrounding their retirement income." He further pointed out that job "stability and job security, especially for men, . . . also declined" and the "long-term shift toward more nonstandard work arrangements (including part-time, temporary, and contract work) explains part of the rise in job instability and job insecurity." Employment quality was on a three-decade slide and the deterioration was ripping away workers' "attachment to their employers."[40] Contrary to conventional wisdom, it seemed that for some large employers capitalism was working just as they hoped. In 1996 AT&T vice president for human resources James Meadows suggested jobs were a quaint idea: "In AT&T we have to promote the whole concept of the workforce being contingent, though most of the contingent workers are inside our walls. 'Jobs' are being replaced by 'projects' and 'fields of work,' giving rise to a society that is increasingly 'jobless but not workless.'"[41]

Employer power and political enabling kept driving job quality down. A 2019 Russell Sage Foundation report cited substantial evidence that a "shift in bargaining power toward employers has been an important part of the post-1979 collapse in job quality." In language that would resonate with my students, the authors made the case for doing something to abate the damage done to work's lofty status as the path to prosperity. "Given the centrality of work to human welfare and the functioning of organizations and societies, enhancing the quality of jobs is a pressing issue for public policy."[42]

In 2022 questions about job quality captivated national discussion as millions of workers quit bad jobs and looked for better ones. In June the Department of Labor (DOL) held an extraordinary one-day conference about job quality as part of its "Good Jobs Initiative."[43] Cosponsored by a coalition of twenty philanthropies, this was the first time the federal government had held a summit on job quality. The historic day of plenaries and breakout sessions featured staff from DOL units, state and local officials, private nonprofits supporting studies on job quality, business leaders, labor organizations, and invited academics.[44] Beyond the national focus, Illinois went further than any other state in establishing a Future of Work (FOW) Task Force to examine workforce needs. The task force, which I sat on, issued an eighty-page report that included a definition of a quality job along with a seven-component and multidimensional metric to assess a job's quality. I was one of several researchers affiliated with the Project for Middle Class Renewal at the University of Illinois who constructed the yardstick. The task force also recommended adopting the statewide job-quality measurement as a tool to determine public expenditures. I'll revisit the FOW Task Force in the conclusion, but for now I cite it as an example of how questions about the ontology of work under capitalism remains as vibrant today as it was at the dawn of wage labor.

Work has one other timeless dimension that psychologists, sociologists, anthropologists, political scientists, philosophers, economists, and historians continuously investigate. It goes to the heart of what it means to be a human being. Do we labor for our own good and personal growth? Or do we sweat by our own brow on behalf of the general welfare? Are we socially oriented or personally oriented beings? Perhaps it is and must be both. Abraham Maslow identified self-actualizing and self-transcendence as the ultimate goal of a meaningful life, and Aristotle held the "virtues" to be a roadmap to "living well."[45] The work we do features prominently in both accounts. Professor Barry Schwartz answers the question, Why do we work? by claiming it isn't for pay, even for "soul deadening" jobs.[46] "Almost every job," he contends, "gives employees the opportunity to make someone's life better."[47] Adam Smith agreed but not necessarily for beneficent reasons. He held that self-interested laborers would generate benefits for others and offered the example of a "pin factory" production system to make it so. Marx deconstructed that system and found it alienating. Marxist theoretician David Harvey explained that capitalist social relations produce "alienation in both its objective and subjective garbs."[48] Let's return to the phrase "wage slavery" for a moment. According to the Google Books Ngram Viewer, printed use of the term crested in 1921 and then receded for nearly fifty years (with the exception of 1936), before shooting back up in 1970. Its textual appearance in 2019 was equivalent to its use in 1901.[49] Truth is that work and its' meaning are and have always been deeply contested.

The substance of work and how it impacts the people who do it and the society that depends on it is essential to human flourishing. A quality job and meaningful work should not be treated as a preference in the labor market. Instead, I agree with Ruth Yeoman who posits that "state intervention aimed at promoting the social and economic conditions for widespread meaningful work" should be "understood to be a fundamental human need, which all persons require in order to satisfy their inescapable interests in freedom, autonomy, and dignity." Truly understanding the meaning of work in the lives of people who labor for a living and depend on it, is a prerequisite for creating the conditions to "allow as many people as possible to experience their work as meaningful through the development of the relevant capabilities."[50] The point of presenting how workers experience and understand their labor, to paraphrase Marx's famous statement about philosophy, is not to just interpret what work is but to change it.[51] It is ultimately an object of political action.

Working Together

One last thing. Hours of discussions with workers has taught me that work is interdependent. Nobody's work independently originates. Everyone's work is the product of causes and conditions that are themselves a result of other causes and conditions. These words you're reading were typed on a laptop that was manufactured by people using materials that were mined and designed by others. And those who did the mining and engineering used tools that were made by other workers. And a truck driver drove the laptop from a warehouse to my office after another worker completed the paperwork and somebody else paid for it. And all these people were taught by a teacher or trained on the job how to do their work.

So many hands, minds, hearts, and, if you believe, souls sitting on my desk. Each of us doing our work like ghosts to each other in separate places and at different times. It's truly amazing the ties that bind the working class. Illuminating those invisible threads requires knowing what work is. American citizens should take seriously what workers say "work is." Their subjectivity developed through the work they do is a powerful guide to how we should protect, nurture, and honor work in the society under construction. The reality of work won't be changed unless we recognize what a complicated, contradictory, glorious and poetic experience work is. To change what our society does with work and to workers requires first understanding how workers experience their labor. The union workers in my class have a great deal to say about work, and their experiences about what work is can serve as a model of what work should be for all in society. In shaping the future of work, their voices need to be taken seriously, because as articulated in powerful six-word statements, they speak up clearly for the dignity of work in all its dimensions.

CHAPTER 1

The Time of Work

ONE PROVOCATIVE ESSAY—"Work is now and forever"—expressed what many workers wrote in different forms. It forcefully spoke to how workers experience work, as having a permanent hold on their time. Consider the essay's structure. First, there is the temporal recognition of a constant "now." It is followed by the sense that the work, which is done "now," is unyielding and will become work done tomorrow—even if it's a different job. Additionally, the essay allows for no uncertainty about the use of time; work is predetermined. The time at work can also be an investment in life or a form of deprivation. "Work is time off to play," but also "Work is losing time with family." No matter the meaning imposed, with each unit of expended time, work becomes in another worker statement "what keeps us living shorter lives." My students know something about work's hold on their lives.

Americans work a lot. And they're often trying—sometime desperately—to work more, not less. Working is so encouraged that, unlike at least 134 countries that have laws mandating paid time off, which reduces the required annual hours of work, the United States has no such mandate. American employers are alone among their advanced-economy peers in not having to provide a single hour of paid vacation or sick leave. National, compensated maternity and parental leave is also common for parents around the world. Unless you are unfortunate to be a new parent in Lesotho, Swaziland, Papua New Guinea, and—inexplicably—the United States. Daily labor for adults is also free of any legal caps, unless you are lucky enough to work under a union contract. Time-use studies done in the country regularly show that Americans spend roughly one-third of their day on the job. Only "personal care activities" took a bigger chunk of the day.[1] The work ethic is accepted as an American value, and there is little societal resistance to spending more time working.

According to the World Economic Forum, in 2019 workers in the United States clocked an average of 1,779 annual work hours. All that time consumed by work. Time spent in work. Time measured in work increments. Hours and minutes transformed into work units, like shifts and schedules. Time artificially and arbitrarily divided into regular and overtime. Some of it is called part-time because it's not enough. Or it can be full time and way too much. Perversely, some can't get a day off, while others can't find work. Paradoxically, Americans are both overworked and underemployed. Labor economists Lonnie Golden and Morris Altman explain that workers are "experiencing underemployment if they are unable to get as many hours of work" as they would prefer at their current job. On the other hand, workers are in a "state of overemployment if they would be willing to reduce their hours of work burden" but lack that option at their current job.[2]

Workers should be entitled to refuse to work overtime and not risk losing their job, but few have such a right. To even raise objections is to invite the employer's wrath. For example, nurses report being forced to log sixteen-hour days to avoid being disciplined at work. Failing to do so subjects them to the indignity of having their professional integrity questioned. Managers at a Michigan hospital owned by healthcare conglomerate Ascension regularly scolded nurses by reminding them that to refuse sixteen-hour shifts "is not in line with our value of dedication."[3] On the opposite end of the spectrum millions of workers struggle with very inconsistent hours and an unfulfilled desire for more work hours. Work schedules can vary from a handful of hours to an abundance of hours per week, a variance that is prevalent in all occupational sectors. Roughly, 15 percent work irregular and weekly changing shifts. An astounding 40 percent of employees regularly or occasionally perform "on-call" work.[4]

Absurdly, the total hours consumed by people at work doesn't appear to be even good for business. Only 43.8 percent of workers feel like they have enough time to do their jobs.[5] The lack of adequate time to complete work assignments is a serious problem for employers, consumers, and employees. There is a positive relationship between the availability of sufficient time to complete assigned tasks and job satisfaction. Numerous research studies have confirmed that workers who are satisfied with their workplace miss less work, are more likely to be at work on time, and outperform their dissatisfied colleagues.[6] Worker happiness is rarely, if ever, more than an instrumental concern of employers. However, since it is the employees' laboring time that is responsible for producing the profit that capital draws from the workers, the nexus of time and employee satisfaction should register serious employer attention. Research has also demonstrated that unhappy employees—particularly nonunion workers—continuously look to exit their workplaces. The result is a high turnover rate that can affect the profitability of the organization, because hiring new workers is costly.

Juliet Shor points out that an obsession with work "has created a profound structural crisis of time" among the populace.[7] Adam Smith in the *Wealth of Nations* saw the coming penurious impact of runaway work time: "The innate human desire to improve one's lot is strong enough to make workmen apt to overwork themselves and ruin their health and constitution in a few years."[8] It's not just a psychological attachment or an individual drive to be gainfully employed that puts workers in harm's way. Few workers have any real control over their time. Most employers require workers to be, in effect, constantly available. Employees know the difference between work time and being "off the clock," but it can feel undifferentiated. As Trinidad Sanchez Jr. said "Work, work, work, not easy to define, but easy to delineate by those standing in line to punch a clock."[9]

You're either starting or ending work, but the twenty-four-hour cycle revolves around a job commitment. And frankly, workers know that if they want to keep a job, they are expected to potentially give all their time to their employers. "Work is all the time." Not just in the present moment, but "work is the rest of my life."

A prolonged 2022 dispute between railroad employees and large freight carriers centered around workers' lack of time off to tend to routine health concerns. An Idaho engineer summed up the feeling of an all-consuming job in the following way: "The way the railroad treat us, their opinion seems to be that our lives belong to them."[10] While the Thirteenth Amendment ended involuntary labor, our country's employment policies practically force people to stay on the job. The United States is one of only seven countries in the United Nations—including some island jurisdictions—that has no federal paid leave law.[11] Among the forty-one Organization of Economic Cooperation and Development countries, the United States comes in last at zero weeks of federally guaranteed paid leave. In comparison, countries like Estonia, Bulgaria, Hungary, Lithuania, Austria, Slovakia, Latvia, Norway, and Slovenia offer over a year's worth of paid leave.[12] As one student essay proclaimed, "Work is dominating my life." Even the best of jobs, according to Duke University Professor Kathi Weeks, "is a problem when it monopolizes so much of life."[13]

Workers are of two minds about work and time, or maybe it's just one mind that holds contradictory thoughts in a delicate equilibrium. Work is an absolute necessity. My students consistently stressed that they saw no option regarding the need to work. None of them were going to live off stocks, rents, interests, or profits. Workers had only their labor power to sell, and that meant finding a buyer. The deal had a raw, unsentimental quality. "If labour could be had without purchase," John Stuart Mill quipped, "wages might be dispensed with."[14] Adam Smith, universally cited as the founder of capitalism, was scathing in depicting the motivations of the employer: "Whenever the law allows it, and the nature of the work can afford it, therefore, he will generally prefer the service of slaves to that of freemen."[15] But since workers can't be owned and wages must be paid for time worked then "eight, ten, twelve, fifteen hours of his (i.e., worker) daily life belongs to him (i.e., the employer) who buys them."[16] Work was "exchanging my time for your money." Time was a value owned by the worker, and it had currency as a means of exchange for the wages paid by the boss. Labor in use is always being expended and most often measured by intervals of time. Time then appears as both a measure of value and as something real in its own right.

With each ticktock, clock time is a steady instrument the employer uses to measure the exchange value of work. In doing so, clock time is transformed. Workers in my class knew that time was not a universal concept. They even renamed it. Work is "labor time to complete specific tasks." Not standard or daylight-saving time. Time wasn't a neutral unit of measurement. Time was when a person started to produce, began to serve, commenced to "get shit done." Consider my father. He didn't like the morning 7:00 a.m. shift at Republic Steel.[17] But he had no problem with regular 7:00 a.m. It was labor time 7:00 a.m. that his body fought against. Why? Because 7:00 a.m. was no longer merely 7:00 a.m. It was now the first hour of his body in motion that had a dollar value pinned to it. Dad's time, like the workers' time in my class, measured the price tag attached to labor. On its own, 7:00 a.m. just measured a unit of time. Dissociated from any activity, 7:00 a.m. relentlessly moved forward into 8:00 a.m., 9:00 a.m., 10:00 a.m. until the day was over. But Republic Steel 7:00 a.m. time was the beginning of the company's command of my father's labor. It was time cleaved to work.

Holding a job was inevitable if you wanted to live a decent life. Having a job, though, wasn't enough. Workers noted that work is "day in and day out," and usually, the more the merrier. Too little work was almost never a good thing. Leisure was appreciated, but it was principally a by-product of labor. We'll focus more on the purpose for work in chapter 4, but workers treated labor as a foundational activity, as the natural and preferred state of a person. We work, therefore we are human. They have a point.

While I'm certain only a few of my students would have been familiar with Marxism, their reflections on work's essence were pretty accurate descriptions of Marxist thought. In an essay written by Marx's lifelong collaborator

Frederick Engels, he says, "[Labor] is the prime basic condition for all human existence, and this to such an extent that, in a sense, we have to say that labor created man himself." After creating "man" (i.e., people) labor then gave cause to form society because it "brought people together under conditions where they had something to say to each other."[18] The ability to work, then, was an essential attribute of the self and society. Work helped to "establish the regularity of life, it's basic rhythms and cyclical patterns."[19] That all sounds very significant, and you might have figured that what logically follows is that a person's labor is primary to any other social good. But the workers in my classes knew differently.

In their lives the labor they performed was more like Aristotle's prioritization of leisure over work. To Aristotle leisure is not mere amusement but the intellectual pursuit of higher order goods, like understanding the essence of beauty, goodness, social order, truth, and justice. Leisure is an "end of all practical activity" and "a sort of mastery over and thus independence from work" which is "oriented towards the material sustenance of life."[20] Workers repeatedly stressed that their labor time was a means to an end. Sometimes the ends were grand, like taking care of family; mostly, though, the ends satisfied extrinsic material needs, like paying bills. For Aristotle and my students, leisure only becomes "possible after sufficient work is done to sustain life." In other words, work time comes first, and as one essay explained, periods of leisure are derivative of "putting hard time in." Not because work activity is of the highest value but because unless you are an owner of the means of production, labor is the primary and necessary cause of all that follows.

Workers understood their labor as a commodity, and in Marx's words, a "mere exchange value for the worker," meaning workers knew they had to work and that it was in exchange for a wage.[21] It didn't take an extensive dive into dissecting capitalism for workers to understand that work is "how I put gas in my truck." Marx put it this way: "Labour power (i.e., the capacity to work) is a commodity, the wage-worker, sells to the capitalist. Why does he sell it? In order to live."[22] No matter the occupation, the actual labor performed, or how much gas it allows for, the worker uses up hours of her life. Determining how many hours, according to Marx, was based on the "necessary labor time" it took to do the job.[23] Putting it bluntly, work is "selling my time for money." It was a simple but deeply personal tradeoff: "my time for money." The employer desperately needed the workers' labor power and workers had to have a job. So my students sold off their capacity to create wealth in "temporal packets."[24] One way to accept the loss of time was to view the iterative work commitment as "just a couple of hours." Workers sometimes questioned the moral value of having to trade away their time but accepted that it was all about the exchange rate. Being in a union raised the worth of their time, and they regularly praised it. For example, an essay stressed that work is "better in Local 150."[25] But even at a premium rate, that time sacrifice comes at a cost. Work's impact will be addressed more directly in chapter 3, but it's self-evident that workers give up some quantity of freedom as measured objectively in units of time when they trade their labor for a wage. Perhaps they give up everything. The vast expenditure of time and the reoccurring requirement to expend it left workers wondering if "work is selling yourself."

So how do work and time intersect in the lives of workers? There is an extensive field of literature examining theories of time. Philosophers like Aristotle, St. Thomas Aquinas, David Hume, Descartes, Sir Isaac Newton, Whitehead, Kant, Spinoza, Bergson, and Albert Einstein have weighed in on the topic.[26] I won't explore these competing ideas here or attempt to situate any worker beliefs into the realm of theories. For all their erudition, the philosophers didn't seem to consider the ways that working would define time as a concept or be experienced by workers. The poet Naomi Replansky evocatively expressed how a person's work was paced in metered breaths. "The too-bit cut, the metal curled, / the oil soaked through her clothing. / She made six hundred parts a day / And timed herself by breathing."[27] Workers weren't interested in conceptual notions of time. Nevertheless, the idea of time was an unmistakable, dominant, and pressing matter weaved throughout a worker's understanding of what work is.

To begin with, as previously noted, working time means having an obligation to the employer. What's on the clock belongs to the owner, or at least the renter or user of a worker's time. Work happens on the job and is "an opportunity to serve with pay." However, the time before or after reporting to work, at least in common understanding, belongs to the worker. In the late nineteenth and early twentieth century, labor unions marched militantly by the thousands behind the banner of "8 hours of work, 8 hours of rest, 8 hours for what you will."[28] The length of the working day or week used to be a central mobilizing issue for the American labor movement.[29] Work weeks averaged sixty hours, and before the labor movement the weekend wasn't even a thing. In 1893 the first president of the American Federation of Labor (AFL), Samuel Gompers, explained the ambiguous relationship between time and worker aspirations. Framing his comments in terms of what workers want, he proclaimed, "more constant work . . . more leisure."[30] Working regularly was seen as providing opportunities for leisure and play. Too much of the former got in the way of the latter. In the playful words of a student who loved the outdoors "work is keeping me from fishing."

Assuming you only needed eight hours to make a living and could get eight hours of sleep, your discretionary time and the boss's time were treated equally. In practice, it never worked out that way. Time allocation was never balanced between laboring for a dime and fishing, reading, dancing, or making love. If it were, workers would never write that "work is why I didn't sleep in today." While the average work week has fallen by half and leisure time has greatly expanded since the 1850s, any movement toward a shorter workweek has completely stalled.[31] In the 1930s the labor movement backed a national bill to establish a standard thirty-hour workweek.[32] In 1933 AFL president William Green stood before a crowd of union officials in San Francisco and declared, "We stand unflinchingly for the six-hour day and the five-day week in industry." The labor movement was advancing on an hours' reduction law as the Black-Connery bill had comfortably passed in the United States Senate. Green was trumpeting the measure's affirmation of an official American work week set at five days and thirty hours, with, importantly, "severe penalties for overtime work." Economist John Maynard Keynes predicted the inevitably of an even shorter fifteen-hour workweek. He wrote in a 1930 essay that "For the first time since his creation man will be faced with his real, his permanent problem . . . how to occupy the leisure."[33] Franklin Roosevelt and Labor Secretary Frances Perkins initially endorsed the Black-Connery bill. However, the president gave in to pressure from the National Association of Manufacturers and pulled his support. The bill was subsequently defeated in the House of Representatives.[34] Some unions, like the United Auto Workers, tried unsuccessfully to negotiate thirty-hour work weeks into their contracts. In truth, the forty-hour week is no more than a legend. Since at least 1989, the mean number of weekly hours has exceeded forty every year.[35]

Economic theories assume that workers develop their personal desired number of work hours based on how much they are compensated, other sources of wealth, and innate preferences for work and leisure. Their hours are also determined by inflexible work arrangements set by employers. A major reason people work as many as hours as they do is involuntary and outside their direct control. The most egregious account of compulsory labor I heard was from union workers at the aluminum manufacturing firm, Arconic. Employees were required to work sixty-four hours between Monday and Friday. Meeting this threshold meant working at least fourteen hours of overtime. If during the week a worker missed an eight-hour shift, they would have to work an additional shift on the weekend. Incredibly, many employees in one department were required to work consecutive days of sixteen-hour shifts. According to union officials, 90 percent of the company's employees regularly worked at least one mandatory hour of overtime every week. Involuntary and voluntary overtime was so extensive that workers treated it as part of their standard pay. Roughly, 50 percent of their weekly earnings were dependent on overtime hour earnings.[36] It is no surprise to me that in anticipating such a grueling life-consuming work schedule my students agreed, "Work is ok—on Monday, and payday."

Today, even when workers have the right and opportunity to step away from work, they rarely do. Most Americans who have any paid vacation or earned time off use only a fraction of it.[37] There used to be a cost disincentive for employees overworking people, but no longer. Employers and workers now place a premium on being overworked. Speaking in terms of what is happening to all workers one young electrician offered a dark and damning reflection on how working people experience the passage of time: "work is extorting our time." Workers can feel forever tethered to work time long after the workday ends. In the poem "Factory Time" Tom Wayman expresses this permanent state of attachment to the work schedule.

> But even when I quit
> The numbers of the minutes and hours from this shift
> Stick with me: I can look at a clock some morning
> months afterwards, and see it is 20 minutes to 9–
> That is, if ever out of bed early—and the automatic computer in
>   my head
> Starts to type out: 20 minutes to 9, that means
> minutes to work after 9: you are
> 50 minutes from the break; 50 minutes
> of work, and it is only morning, and it is only
> Monday, you poor dumb bastard[38]

No matter how we parse time as a genre, time itself consumes life. Particularly work time. The derivation for my students is, as follows: "Work consumes my life." But how do workers experience the intersection of work and time?

Work as Time in the Present

Work is understood simultaneously as unfolding in multiple time dimensions: present, future, and past. In the present, work is "what I do every day" or "almost every day." Work is felt immediately and "takes up time." Spending time working is how a worker's day makes sense. Workers experience the passage of the day in the moments they worked. Those days add up. Work is a "Monday through Friday, sometimes Saturday" activity. It is as if there is only work time: "Something I'm always doing." While not literally true, work feels like it "is all I ever do." Work is always being done and never really completed; it is merely paused. The next day it repeats. A twenty-four-hour day may rule our calendar, but workers consume time in smaller segments.

There's "getting the job done" and going home. When is the job done? That depends. For building trade workers, the job often stretches over several days, if not weeks and months. But a store clerk is finished after every shift. A manufacturing employee produces some tangible object and then does it again and again until it is time to stop. Now a teacher's work time is ubiquitous. You instruct each day while school is in session and then work comes home with you and becomes "a part of my personal time." A study I did with colleagues about the time Chicago K-12 public school teachers spent doing their job amounted conservatively to fifty-eight hours per week.[39] Teachers on average work a ten-hour and forty-eight-minute standard school day. A second analysis of Illinois teachers found that 16 percent of them invested over fifty-five hours in school related work.[40] My wife, Lynn, was a middle school teacher for decades, and while at home after school ended, she would work on her class for hours. However, students are in the classroom for the better part of nine or ten months, so the job isn't done when the daily afternoon bell rings. It seemed to me that Lynn was always being a teacher. She loved teaching, but her all-encompassing time commitment was not unusual. Every teacher knows the trade-off. Which raises a compelling question. When is a teacher not being a teacher? Didn't the job time requirements nearly completely define my wife's identity?

Questions about identity are interwoven into how workers used their time. The force of work in the moment helps to shape a sense of self, in the way a chisel pounding on a stone sculpts an image. Work is "what I make each day." Whether the job is defined in outputs, projects, shifts, or annual growth it's understood as happening in and shaping the present. My mother and her customers knew this very well. The conversations I overheard from the women who visited my mother's basement-beauty shop were tailored by the passage of work time. References to how layoffs in the mills had created family hardships were common and laced with uncertainty about "getting by."

Recalling these lamentations from working women sparked a creative writing moment later in my life that produced an original poem. I titled it, "In the Conversation of Women," and the poem included the following two lines that revealed how time was talked about:

> Someone mentioned that poor ole dad
> had not worked a day in thirty

In the second line I'm expressing the condensed time frame that workers typically experienced their lives. Work was measured in allotments of time that often mirrored looming due dates. Thirty-day mortgages and rents, bills paid on the first of the month, installment payments, interest owed on borrowed money, and as was the case with my family, paying the monthly tab on groceries. Many of mom's customers were also employed, and they talked about balancing the hours at work with the time away from work. Only they never really said "balancing." Between washings and colorings, women told stories about barely having the time to go from the job to the supermarket or doctor or a friend's wedding. They explained, complained, and joked about being consumed with things needing to be done and too little time to do them.

Students in my class were no less able to point out that the day revolved around their job. They literally set their clock by the time they needed to be at work. "Work is to be on time." Getting to the job was meticulously planned and timed. Traffic congestion, finding parking, the train schedule, catching the bus and walking to and from the job were all factored into the day's movements. This was all part of the "8 for what you will" and the minutes added up. Time required to be ready for work was time connected to doing work. Breaks for rest and lunch were usually also allotted and when the workday ended work was "the time I put in." To workers time is experiential and immanent. Workdays amounted to points on a continuum that opened and closed according to the hours employed. The labor endured just as long as it took to be consumed and exchanged for compensation. The immediacy of the work is underscored by the compensation workers got with each paycheck. Most of my students were paid by the hour. Therefore, time most often passed in sixty-minute segments. Labor inputted and payment received. This for that. This because of that. The loop is closed. And then repeat the cycle the day after and the day after. Time for workers in the present was of relatively short duration and defined by measures endlessly recreated. For workers in my classes the material need to labor produced an acceptance or resignation that work time was inevitable. One worker described the work-time nexus in precise measurements: "Something I'll be doing for 30 more years." Whether exact or approximate, the influence of time doesn't end there. The hours, years, and decades of work endured and were indivisible. Work, every worker agrees, is at its essential core "time consuming."

Work as Time in the Future

Workers' experience of time was not restricted to the present moment. They also spoke of work in the future tense, as in work is "what we will do." My students were honest enough about their socioeconomic status to admit they were dependent on wage labor. Folks never really expected to hit the lottery, inherit riches, or be socially mobile enough to climb into the upper class. They accepted the need to sell their labor to live comfortably. "Work is trading time for money." But not just to get by—not by a long shot. Work for them was also an investment in the future. Workers made it obvious: work is "the future." It is the activity that is "going to get me places." A hard day's labor may build the day, but it also determines numerous tomorrows. "*El trabajo es lavida y unbuen future* (work is life and a good future)." My students held a kind of Aristotelian version of "efficient causality" toward work. Aristotle laid out an "if . . . then" explanation for why things change.[41] A worker expressed the same idea this way: "Work is a step in the right direction." Another student identified a path-dependent quality of work by adding, "Work is paving the way to the future." Workers always have in mind the long-term effects of their labor. Vaccinating a patient is not only good for the patient's current health; it's also a way to keep them from suffering a disease that may cripple them over a lifetime. A teacher teaches a child to write from 8:30 a.m. to 3:00 p.m. so that once the child becomes the adult, she can fill out a job application or write a poem. An electrician wires a building in the spring so that a family stays warm when the winter chill sets in. Work is "doing something that will last."

In recognizing the future time horizon of a job, it's helpful to appreciate why or for whom the worker is working. "Work is the foundation of my children's future," "the way my kids go to college," or "how I live a better life." Here, the focus is on days yet lived. Maybe even days never lived. Your labor outlives you. Hammering a nail today produces a better life for your daughter. Checking out a customer at the grocery store helps you to eventually buy a house. Driving products, like home appliances, across country to stock stores contributes to people getting the things they need to sustain their lives. Teachers leave no doubt about their sense of work time: "an investment in a child's growth." Work evokes a sense of time that is "for generational support." In the elegiac words of one student, the prospective sacrifice of time laboring in the present was motivated by a desire to give birth to something that would last for multiple lifetimes: "work is planting a tree for your grandkids."

My dad thought about what his work time was worth. Despite being part of the unionized working class that built the country's infrastructure and lifted millions of workers' living standards, he never really saw his labor in a utilitarian sense. In the hours of conversation we had together, there was one bittersweet moment that haunts me still. I asked him if he ever wanted his sons to go into the mill, like he did. I'm the oldest of four sons. Along with me, two of my brothers did a little time in a steel mill. My youngest brother, Rick, spent less than a month. His time was brief because one of his assignments was to work on the coke batteries, and Rick decided that was a god-awful place to earn a living. He was being generous in his description.

The coke batteries or ovens are essential to the steelmaking process because they convert coal into metallurgical coke that is then used to heat the blast furnaces. Steelworkers, particularly Black workers, will tell you that working in the batteries is the dirtiest, ugliest, hottest, and most unhealthy job in the mill because it generates toxic gases involving tar and ammonium sulfate. Working there was considered so onerous that black workers were often segregated into the coke ovens because white workers refused the assignments.

After coming home following what turned out to be his last day in the batteries, Rick told my dad, "I'm never going back." He was worried that Dad would be angry that he quit the job. Instead, my father was relieved. Dad never tried to prevent any of his sons from taking temporary factory jobs, but he was adamant that none of us should pursue careers as mill employees. When I asked him about his sons following his footsteps into the mill, he defiantly answered: "No, I never wanted you guys to work in the mill." I was a bit surprised by the swiftness of response, but it was the second half of his answer that took my breath away. "If you did, then what was the point of everything I did?" Dad's reply unmistakably signaled for whom and what purpose he was working. But it was how he marked time that left me deeply reflective. The biggest part of "everything I did," he said, was the thirty-seven years he worked at the plant. Every day when he headed to the Youngstown, Lansingville Plant of the Republic Steel Company, he was doing more than working rotating eight-hour shifts. He was walking into the future. Not his, but mine and my brothers.'

Dad never warmed to shifting two-week work schedules. It unsettled him. He hated the 11:00 p.m. to 7:00 a.m. shift because he could never sleep during the day. The 3:00 p.m. to 11:00 p.m. rotation wasn't much better. It played havoc on things like going to friends' weddings or your sons' ball games. Now, the 7:00 a.m. to three in the afternoon rotation was good for family events, but you had to get up early the following morning, which meant being home and in bed earlier then you sometimes wished. My father wrestled for over three decades with a wicked contradiction that shapes most workers' lives. They have to work, and in doing so sacrifice opportunities to do other things and be with people they love. "Work is not a day at Great America."[42] However, because they were employed, their time away from the job was more highly valued. A worker put it this way: "Work is a way to enjoy my time off." No matter the work schedule, time was compromised. Workers in my class shared a disquieting truth: work "meant time away from home."

Dad shared with me that some of the happiest moments in his life were watching his sons play sports. My brother Jeff was an outstanding high school quarterback. The rest of my brothers and I favored baseball. Truth be told, Dean (the third oldest son) preferred fishing, and my father liked sitting in the boat on a quiet lake. Football games were played at night, and baseball was finished before the sun went down, so as long as dad wasn't on the 3:00 p.m. to 11:00 p.m. shift he could attend. Of course, every two weeks he was pulling down those midday to late-night hours, and sometimes missing a game really upset him. I still recall the anger he displayed when he heard that I had hit my first Struthers Boys League home run. On this occasion he missed a game not due to a scheduling conflict but because on one of the days that he was off, he chose to do some work at home. For my parents, time off from paid labor usually involved a fair amount of unpaid household labor. Mom always cooked, cleaned, and handled kids' appointments. Dad repaired stuff, cut the grass, and upgraded the structure of our home. Choosing how to best use the precious time off from productive waged labor was a Hobbsian choice. Taking care of familial chores often meant not attending to children's activities or going on vacation. I don't recall any extended family vacations. At best we spent an occasional weekend at a nearby resort with an indoor swimming pool. The one exception was a trip to Niagara Falls. Mom made more of my athletic and extracurricular activities than dad, but the diverse needs of the inhabited unpaid labor space were unrelenting. There was limited free time in the day, and the back side of our house at 421 Wilson Street badly needed repainting. Dad had ignored the peeling and graying of the wood for months. On his day off, he worked well into the evening, and when mom and I arrived home after the game, we found him at the top of a ladder, a paint brush in his hand.

As I recall, it was mom who broke the exciting news of my baseball milestone. My father's reaction still reverberates in my head. He cursed. A very bad word that I had never heard him utter. His profanity was accompanied by a violent slap of the paint brush against the house which made a sound like a sonic boom. Dad's anguish reflected how it feels to a worker when "work is time away from the important things." To me, the home run was a joyful boyhood moment, but to dad it was stolen time. It was, as one worker explained, "time I owe back." Owe back to whom? Mostly to family. In my dad's case, to me. When you worked for a living, your time wasn't your own to spend. My father worked and sacrificed his time for his sons. He was, as one of my students noted, showing his "kids a different path." I'm grateful beyond words, but I also admit to feeling a bit of sadness. In trading his time for a better future for me and my brothers, dad didn't think enough of what he did for a living to want his kids to do the same thing. To dad, he just did the job of a millwright. To me, he built America, one minute at a time.

Workers know they aren't going to live forever or even for very long. Truth is, they're not living any longer than the previous cohort. In 2020 the average life span was 77.48 years. About where it was in 2003.[43] Prior to 2010 life expectancy had consistently climbed, but it has stalled.[44] Life will end, sooner or later, depending mostly on your class status, but work itself has no shelf life. It is eternal. And aging doesn't mean less of it. In the United States there are forty-one million workers over the age of fifty-five: thirteen million are sixty-five or older. According to the US Bureau of Labor Statistics, roughly half (3.8 million) of the 7.7 million workers expected to be added to the economy by 2031 will be older than sixty-five.[45] By that time, workers older than fifty-five will account for 25 percent of the workforce.[46] The kinds of employment will change but my students knew that "work is the rest of my life" and there would always be a job for a worker to do. "Work is going to outlive me!" Work is the brutal and beautiful instrument that creates the future even when there is no aspiration or intention for labor to accomplish more than a way to grow old. By adding up the working days over a lifetime, a person invests in "making a living." The "daily grind" is necessary and predictable. And it's usually felt as "hard time for good time." Rest might be alluring, but time off from work risks a loss of agency in having some input into how the future unfolds.

After years of evocative conversations with workers, I was struck by another aspect of time that grew out of this "doing time" perspective. When workers spoke about their work as a use of time in the present to create the future, it was shadowed in uncertainty. The present moment was a given but little more. Workers viewed work as necessary but unpredictable. A nurse could work fourteen hours a day to create a better life, but work tomorrow was no more certain than it would be if the person had labored for just two hours. Feeling insecure can extend to even the most educated professional employees. University professors in my classes who held adjunct positions cobbled together teaching assignments at several colleges. Adjuncts are not tenured instructors who have a high degree of job security, pay, support, and institutional respect. They are akin to "gig" academics and make up roughly 70 percent of all professors.[47] The sense of present-day unknowing discounted the value workers attached to the passing of time. There was a now-then tension, which national survey data broadly reflected. About half of US workers describe their job as a career, while another 18 percent consider it as a stepping stone to a career. But three in ten workers say their work is "just a job to get them by."[48] My students expressed diverse feelings of job satisfaction and purpose, but rarely did any worker refer to their job as a career. Work could be a powerful calling to serve a higher good or God, but it was still a job and hence firmly rooted in the moment.

There is a real urgency to work in the present because allowing for age, physical decay, and bad luck leaves workers with a pressing understanding that today's labor is all about tomorrow's life. "The road to a good life" and "part of life's steps." Laying a cable, paving a road, pouring molten steel, or cleaning a hotel room is a deposit into a savings account. A worker's hopes, dreams, and fortunes mix with his or her labor to shape the quality of time spent at work. Labor, then, becomes an expenditure of a certain quality of time. Work is and is not merely an expenditure of "time." At its basic level, it is unquestionably a consumption of time. But when done with a purpose, it is time consumed with "dedication and sacrifice." It becomes a "vessel to future days." Yes, work is definitely taking care of the right now—the present moment—but it's no less an investment in the future. "Work is money in the bank."

Work is a cause for a set of conditions not yet realized. It is "for reaching your goals in life." The focus on personal aspiration reflects that workers know they are not merely a cost of production. Despite the way that labor markets function under a lightly regulated form of capitalism in America, workers know they cannot be reduced to expenses on a spreadsheet. They are unlike the other material means (e.g., natural resources, machines, and tools) that are essential to create products for sale and services to offer. Workers are subject to exploitation by their employers and have ownership over their labor. Importantly, workers act intentionally with a purpose in mind. They work to create a life that is somewhat in their own image. Labor is in this respect a "way to create your legacy." It is a "time to strive for greatness." Like a hand pressing firmly on the back, workers feel the future in the rhythms of the present workday.

Work as Time in the Past

As they are laboring in the present with regard for the future, workers feel the weight of the past. Work is "what my father did." Here the legacy of the past shapes how workers approach their jobs. Some are earning a living at what their family members have always done. Others intentionally pursue a different employment path. I would fall into the latter group. My grandfathers, uncles, and father worked in a steel mill. I did too for one summer. One long, insane summer. Every summer the steel companies would need people to fill in for regular employees who took vacation days. There was always plenty of work to be had in the mill for someone young if you didn't mind doing dirty, unskilled, beast-of-burden labor. Oh, yeah—at union wages. Perfect for me.

My uncle Frank got me in at United States Steel's (USS) Ohio Works. He worked there for decades and arranged for me to fill out a job application at the industrial giant's main office building on Salt Springs Road. Before the ink on the form was dry, I was hired and sized up for steel toed boots and a heavy-duty metal lunch box. The superhero lunch containers that carried my bologna sandwich and chips to St. Nicholas Catholic Elementary School would no longer suffice. Lunch in hand, I reported to work the next day. No time to waste.

Once hired I was initially assigned to a crew of bricklayers who were principally responsible for keeping the open-hearth furnaces operative. We worked a lot of graveyard shifts—midnight to 8:00 a.m. I also moved around the mill wherever an unskilled hand was needed. While the spaces I worked in varied, the hours I put in were constant. Week after week I worked seven days and many of them beyond the standard eight hours. For about two solid months I worked constantly. In a very brief time, I had become a "mill rat." Somebody who was more alive at work then at home. If you can call working nearly every waking hour living.

For me, of course, it was just a money-making venture to pay for college. Anybody could do it for a short time, as long as you knew it wasn't a permanent gig. But the workers in the mill and my students in class did need to work beyond a summer job. Many workers spend five years or less in every job they hold, but as you get older job tenure increases. Between the ages of forty-five and fifty-four, the median tenure at a job was 7.6 years. However, median tenure rose to 10.1 years for workers aged fifty-five to sixty-four.[49] Those jobs add up. According to a 2019 Bureau of Labor Statistics survey, the average number of jobs a person will have over a lifetime is twelve.[50] And few workers would turn down the chance to work extra hours, even if it shortened their lives. Manufacturing workers, for example, clock on average 3.3 overtime hours per week.[51]

I only spent one summer at the Ohio Works. Uncle Frank stayed until the company shut down the plant in 1982. They did it with a grotesque flair. In front of a large crowd of people and cameras, USS proceeded to make a gut-wrenching spectacle of blowing up four blast furnaces in one nerve-shattering sequence. A mill that stood for a century was gone in seconds. Talk about the effect of time. Uncle Frank couldn't believe it. He thought those furnaces would last forever. Local folks who stood motionless not believing their eyes had the exact moment those furnaces crumbled to the ground seared into their brain. For those who couldn't bear witness to the actual event, it was captured for a national audience. A documentary that in part chronicled the demise of the steel industry and resiliency of the community, *Shout Youngstown*, opened with the four monstrous stacks being demolished accompanied by an ominous countdown.[52]

Most workers are just doing the work that's available. However, whether it's meant to be for a short duration or a lifetime, when asked, they quietly told me about their reverence for what came before. You may change jobs many times, but you don't forget the last one. And if your employment history is like that of my dad, my Uncle Frank, and a lot of my students, the work you do comes loaded with precedent. When I worked that brief crazy summer as a mill hand, I knew that I had stepped into a trade that had a long legacy. And every day as I schlepped brick and refractory materials, I heard from the "lifers" about how the job was rightly done. Time stood still with each punch of the mill clock.

As I listened to workers ponder what work is, I realized that history came alive in their work, no matter the skill level. There is a pride in one's labor that comes from an appreciation of the work itself. Work for many is "a craft I have mastered." To many workers their job is the embodiment of years of training, education, practice, principles, and values. Building trades workers are typically apprenticed for three to seven years. The work is highly skilled and takes time to master. The point is that the actual craft of an operating engineer doesn't start with each new hire. It is continued and carried forward from the past into the present. When carpenters attach a roof, they are the inheritors of an industry tradition. How they do the job evolves from one generation to the next, but there is always a "right" way to do it. The bricklayers I worked with at USS knew it. In this situation the past lays claim to the skill required to do the current job. You're preserving a trade as much as working a job.

On the other hand, a lot of work is just plain earning a living. Not much tradition in the work. All jobs require some skills, but many occupational tasks return very little personal satisfaction. National surveys reveal that roughly a third of workers view the work they do as "just a job to get them by."[53] The numbers are higher for folks without a college degree and working in nonmanagerial professions. Those who work at manual or physical labor—the majority of the workers in my classes—express dissatisfaction with their work. Still, in these jobs the past serves a constructive purpose. It functions as a series of steps on an employment ladder. Hotel housekeepers do backbreaking work cleaning up after the mess of others. They do it to pay their bills and maybe save a bit for tomorrow. Workers daily calculate a temporal exchange. Work today is "time given to earn time later." Putting the time in now conjures up a more valuable time available to the worker in the future. Showing up for a work shift is "a chance to get something better." To be in pursuit of "something better" is to recall a "less-better" time, a previously held job, perhaps. The unpleasantness of a past work experience fortifies a worker's resolve to find something better paying, safer, more satisfying. Past work experience—good or bad—is emotionally recorded and felt in the present. How much of the past is felt? Nearly all of it.

As part of the "What Work Is" exercise, workers recalled all the paid jobs they have had in their lives. Babysitting, paper route, working on a farm, waiting tables, cleaning dishes. How many? Three, six, eight, ten, more? Amazingly, workers could describe every job they ever had. And remembering was not just recounting. With each job there was a judgement rendered. This one didn't pay well, that one had a nasty supervisor, another was kind of fun. Provocatively, workers thought of jobs in relation to other jobs they had held. The sentiment that work is "one bad job after another" expressed a lingering attachment to the past.

Workers still carried the effects of previous jobs. Their bodies were stamped like passports from the labors they once did. Memories of past employment amounted to a cacophony of attitudes and opinions about working. Bits and pieces of past work accumulated in their minds, informed them about what work is now, and what it needed to be later. Driving a bus came after working in a factory. Working as a police officer came before being a teacher. For many workers it was a job yesterday, a job today, and likely a job tomorrow. But others worked careers or at least toward careers. Either way, workers held fresh in their consciousness the work and time before the jobs they were currently doing. Recalling previous labor served a clarifying purpose. Holding firmly to the past, while repairing an engine today cleared the mind to imagine a path toward where a worker wanted to be in life. Many workers summed up the utility and interdependent nature of their working careers this way: "Work is what makes my life continue." Life begins and evolves through and because of work.

Their labor also revealed an awful truth about their working time. Time worked was equal parts life taking, life enhancing, and life making. And a life of work, even the kind that is self-actualizing, came at an eternal cost. Consider this workers' poignant and counterintuitive expression of work's temporal impact: "Work is sacrificing yourself for time put in." I have always felt the complicated mix of grateful and angry emotions over my parents' sacrifices. Mom worked all the time. She labored in factories, offices, and the basement beauty shop, while managing the home and her children. For much of that time she suffered from different ailments. Despite sacrificing herself, she never wavered from caring for her family. But the cost was personal. I tried to depict how time spent laboring for others was, in part, a diminution of what my mom imagined for her life in this opening stanza of my poem, "In the Conversation of Women:"

> I heard them speak
> about times with less
> then forgotten sidewalk pennies
> fallen from their pockets. Delaying dreams
> cultivated as little girls
> in miniature versions
> of blue-collar wives
> and mothers.

On one particularly scary occasion my father's work also left with me a feeling of dread about the loss of time. I was living in New Jersey and attending a doctoral program at New York University. The phone rang, and it was my mother. She was upset. I knew that because after saying hello she took a while getting the words out. "They found a spot on your dad's lungs." "They," being the doctor and radiologist. A fairly large dark something was resting on my dad's left lung. There were other smaller ones spaced out like crumbs on a countertop. Until the spot was further examined, the doctor didn't know what it was, exactly. But my mom knew. After all the years that my dad worked in that dirty, toxic mill, how could it be nothing? She just knew. Dad had to have lung cancer. Mom was always a bit of a worrier, but her words grabbed me by the throat.

Dad had long since retired when I spoke with my mom about his health. He had put thirty-seven years of his life in the mill. It wasn't unreasonable to assume the worst, and there was plenty of evidence that the worst was happening. While doing research at home for *Steelworker Alley* I was obsessed with the macabre practice of checking the obituary pages of the local paper, the *Youngstown Vindicator*. I began to keep a running list of the deaths of steelworkers. There were a lot of them to record, and one noticeable and curious fact that appeared in many of the notices was the ages of the people when they died: Most were in their fifties and sixties. Only a few made it to the average life expectancy. Work, according to one of my students, was "a ticking-time bomb." Thus, my family's assumption that my dad had a health problem was not overly speculative. His threatening, if unconfirmed, medical diagnosis inspired me to put my feelings into another poem. I titled it, "Plant Disease."

Heard from mom he
grew a dark spot
someplace close to the lungs

I remembered the nights
he staggered out the door
black lunch box cuffed to his wrist
every time the porch light
went out sadness appeared

Steel prospered when he was young
money paid for Italian loafs
and penny cupcakes at the bakery

Work was hard, dirty and regular
for a boy wanting to help
the open hearths, coke plant, rolling
mills were industrial plantations
consuming coal, scrap metal and people

He swallowed waste for thirty years
inhaled soiled air on every shift
but I never saw him choke on it

When he retired the lunch box
disappeared so did the penny cakes
the dark spot remains
perhaps science will save
what the plant tried to kill

Reading the poem today I'm drawn to the relevance and juxtaposition of the time penalty and personal sacrifice reference. Swallowing waste for three decades was no literary flourish. Dad exposed his health to risk for a long time in order to bring a paycheck home. If this isn't "sacrificing yourself for time in," I don't know what is. Time is not, as we would expect, the input that it takes to build a life. The conventional wisdom is that you work hard, put your time in, and reap the rewards. Instead, workers see time as the thing purchased by self-sacrificing labor. Here is what the equation looks like: a human life minus the labor you use equals a life lived. Provocatively, it is not a worker who fulfills some need within the time he or she has; rather, time subsumes the worker. It amounts to work for work's sake. Workers know the deal. In exchange for the work that consumes the precious time they have on this earth workers ultimately construct a life. Work is, as poignantly expressed by a student, "an exchange of life for resources."

Some of that time comes with compensation for services rendered, but work is always "trading time." In this perspective, work may prove to be satisfying and perhaps a path to self-actualization. However, whether or not workers experience their work as satisfying there is unanimity among them that it is the only "road to a better future." But in its daily stripped-down- to-the-roots application work is understood as a brutal act of self-sacrifice. "Work is a sacrifice for a better tomorrow." Some workers think of their labor as ennobling and uplifting. Others express regret for the lost time. My mom's patrons were prone to feeling remorse. I heard them questioning the utility of the time they invested now that it seemed too late. My poem stated it this way:

> Me and dad work all our lives
> to wind up here bleaching white
> as the bedsheets hanging on the line.

When time felt wasted, workers felt used. They maybe even felt stupid for believing that "putting in time" could have ever paid off. At its worst, work can be "a repetitive waste of life."

Nonetheless, without work there would be no past to build on, no present to embrace and no future to imagine. Work is a mundane "part of everyday society," but it is also a sublime generator that "keeps the world turning." From the conversations I had with countless workers, they experienced work as timeless and omnipresent. "Work is something expected of you." Except during a hoped-for restful old age, every worker thought they would always have to work. Work and working time were eternal. What is work? Work is "life." In this way, workers' conception of time was collapsed. Work is never ending and never beginning. It just is.

CHAPTER 2

Work and Space

IMAGINE A PLACE where you go every day. Depending on the circumstances, you stay there for a few hours or for many. This location may be stationary, for example an office or factory. But it could also vary if, for instance, you were a delivery driver, landscaper, residential plumber, or police officer. When you get there, you begin to work. Some people manufacture big things, others fashion small items. Some provide a personal service, while others help shoppers buy the things they need or want. This place can be either gigantic or intimate. It can hold just a few workers or thousands. One student working remotely knew just how informal the jobsite could be: "Work is within my house." People can labor inside a building or be outside and exposed to the elements. "Work is cold weather or hot and rainy." The space can be a warehouse, a school, a vacant lot, inside a truck, a table in a restaurant, a kiosk on a street corner, a water tower looming over the horizon, or your kitchen table. What these environments have in common is that they are all places where people work. The spaces are constructed by bricks and communal stories. They are also, according to a common essay "where people come together to sustain life."

Wherever you look, you can find a location filled with the labor of folks. Nowhere is there a place where people don't work. We have allotted near universal spaces for people to work. You can't separate the work we do from where we exercise our intellectual, emotional, and physical labor. In 2011 I participated in the Smithsonian Institute's Museum on Main Street's traveling exhibition titled, "The Way We Worked."[1] The exhibition of photographs, manuscripts, personal letters, and artifacts was drawn from the National Archives. It explored how work became a central element in American culture by tracing the many changes that affected the workforce and work environments over the past 150 years. I was asked to be an "Illinois Scholar" on the project and a keynote speaker whenever local historical societies hosted the exhibition.

In addition to having the once-in-a-lifetime chance to be called the "Illinois Scholar," the assignment gave me an up-close view on the importance and universal nature of workplaces. Each opening of the exhibit was molded to fit the localities' particular work history, but the accompanying educational programs all followed a standard outline. Section two was titled, "Where We Worked," and the program included the opening statement, "Where we work affects us deeply. A workplace changes over time, creating new experiences and challenges. We either mold it to fit our needs or adapt as best as we can. Where we worked may seem obvious but start counting it up. Americans work just about everywhere!" The script went on to prove that last point by situating labor within the basic dimensions of the planet. "In the Elements: Americans work the land, on the seas, deep beneath the earth, and sometimes even in space." We also work in less awestruck vistas, for instance, "Within Four Walls: With the increasing emphasis on manufacturing and the rise of white-collar work in the early 20th century, more and more Americans stopped working on the land and began working indoors."

Work happens in other physical configurations. For example, "In Our Communities," where "Americans rely on the efforts of public service workers. From teachers to sanitation workers, from the postman to highway workers, it is difficult to imagine life in communities without their contributions." And those workplaces are used not only "within the bounds of daylight, [and] weather," but "workers moved into an environment where work could take place at any time—day or night."[2] The exhibit came with an introductory video that I played for students after we discussed what work is. Workers were often the most animated when reflecting on the film's presentation on where people worked. With little to no prompting they offered long detailed soliloquies of the places they occupied while working.

Where people work is also a site of contention and struggle. At work power and authority are asserted over the use, treatment, and compensation of labor. Decisions about working conditions, hours, technology, product design, and services are made within a set of structured social relations that unfold in part at the point of production. Where you work then cannot be divorced from the kinds of conflict that are related to employment. Workers often develop a very protective job consciousness that is heightened if the workplace is unionized. In nonunion workplaces employees are classified as "at-will" employees. Except for legal prohibitions based on protected status (e.g., age, disability, race, gender) that have not eliminated workplace discrimination, the employee labors at the will of the employer. Without a union contract, employees can be fired from their job without "just cause" (i.e., a legitimate reason related to job performance or behavior). One student adamantly asserted that "work is a joke without a union." Absent a union agreement and depending on the level of government regulation, the terms and conditions of the work relationship are unilaterally determined and imposed by the employer. Who works, gets access to a job, and is excluded from an occupation is all subject to the discretion allotted to the employer. At work is where most people confront the most "unambiguous and tangible relations of power" in their lives.[3] While mostly working in unionized settings, my students were not oblivious to the power dynamics at work. The site of production, as one worker framed it, is "me doing what I'm told."

Nonetheless, workers sitting in the cab of a dozer, standing on an assembly line, leaning over a wooden joist, digging a hole in the ground, processing an intake form in a state government office, or moving around a classroom acted on and within defined spaces. Despite the employer's legal ownership of the workspace, my students asserted that they did more than occupy and use the jobsite; they modified and created it. The space was initially designed to be used in a particular way, but when interacting within a work environment workers draw their own perceptions of where they produce value. And once modified or created, those spaces formed and housed a worker's life. Whether labor was permanently anchored to a spot or unfolded across the landscape, the space worked in was regenerated by the workers "setting in motion arms and legs, head and hands."[4] In the words of one of my students, "Work is a place of constant change."

In this chapter I will explore seven ways that my students' work shaped a lived understanding of space. First, as a place of action where things get done. Second, as a site where workers authentically exist. Third, as a location to learn and apply skills. Fourth, as a site of enjoyment and reverence. Fifth, as a place of danger. Sixth, as an ideal-typical space. Finally, as a site that obscures. Before going further, however, let me point out an inherent problem that hinders workers' ability to realize how their labor is manifested in the places they encounter.

What work amounts to is a complex bundling of worker engagements with materials, natural resources, equipment, tools, the employer, and other workers in particular settings. The outcome of work is everywhere, but the material outputs (i.e., commodities and services) available for sale in the market or accessible as a public good are not the possession of the worker. What the worker produces belongs to the employer. So do the means of production and importantly, the work site. Workers almost never own where they labor. They spend a lifetime at work. They master the tools of the trade related to their worksite. They typically arrange their workspace. They are responsible for the efficiency of their jobsites. They make the products and provide the services that everyone including themselves consumes and uses. And most often they work alongside one another, or at least have a lot technically in common with other workers. But none of these activities belong to the workers and that potentially sets them adrift from each other and their own labor. The structural conditions that workers experience under capitalism produce what Marx identified as "alienation" or more specifically "alienated labor." This refers to work in which the worker finds no meaning or has no control over it. Working is instead reduced to an activity that belongs to a boss and, from the workers vantage point within the employment relationship, is simply a means to earn a wage. Under these conditions, alienation takes four forms: (1) alienation from the act of production, (2) alienation from the product of labor, (3) alienation from a person's true nature (i.e., "species being"), and (4) alienation of one person from another. In each case a relation that distinguishes human beings is severed, and the worker is separated from an essential element of their own nature.

The rendering of workers from their constituent parts has both an objective and subjective side. Although alienation may be felt, it is not merely a subjective feeling where the worker "does not feel content but is unhappy."[5] It is also an objective structure of experience and activity that organizes work in capitalist society. From this perspective, individuals work under alienated conditions regardless of how they feel about their job. But work can also be psychologically or emotionally estranging. Marx wrote of the worker whose labor "mortifies his body and mind."[6]

Alienation from the state of production and the product of labor bears some relevance to how workers conceptualize their workplace and the community spaces their work has shaped. Both forms are a challenge to how workers understand the spaces that they occupy. Marx described the consequences of alienation for worker identity in the following stark way:

> The less you eat, drink and read books; the less you go to the theatre, the dance hall, the public-house; the less you think, love, theorise, sing, paint, fence, etc., the more you save—the greater becomes your treasure which neither moths nor dust will devour—your capital. The less you are, the more you have; the less you express your own life, the greater is your alienated life—the greater is the store of your estranged being.[7]

Despite the objectively alienating conditions, my students recognized that it is through their work that they integrated themselves into the world. While some workers did have deeply dissatisfying experiences with work, for most of them their subjective feelings were more complex and less unitary. If, for instance, you had a good feeling about what you did and liked the people you worked with, going to work was "fun." But if not, getting paid was the only reason "to be there." Work could be a "retreat" but also a "prison." One student saw the duality in her workplace: "work is freedom yet, incarceration." The nonalienating coexisted with the alienating. Sometimes during the same shift. One day the workplace is a joy to go to; the next it evokes a sigh of resignation. It was always, however, a worker's productive activity that constructed interlocking relationships with their worksites, tools, one another, the labor process, goods and services, the community, and the natural world. The answers to "what work is" reveal that workers are more than passive creatures of their work environment; they are active interpreters and creators of it. Since doing work meant being at work, work was a profoundly important destination. "Work is," as one essayist wrote, "where I go every day."

A Place of Action to Get Things Done

Work is a space where workers went to do things and get things done. Nothing poetic here, just pure function. "Work is action," and "work is getting it done." Work activity was intended to construct useful and durable objects as well as provide services that people needed. According to a worker statement, "Work is building something awesome." A prerequisite for fulfilling the object of the action was a space to act on. Prior to and during the pandemic a minority of workers were able to do their job and not go to their employer's designated workplace. In 2015 roughly one in four workers worked at least a single day at home.[8] Few of those folks then or in 2020–21, however, filled the face-to-face, essential, or frontline occupations that were regularly represented in my class and made up the majority of the labor force. One 2020 estimate found that 37 percent of jobs could be done at home.[9] They were overwhelmingly professional positions. Importantly, many who worked remotely during the coronavirus health crisis, as did teachers, felt safer but acknowledged that virtual work was not the best site for applying their talents.

Conversely, for the hourly employees who had to sell their labor in-person during a pandemic, being in a designated workplace was paramount to keeping their jobs. Failing to be at work was job abandonment. In a twisted manipulation of class status that challenged the concept of "free labor," workers were so "essential" that they were given special dispensations. Some factory workers in Indiana had a dilemma. In March 2020 they were ordered to report to the worksite, but the state had a travel ban to limit the spread of COVID-19. To accommodate workers traveling to work—or to insure they had no excuse keeping them from showing up—firms provided their employees with a letter granting them "priority access and exemption from shelter-in-place requirements, as well as community health support, so they can perform their duties."[10] Workers were told to keep the letters in their cars in case they were stopped while in transit. Here one might say, "Work is a place that supports my family." But only, as is the standard for my working-class students, if done where the employer dictates.

The job happened at construction sites, inside operating rooms, down hotel corridors and preferably in front of white boards. Workers understood the shape, size, and location of their workspace, as well as its expressed use. Sociologist Arthur Stinchcombe refers to this as the job's "formal code." He also describes a "restricted code" that determines how space is modified and used.[11] Worker essays revealed that each of them converted the spaces they utilized whether they applied their trade inside four walls, standing on a ladder, sitting behind a wheel, or in a "big hole in the ground." Workspace had to be arranged so that a worker could act and get the job done.

Their space was organized with utilitarian precision. Tools laid out in an orderly manner, the area meticulously prepped and people assuming their proper stations. Everything where it belongs. Everyone where they need to be. Whether a restaurant, department store, office, or warehouse, working unfolded in relationship to a particularly designed space. Importantly, students stressed that when laid out correctly, where they worked turned them into "a high functioning machine." Many conveyed the idea that the space they worked in became an extension of the themselves. The "jobsite" or "going to work" reflected their identity.

Work was where important life-enhancing events unfolded. The jobsite ensured that "money got made." It was "a place to make money," "for decent wages," and "good benefits." Workers said they went to the factory and office "to earn." While work was something the person did, it was often defined not as an activity but as a space: "Work is where I earn a living," or "my place to make a living." At work, workers earned the wages they needed to buy things that sustained life. Not just for them but, as one student put it, "for my family." Nothing of real value was free. Students were aware that a person could choose not to work. Crime, begging, and relief programs were options. But poverty was debilitating and welfare support minimal and degrading. In America there are no federal constitutional rights to food, clothing, housing, medical care, employment, or education. My students are always surprised about that last one. How can there be no US constitutional right to an education? Shock aside, the education you got was the education you paid for through tuition or property taxes. And the ability to pay in either case came from your job or capital earnings. Which is why a student declared it was important that work was "a place where I make money."

Work was serious. The jobsite was too. Being at the workplace provided individuals with an opportunity to put in "a full day's work." No one treated their worksite dismissively. Workers described a multitude of tasks they executed on the job. The labor process for many was very mechanistic. Tasks were often repetitively performed. Workers stressed that doing things right required doing it the right way every time. Repetitive was not the equivalent of tedious. Work is "doing a good job each time." Being "at work" meant abiding by rules and norms. The job was structured so that work could be done by anyone properly trained. It wasn't alchemy. Nor was it strictly paint by numbers. Work, as we will see, was also a creative act. In fact, in talking about their jobs my students often used the words *work*, *labor*, and *creativity* interchangeably. Activity could become art within the spatial boundaries of the job. "Work is a place for creativity."

Work and, more to the point, the workspace, did come with certain prescriptions. A plumber arriving at a jobsite had certain well-defined steps that had to be completed in proper order. When finishing the job machine operators were required to adhere to rigorous "tag out" procedures. Teachers had a lesson plan and a curriculum to follow. Most actually disliked the proscribed nature of the job. Teaching for them had become too mechanistic. Too dictated. Assembly line workers followed a series of actions that were interdependent with other actions. Yes, the job could get monotonous, but work is "being disciplined and baking the donuts."

Space to my students was not randomly arranged. Work taught them that space was a scientific equation designed to maximize production. The spaces were purposeful. And the purpose was determined by the employer. Jobsites were designed to be functional. That functionality raised efficiency. It also reduced workers to costs of production. Firefighters and home care childcare workers alike knew that they were part of the employer's crude economic calculation. How to get the most work done, and create the most value with the fewest workers? Or as one student put it, work is "figuring out how to pay less." The endemic pressure to do more work with and for less was a sobering hedge against workers seeing their places of employment as friendly confines or neutral laboratories. Instead, they understood that the spaces they worked in were necessary "profit surfaces" arranged to generate wealth and income. Work climate and environment could be good, but the workplace was still a fulfillment center. Only the orders differed.

A Place of Being

Nearly every worker could easily tag their labor to locations. No one worked just construction or in manufacturing. But instead, geography mattered. Take those working in or near Chicago. Workers labored "downtown," "on the pier," "the blue line," "O'Hare," "back of the yards," "McCormack Place," "Halsted and Archer," in the "west loop" and on the "roads of Chicagoland." Teachers worked at Walter Payton High School, nurses at Stroger's Hospital, musicians at the Goodman Theater. They also worked in suburban villages and neighborhoods all around the state. Some were "tri-state" employees, others were "collar county" and still some, "downstate." There were those who worked in "vast open green spaces," "along the side of the road," and "underground in a mine." Each space was a notable location and a node within the geography of labor. Workers could name check something unique about where they worked. It was as if the shorthand reference to place elevated their work from human activity to something instantly recognized and valued. Like being at Wrigley field during the Cubs World Series run or in Grant Park when Barack Obama first stepped onto the world stage as America's first Black President. Workers in one class were ebullient in explaining how Chicago's whimsical "Cloud Gate" sculpture in Millennium Park was constructed. Known as the "Bean" because of its kidney bean shape, Chicago iron workers welded and polished the 168 steel panels into a seamless finish on the site of the iconic piece.[12] Welding wasn't a glamorous job but using a blow torch on the "Bean" was putting an unmistakable property stake in the ground.

The workplace was familiar territory and took on human characteristics. Workers spoke about their jobsites in anthropomorphic terms. The office could be "tense," "playful," and "relaxed." Construction sites were "challenging" and "dangerous." Schools felt "inviting," "warm," "chaotic," and "exuberant." Factories and warehouses were "stressful," "depressing," "lacking personality," and "mean." Space at work could be a refuge—"Where I go to find meaning." It could also be a confinement. While work is "not supposed to be a jail," it could be "a punishment for not having money." The workplace could be intimate ("me and my brothers and sisters") or socially distanced ("nothing but me making money"). A student needed eight words, but the essay claimed that work added up to "more than a place to collect a paycheck."

Workers also took pride in how their labor infused the spaces they worked with meaning. A housekeeper was responsible for the four-star rating a hotel received, a United Parcel Service driver embodied the reputation of the firm, an iron worker made the awe-inspiring building that framed the skyline. Where they worked is also where the workers fused their identity with what they made. When a building went up, electricians became a part of the structure. When a student learned to read, the teacher's instruction was embedded in the letters the child learned. The world the workers made was proof of their salience. Every space bore their mark. A worker's presence was undeniable if most often ignored. Work not only gave birth to places appropriated by consumers and citizens but it also provided a site for workers to be fully human. In creating the conditions for living authentically, it was wholistically "a place of empowerment."

At work my students participated in an activity that was the primary means through which they could express and develop their intellectual, physical, and emotional capacities. In other words, it was at work that they could think, conceptualize, create, problem solve, and build relationships. Work is "a place where I have agency" and "a chance to live well." The job enabled them to use the powers that Marx claimed was innate to their "species being." Workers were not animals or machines. They were not social security numbers, digits on the expense side of a ledger or the means of production. The worksite needed to be more than a means to stay alive. It had to provide a person with an opportunity to exercise their full humanity. Numerous students realized the same thing. Work was a "place to build a life." When work equated with being treated respectfully, it was not alienating. However, when work was being sentenced to "years of hard labor, then death" it was thoroughly alienating.

As a kid I recall that my parents would take me and my three brothers to a restaurant in downtown Struthers, a working-class town where my dad still lives. The Wagon Wheel was a favorite and had a reputation for serving a good cheeseburger. After dinner my dad had a routine that I'm not sure my mother appreciated. He would walk me and my brothers up real close to the train tracks. Freight trains would rumble day and night through Struthers along the Mahoning Valley River. At least they did during good economic times. Train cars would bring tons of coal into the mills that lined the river and export finished steel products on the way out. As the long flatbeds piled up with steel pipe charged through town, the sound of the metal banging and the bouncing railroad ties made a thunderous roar.

It must have worried my mom a bit that we seemed to be standing perilously close to the tracks. In truth, we were never too close to get hurt, but we were close enough for what my dad had in mind. With each passing car he would point to some spot at the end of the pipe and proclaim, "I made that, I made that" over and over again. Now, the trains went by too quickly for any of us to see what his finger was pointing to. But he saw. On the end of each pipe was a stamp that indicated it had come from his mill. My father rarely showed much overt pride for his work. In this instance however he knew that his labor had "congealed in an object" and contrary to Marx's fear that once objectified in his or her labor the worker would lose a sense of reality, my dad was never more aware of what was true in his life.[13] Going to the mill was not a calling or an act of noble sacrifice; it was a tough dirty job that paid the mortgage and kept food on the table. But here, a more profound quality in work can be found.

The steel company had family appreciation days at the mill where workers could bring their kids and tour the property. Never my father. The first time I set foot in a steel mill was when I was earning a paycheck from it. To my dad, the workplace deserved respect, but was not worthy of personal celebration. Except when he stuck his swollen, scarred finger at that traveling pipe. Then he had a pride of place. For a fleeting moment what came from Republic Steel was beautiful enough to share with his sons. The pipe, it seemed, was an expression of my dad's life. I imagine his satisfaction was comparable to what one student meant when she explained that work was a place for "turning labor into something good."

In my students' interpretations, the workplace held the "process of making worthwhile things" by extracting, manufacturing, and converting things without value into something of value. Work was responsible for the built environment and the people who inhabited the community. Each person and each thing held "within itself a piece of an interconnected web of production."[14] Workers are most aware of their individual agency at the point of production. Whether in a classroom or boiler room, they act on the job; it is where they use their basic human power. In contrast, the employer and consumer see the workers as abstractions. Except for those in the caring professions, the worker at work and at the point of his or her highest achievement is treated one-dimensionally. They are human bodies compelled to work and to keep them working under capitalism they are converted into "waged bodies." From the employer's side workers are reduced to labor costs. But from the workers' vantage point the workplace is the site of creative human actions that produce the material world and nurture community. It is "*donde todo el mundo se conecta* (where everyone connects)."

Workers know that the job, and particularly where they do it, is the wellspring of a purposeful life. That's why when asked about what work is, workers said, "a place you create your legacy." Imagine a place that embodies a life's work passed down from one generation to the next. A space where a worker accumulates a record of achievement. The post office, the department store, the construction site, and the school were not merely places of economic exchange; they were repositories of good works. Workers became identified with where they worked as much as by the job they held. It was "where you leave your mark."

The workplace of course never legally belonged to the workers, but in listening to my students talk about their employment, something intriguing emerged. Most workers spoke as if they had some ownership rights to the workplace. They shared a sense of property entitlement. Workers never spoke about the jobsite as an alien territory. How could it be? It was "where I go every day." Workers were not formally in charge of the office, store, or bus depot, but they described workspaces that were so extensively used that they conceived of the property as their possession. By their accounting, time and utilitarian purpose conveyed some rights to decide how the worksite was to be appropriated. It was a property entitlement born not of a legal deed, nor a bill of sale or registration, but from productive use.

The memory of past work and where it happened was particularly strong. Workers could easily recall the details of past jobs. Many had been doing paid labor since they were kids. The average student had five paid jobs, while many had seven or eight. Many had more than a dozen. One, by age fifty-five, had been paid to do twenty-four jobs. The nature of the work, where they did it, what they were paid, and how the work made them feel were all live sensations. A paper route was chronicled as vividly as the job they currently held. Bad jobs were readily revisited. Working nonunion jobs really left a scar. I repeatedly heard that work is "bad if its non-union." Students excavated every old job from the past, but none of what they surfaced was merely history. Work simultaneously eroded the body and left enduring signs of the individual's presence. For some workers the workplace conjured up more than self-awareness. One essay delivered an emotional wallop. It made me proudly aware of the evocative quality of my teaching: "Work is where I'm reminded of my father." My classrooms are vastly different from the spaces where my parents sold their time, but when I stand before a class of workers I feel as if my mom's and dad's labors are alive.

While workers' current job tenure varied substantially, it was the exception for a student to describe their work as ephemeral. Even six months on the job were enough to leave a permanent impression and expectation. Work is "a place to create a future." The jobsite was "where you built a better future." And students with longer terms of employment in an industry or occupation hung onto what previous work had accomplished. "Work is an opportunity to grow." For younger workers it is also "a place to grow and mature." Students reflected on the alchemy the workplace produced. It "made my family possible." To them, work was "me spending my best years digging." Digging, painting, driving, serving, nursing, teaching, and rigging all occurred on the job at some jobsite. Work is "where and how we exist." Place and activity are a powerful determinate of personal identity. It's, as one student said, where "work made me, me." And in return another said, "Work is a place where I am respected." The workplace is not simply a receptacle for intentional activity ("where I pour my life into") and profit making. Space brought people together and forged bonds. "Work is where friends are made" and a "place to see friends." It also created opportunities for social judgement and self-definition. Few, if any, of my students performed the tasks they did as electricians, carpenters, and truck drivers in isolation. They labored in the company of electricians, carpenters, and truck drivers. It was on the job where "people grow their skills together." Work consequently was a social act, and the jobsite was "where value is determined by others," meaning by people like you. Work was interdependent with the space for doing it in. One required the other. Workers forgot neither. Nor did workers have any illusion that "work is where you have to go."

As a Place to Learn

On the job was where a worker learned to be a carpenter, a clerk, a bus driver, a firefighter, and a cook. It was a "place to become more educated" and where "you get an education" and "equip people with knowledge." Workers understood that their jobs required general and specialized knowledge. Every job tapped into a deep reservoir of intellectual skills. Workers in my classes objected to the idea that they were not "smart" or that any job was "unskilled" or "low skilled." No job was without skills. In fact, the intelligence embedded in the work done by my non-college-educated, hourly wage "blue collars" students, is undervalued because it's largely unseen.[15] Work unfolds in spaces that are both in the "front" and the "back" regions of our lives.[16] Most of our labors, though, happen "backstage" out of site of the consumer or public. A patron sees the waiter carrying a tray of food, but the kitchen where the meals are prepared is hidden. The UPS or Amazon driver drops packages at our doors, but we never catch site of the multitude of complex actions and decisions the driver must perform before ever stepping foot out of the truck. To our and the worker's disadvantage, we miss a lot. By concealing where much of the work is done, the skill of the worker gets dichotomously defined as either the kind that "make(s) a good impression" or is "unimpressive-looking labor."[17] What's not viewed is not appreciated and, hence, called "low skill," warranting minimal societal respect. In this way, because of where some of the labor happens, the aspect of work that people directly engaged with becomes a "performance" to the person benefiting from the labor. Affinity for the millions of folks whose viewed labor is "unimpressive" is difficult when so much of their labor is spatially oriented. Even the college-educated labor done by nurses and teachers is mostly invisible to the community. Author Mike Rose laments that our cultural iconography celebrates the "muscled arm, sleeve rolled tight against biceps, but no image that links hand and brain."[18] He dissects the false divide of work into "neck down" and "neck up" occupations.

It's important to ask, What works? I put the question before my students, and they offered clues in their answers. "Work is hard on the body." "Work is frustrating." "Work is mentally challenging." "Work is enjoyable with the right mind set." It was self-evident to them; they labored with their bodies, minds, and emotions. All work involves mental processes, and the interplay of hand and brain, body and mind, thought and emotions signifies substantial intellectual capacity. Antonio Gramsci asserted that "one cannot speak of nonintellectuals, because nonintellectuals do not exist. . . . There is no human activity from which every form of intellectual participation can be excluded: homo faber cannot be separated from homo sapiens."[19] In *Zen and the Art of Motorcycle Maintenance* author Robert Pirsig beautifully lays out the relationship between the mind and parts of a bike: "John looks at the motorcycle and he sees steel in various shapes and has negative feelings about these steel shapes and turns off the whole thing. I look at the shapes of the steel now and I see ideas. He thinks I'm working on parts. I'm working on concepts."[20]

Labor forms an indivisible cognitive and physical unity. "Work is where your thoughts guide your achievements." The assertion of body and mind in the harmonious use of a hammer, dry erase marker or washcloth amounts to what Aristotle referred to as "instruments of instruments." It is an evocative phrase that places the workers intentional action as the first cause of all production processes. No medium uses itself. It takes a conscious and skilled actor to get work done. Here is an example of the extensive intellectual and technical skills one group of two dozen support staff, mostly women, exercised across multiple departments:

> Effectively communicate with diverse groups of people, in person and written form; have good social-emotional awareness; have good editing skills; good relationship building skills between depts; positive attitude; have artistic skills; producing high quality presentation binders, flyers, workshop packets, forms; have good oral communication skills: use various programs, including database, Microsoft office suite, Windows, Zoom, Bluejeans, Dropbox, Teams, Sharepoint, Adobe, copiers, digital platforms;

mechanical skills; run and maintain operation of machines, including computers, printers, copiers, postage meters, folding machines; good research skills; search for materials and sources for members, vendors, products; organize complex activities for members, including new member materials, meetings, workshops, training, and conventions; works independently with minimal supervision, responsible for routine decisions, manage office operations in absence of professional staff and management, schedule building and equipment repairs, maintenance, and inspections; express and develop new ideas and suggestions; handle multiple tasks/projects simultaneously; organizational skills and dedication to complete projects in a timely manner.

The list of skills required for folks officially classified as "support" undermines the conventional dichotomy between skilled and nonskilled jobs. It is an error of logic to claim that any work could be done without any skills, and even "low-skilled" is a nonsensical designation. Every job if dissected closely enough would reveal a host of mental and physical calculations and manipulations. In an essay drawn from his book *Shop Class as Soulcraft: An Inquiry Into the Value of Work*, Matthew Crawford notes the cognitive aspect of manual labor: "The physical circumstances of the jobs performed by carpenters, plumbers, and auto mechanics vary too much for them to be executed by idiots; they require circumspection and adaptability."[21] As a kid I recall my parents pointing out how important it was every time the "garbage man" showed up outside our home. Trash hauling is unappealing to many people. The work literally stinks. However, it's essential to a community's health to keep germs from spreading that the work be consistently and well done. But on average because the job is defined as "low skilled" it only pays about $40,000 a year. Childcare providers watch and take care of society's most precious form of human life—young children. PreK teachers educate our most vulnerable people. And yet these teachers are paid—even with a college degree—roughly in the mid-$30,000s, while the banker who takes care of money he or she hasn't earned is rewarded with millions.

The reality is that skill labels are ideological terms meant to justify creating an elaborate occupational scale of worth. Conventionally we use education levels and intellectual versus physical labor as proxies for what a job is worth. The more years of education a position requires the greater a job is worth, even if the link between the two is tenuous at best.[22] Concurrently, the more advanced and complex the thinking required to perform the task, the greater the value of the labor. However, job skill designations have never been a purely technical assessment. A job doesn't get a skill label through the application of some objective metrics. Instead, skill is socially constructed.

Labor unions, employers and political parties contest and determine how skill is defined and more importantly, who has the power to define it.[23] The final calculation will change based on the relative power relationship among workers, capital, and the state. Over the past forty years as unions lost influence employers have had the near unfettered means to "fissure" the workplace and stratify employment in ways that legitimate the exploitation of labor by gender, race, immigration status, and disability. Writing primarily about the exploitation of immigrant labor but with implications for workplaces everywhere, Professor Natasha Iskander asserts that skill distinctions serve the material interests of capital. To be coded as "unskilled" in a market economy limits a person's individual freedom, weakens his or her political rights, and reduces a worker to a body with little imagination and desire.[24] In part, the post-pandemic exodus of millions of workers from low quality jobs was a mass attempt to reconstruct the value of labor.

In thinking about where work is done, we could use a different measure of skill and value. Instead of relying on abstract metrics to determine a scale of job worthiness, all workspaces should be appreciated and treated as locations that enable workers to learn how to make things, serve others, problem solve, construct relationships, and acquire new talents. As one of my students said, "Work is where I show my abilities" and "where you can learn to help others." It is according to my students, an "educational place for knowledge" and deserves to be treated with high regard. A close examination of the skills inventory for nearly all jobs would convincingly argue for breaking the artificial link between skill, value, and compensation. No matter the technical job components, workers recognize that to some degree "work is where you create your worth."

Much like the support staff, all my students viewed the space that housed their work as a "training ground for the future." Workers talked about their workspace in multiple ways, but one reoccurring idea was that the jobsite was a "school of hard knocks." It was as much a school for "completing challenging tasks" as an exchange of labor for money. Work creates the complex setting for "life's natural schooling" to unfold. It is "where I come to learn." A familiar "place to learn every day." And the learning came from multiple sources. Apprentice construction operators took direction from more experienced operators. Senior, tenured teachers mentored junior instructors. Catering was a trade handed down from one lead employee to a novice worker. At work you participated in and perpetuated a "tradition of service." Worksites were where workers "stand on the shoulders of giants." The spaces that workers occupied were classrooms where the job was made real. It was where you "could improve your skills," "master your craft," and be exposed to "constant training to better yourself." Developing the craft was a prerequisite to unlocking the workspace's potential in "putting skills to use." My students liked "solving problems," "figuring things out," "diagnosing," and "having a say." The work that unfolded in some workspaces was "always a welcomed challenge." One worker used alliteration to emphasize the subtext of the intellectual labor unfolding at work: "Work is a puzzle of progression." Unfortunately, too few jobs allow workers to do work that is "good for [the] mind." Only between roughly a third and 40 percent of workers equivalent to the ones in my class, report that they "take part in decisions" on the job.[25]

Too many workers are treated like the early twentieth-century steelworker Schmidt in Frederick Winslow Taylor's *The Principles of Scientific Management*. According to Taylor, Schmidt was an employee at the Bethlehem Steel mill and became part of Taylor's experiment to design jobs so that production was maximized, and workers become pliant subjects of management.[26] It was Taylor's belief that workers were "lazy" and naturally looked to evade hard work. Therefore, the best approach is to reduce the jobs to a series of simple directed steps. In Schmidt's case that involved carrying one-hundred-pound "pig" irons. No thinking is required. Do what you're told, and you'll even make more money. Taylor is dismissive and insulting toward the good-natured Schmidt. He excuses this treatment by explaining that with this "type of an ox . . . a man so stupid that he was unfitted to do most kinds of laboring work" it was perfectly appropriate to be verbally harsh.[27] The notion that workers are subhuman has justifiably angered labor union leaders for centuries. In 1984 United Farm Worker President Cesar Chavez gave a speech calling out the treatment of agricultural workers: "Farm workers are not beasts of burden to be used and discarded."[28]

A corollary attitude was that workers were cognitively and morally on par with children and needed to be treated accordingly. Consider Henry Ford's startling offer in 1914 of five dollars a day to work on his assembly line. The five-dollar-a-day rate wasn't guaranteed, but mostly a variable bonus payment with intrusive conditions. The bonus came with character requirements and was enforced by the company's dystopian sounding "Sociological Department." This internal group of inspectors would visit the employees' homes to ensure that they were "avoiding social ills such as gambling and drinking." Workers also had to learn English, and recent immigrants were required to attend classes to become Ford's version of "Americanized." Women were only eligible for the bonus if they were single and supporting a family. Men, conversely, were not "eligible if their wives worked outside the home."[29] In 1893 the first president of the American Federation of Labor, Samuel Gompers, gave a speech titled "What Does Labor Want?" He pointed out that it wasn't just technical work requirements that lead to differing views and treatments of workers and owners: "The separation between the capitalistic class and the laboring mass is not so much a difference in industrial rank as it is a difference in social status, placing the laborers in a position involving a degradation of mind and body."[30] Sadly, workers told me that a lot of work is this way or would be this way if the employer could get away with Schmidt-like abuse.

Laborers eagerly pointed out all the different trades they performed and how skilled they really were. Plumbers described the elaborate training and tests that had to be mastered to be licensed in Chicago and the state. And steelworkers from Burns Harbor, Indiana, broke down the intricate thinking process of tapping an open heart and doing maintenance on coke ovens. Another student detailed the skill required to operate a caster crane in Granite City, Illinois. Whether the jobsite was an office, hospital, commercial building, school, sewer, hotel room or train station it "allowed one to put the impress of mind and skill on the material world."[31] Treating manual labor of any kind as "intellectually substandard" was at worst a denial of the person as a human being and at best terribly dismissive of the workers' minds.[32] Workers made clear that work itself was always an opportunity to create, build, assemble and disassemble, repair, and nurture. It provided, according to many essays, "a place to gain new skills" and to "perform a skill." The workplace was a "continuous learning exercise" where people "*forman metas y habilidades* (form goals and skills)." Jobsites were spaces to personally grow and to, as one student put it, "better myself." Another said, "[It is at work where I can put] my profession in action."

Nearly without exception, my students were continuously learning their trade, and that meant acquiring new skills and adapting to new technology. Workers then held to a "toolbox ideology" where knowledge and use of appropriate technology were critical to job performance. The absence of the right equipment was scorned. My favorite expression from a worker about a jobsite that was considered outdated was "work is a time capsule of the 70s." To every worker, mastery of the tools and procedures meant that work was "doing the job well every time." Herbert Applebaum underscored how the use of tools signified a construction worker's skills that can equally be applied to workers in every occupation: "the tools themselves, how they are used, when they are used, and how they are taken care of, are important indicators of skill and expertise."[33] The tools of a worker reflect the credentials and legitimacy of the worker to be in her workspace.

For some workers that space moved and changed periodically. The spatial frame of reference wasn't fixed and created a chance to experience work for good or bad as "doing something different every day." Housekeepers are employed by different hotel chains, glazers worked on different construction sites, and some factory workers rotate through different parts of a plant. Bus drivers literally propel their workspaces "moving the city forward." Taxi drivers navigate urban landscapes from behind a steering column. An excavation laborer digs trenches for sewers, hauling dirt. Many laborers literally do their work in deep holes in the ground spread across urban and suburban landscapes. No matter the place, work taught you how to solve problems, work with others, contend with difficult people, keep to a schedule, learn discipline and be responsible. Work nearly always involves interactions with other workers. Therefore, laboring, to my students, meant "learning and passing knowledge along." The jobsite provided opportunities for large to "small achievements every day." And most of all, it was while at work that you were, as one student put it, "earning your share." The jobsite operated as a generator for determining what workers were owed for their labor and a place to raise their self-worth by evolving as human beings.

As a Place of Enjoyment and Reverence

The place of employment fulfilled technical and extrinsic purposes, but there was more going on. Being at work could also be pleasurable, even reverential. Jobsites for some workers were "a fun place to be." One student ignored the word limit but offered a rich imagery of his workspace. He said, "[work is] where I get to be the kid in the sandbox, but with a 30-ton machine." Here space was compared to a playground where instead of a plastic shovel the worker operated powerful equipment made from iron and steel. It was where the worker could earn a living but have some fun doing it. The playground equipment associated with emotional satisfaction could even be transported outside of the workspace and still convey a sense of place. International Union of Operating Engineers Local 150 has a nearly one-hundred-year-old Bucyrus-Erie steam shovel stationed in front of its union hall in Countryside, Illinois. It is on a raised platform alongside part of US Route 66. Amazingly, the shovel is still operative. The machine can run on compressed air or wood and coal. On May 19, 2021, the city of Countryside celebrated its first "Steam Shovel Day" where operators and elementary school kids ran the machine. Watching the machine shovel move and the joy on the kids' and adults' faces left little doubt that the location where this work is done, can be a site of accomplishment and even pleasure.

For some, a pleasurable workplace inverts the classic dichotomy between work and a personal nonwork life. Under these conditions the job can be a refuge. One student said, "Work is a place to enjoy my life." Ideally, work should make you feel good and be a "place you enjoy going." A lot of my students did express satisfaction with their work. They liked what they did for a living and were exuberant in talking about their jobs. Some workers went so far as to write that "work is play." The workplace could be "like a circus" with all the confounding, unexpected, risky, and delightful turn of events. Workers did difficult jobs but regularly sought out "pleasures in the exercise of their energies."[34] Many expressed an appreciation for how going to work could be more than earning a living. When I asked students how many of them took comfort from more than the extrinsic rewards of their jobs, nearly everyone answered in the affirmative. For example, workers wrote, "Work is not hard if you love it." They also said "[It is] fun if you like your job." Others scribbled, "Work is a pleasure to do each day." There were also students who made it clear that whether going to work was enjoyable or not depended on the workers' state of mind: "Work is what you make it." Somewhat surprisingly, the level of occupational difficulty or working conditions had little correlation to whether a worker spoke approvingly about their job. Firefighters as well as cashiers had good things to say about what they did for a living. To some the supermarket was as sacred as the firehouse was to others. Now, importantly, that attitude was rarely shared about the employer. Workers were connected to the work, and they felt some entitlement and a great deal of pride about the site of that labor. But how the employer was defined was dependent on how the workers were treated.

In *Steelworker Alley* I wrote about how my father and his workmates transformed their workspaces into miniversions of their private lives. The mill workers fashioned their lockers with family images, cooking utensils, and books. They played dice and card games, told jokes, discussed current events, reviewed sports scores, and shared kids' activities and family tribulations during down periods. My students described workspaces adorned with plants, framed photos, personal mementos, helmet stickers, and flags. In some cases music provided the background soundtrack as workers performed their tasks. Listening to my students talk about where they work, I realized the elaborate ways that they infused their personalities into the work. The space was owned by someone else, but it was partially appropriated by each worker to make it more tolerable and less just somewhere they had to be. More like home.

Unmistakably, the spaces were primarily used for earning a living, but workers spent so much time on the job that many felt compelled to shape their workspaces into something a bit more personal, tolerable, and familiar. Work is, one student said, "more home to me than home." And another called it a "home away from home." Work is even "sometimes an outlet from home." Home and work have conventionally been conceived as separate spheres fulfilling different functions. The workplace was where unattached strangers congregated for the purpose of economic production. As a site of production, it was driven by economic transactions between workers, managers, and owners. Employment was ruled by the logic and force of the market and state. The job was where people, as workers, were formed. Essays that read "Work is where/or how I learned to be a [fill in the missing occupation]" expressed the formative process and site of assuming a worker identity. My father, mother, and countless students were not born as the means of production. That leveling, homogenizing transformation occurred when they punched a time clock in a factory or swiped a key fob to enter a school. Before and after that moment, workers were all the glorious shades of people they chose to be or due to life's circumstances had become.

Work was analogous to a cloak the person put on when entering a defined space that was later stripped off once leaving the premises. It was at home, however, shorn of the work uniform, where the worker was authentic and fully an autonomous and unique individual. As part of the household the person was surrounded by family. It was a domestic domain meant to nourish personal growth and wellbeing. Home has also been ideally thought of as where a person replenishes from the workday and found the means to reproduce what was necessary to go back to work the next day. It was a space of social reproduction supported by the unpaid labor of cooking, cleaning, educating, nursing, child-rearing, and loving. In my male workers' cases, the unpaid home-based labor was mostly done by a female partner, even when that partner was both worker and reproducer.

The female workers in my class did double duty. They were working in factories, driving school buses, cleaning hotel rooms, coordinating interoffice work, helping special education students in schools, and doing the bulk of household labor. Married or partnered students, regardless of age, noted that work was mostly gendered at home. The linguistic differences in how they described home and work belied an interesting convergence. Comments about the household and kids' activities revealed parents dividing labor along gender lines. Dad volunteered for athletics, mom for dance. Mom prepared dinner; dad fixed the garage opener. Both tried to make doctor and school appointments, but mom usually did. Workspace, however, never was referred to in gendered terms. The worksite took on anthropomorphic characteristics, but female and male workers used the same adjectives, nouns, and verbs. A universalized described job environment in no way assumes the absence of gender discrimination or harassment in labor relations. Union contracts should be intolerant of any forms of discrimination, but work environments, like construction sites that typically include few women, are often uncomfortable for women at best and threatening at worst. However, women as well as men who share that workspace by their own accounting come to appropriate and appreciate the space in very similar ways.

Historical and sociological scholarship abounds on the gendered evolution of the workplace and home. Regardless of the worker's gender, many workers seemed to agree with Professor Arlie Hochschild that "home had become work and work had become home."[35] A number of my students acknowledged, "Work is a second home" and "where my second family lives." The workplace was both a site of production and reproduction for workers. Products and services flowed from human labor and personal and social identities were formed at work. The spaces where workers "earned and learned" amounted to something greater than what the boss took as tribute and was consumed in the marketplace. And despite the exchange-value of a work-for-pay system, the jobsite did take on the personalities of the worker.

A job-home nexus wasn't all about personifying the workspace. Workers also, to the extent the situation allowed, designed their workspaces so they could better do their job. Take, for instance, my wife Lynn. She was an eighth-grade literacy teacher for thirty years. She taught kids to read and write. Her plan to help students learn to love reading and become better writers involved turning the classroom into a wonderous, whimsical place. Lynn substituted big cushy pillows and rugs for rigid chairs and cold tile and tabletop lamps with colorful homemade shades for overhead fluorescent bulbs. She had an old, upholstered rocking chair at the front of the room where kids could sit and read. She even had a dressed-up mannequin of a woman to accompany reading and writing moments. On the classroom walls Lynn stenciled inspirational sayings. One of her students' favorite sayings was taken from the movie *Transformers*, spoken by the character Optimus Prime: "The seeds of the future lie buried in the past."[36] Lynn's classroom embodied, like other workspaces, a bit of the divine.

A few workers thought of their work or workspaces in overtly religious ways. "Work is a blessing." "Work is a gift from God." "Work is where I do God's will." Most of my students acknowledged a belief in a deity but only a tiny fraction attended formal religious services or read a holy book. A few even referred to work as an eternal form of damnation caused by impious actions. One worker exceeded the six-word limit, but the essay expressed one traditional biblical view of work's origin: "Work is punishment for sin in the garden of Eden." An alternative religious interpretation was that "work is good for the soul." What no worker ever expressed was the idea that the workplace was a kind of tabernacle where, by working hard, a person would be blessed by God with the joys of capitalism. Nonetheless, something of a secularized faith purveyed how my students referred to their work and worksite. Every worker was appreciative of having a job to go to and some saw it as a sign of divine fortune. The syntax is inexact, but we know instantly what this essay's writer meant: "Work is what allows me to be providential." While there was little hint of formal religiosity in workers expressions about their jobs, there was an unmistakable sense of the sacred.

My dad said he believed in God, but except for parish-sponsored fish fry dinners on Friday nights and holy days like Christmas and Easter, he never regularly went to church. Mom on the other hand, held to a fervent belief in a loving God. She attended Mass and occasionally read the Bible. Neither activity, however, best explained her faith. I learned what really lay within her spiritual nature when I began to question my own beliefs. In college I began to look for answers for why my working-class parents struggled to provide for four boys. Speaking with my mom was part of my quest for answers. We spoke a lot about how arduous it was to take care of the family on her and my dad's modest earnings. She wasn't complaining, you understand. She was trying to explain to me certain realities. Unless you had a college education or were the child of a rich parent who owned a profitable business or commercial property, you were going to have to work a lot to make a good life. There were several notable experiences that mom shared in her storytelling. Dad was laid off a lot. My mom worked several different jobs. There were physical illnesses. My mom had to buy cheap cuts of meat and cook lots of potatoes because they were the least expensive ways to feed growing sons. All these details figured into a survival story.

Feeding the family featured prominently in my mom's accounts. It did also in what my students shared. While work's purpose is more directly explored in chapter 4, recognizing the transitive role of the workspace in providing the means to sustain life is illustrative of why work is as much a destination as a purposeful action. "Work is putting food on the table." Or work is, one student said, simply "feeding my family." One student viewed labor metaphorically as "my breadmaker." No single specific action verb was used more often by workers to define their work experience than "to feed." One essay even equated the English predicate expressing action and being with labor: "Work is a verb for food." Making food available served literally as well as metaphorically as the most evocative reason why a person had to labor. The use of "feed" and "feeding" appeared to be primal in how workers defended the work they did. According to Marx, "All labor is originally first directed towards the appropriation and production of food."[37] You squelched hunger, and then you could get on to satisfying the higher order needs on Maslow's pyramid.

Food acquisition also symbolized how workers psychologically and morally purposed their work. Feeding was biologically necessary, and it also marked the worker as a responsible provider. Through productive action the individual, family, and nation were fed. The workers were also reproduced and prepped to live freely with every meal. "In general," according to Marx, "people cannot be liberated as long as they are unable to obtain food and drink, housing and clothing in adequate quality and quantity."[38] Nourishing the body and brain is unquestionably a reason for working. Talking about food provisions may appear to be only tangentially connected to corporeal-spatial dimensions of work. In my working-class upbringing, putting food on the table was an act of grace holding literal and symbolic importance. I should add that my growing up also featured a healthy dose of Catholicism. The symbolic significance of "being fed" was regularly dramatized through the act of our family receiving communion at every Sunday worship service. The ritual of going to church to consume the blessing conveyed by swallowing a vanilla wafer was similar to my parents going to work and bringing groceries home. Just as the communion service fed the soul, so too did work nourish the body. In both cases a bit of the divine mixed with the mundane. As two student essays put it, "Work is required for the soul," and "Work is applying the gift God gave you." The relationship between work and sustenance was so prominent that it underscored the sacred quality of the workspace.

Reading my students' words triggered a memory of the most prominent story my mother told me about what being working class would require. During periods when dad was not working due to slowdowns or strikes, my parents would supplement the family diet by driving into the nearby countryside where the Amish grew potatoes. As the Amish farmers harvested potatoes and loaded them onto pickup trucks, many would be left behind on the ground. Mom and dad and others looking to extend the food budget would follow on foot behind the farmers and collect the discarded potatoes in baskets. The Amish never objected to sharing their bounty. Many of the potato skins were a little green—mom suspected that's why the farmers never minded leaving them to others—but after cleaning and peeling they were good enough to boil, bake or fry. And to feed four boys, my mom cooked potatoes every way she knew nearly every day.

There were occasions when those free potatoes were an exceptional gift to the family's wellbeing. One whole year stood out in my catechism about the relationship between basic human provisions and having a job to go to. In 1959 the steelworkers' union went on strike. The mills stayed closed for 116 days. Company greed caused my family to lose our first home. With it went a big yard, a dog, and a basement the size of a sports arena. At least that's how large it looked to a four-year-old kid. Before moving into our first home my mom, my dad, and I lived with my father's parents, so we packed things up, sold the new place and went back to live with dad's folks. It would mean less independence for a while, but at least the rhythm of life wouldn't be disturbed. Both my grandfathers were steelworkers, although they did not work in the same mill. There were many mill and manufacturing spaces dotting the Youngstown area landscape, which collectively consumed thousands of human lives. Boarding with the grandparents did have its delights. At night I could look out the bedroom window and marvel at the colors and sounds exploding against the dark sky as the mill furnaces poured out "heats" of molten steel. Fiery gases rising into the air painted a heavenly stained-glass window for a kid to admire. In the morning I'd wake up to grandma's warm homemade Italian baked bread. Butter was meant to melt on the fresh loaves that were lovingly pulled from the oven. Nonetheless, later in life I concluded that a lost home and insecurity were unfair. My mom and dad worked relentlessly, but they would be homeless if not for another steel-working union family.

Thinking about the experience of losing a home or being forced to rely on grandparents for shelter and extended periods of reduced family income fed intense discussions about God's existence between me and my mom. In responding to my own doubts—which bothered her terribly—about either an all-powerful or all-loving God, she urgently interjected a single personal religious belief. "Bobby," she began—it was always the intimate version of my name when she wanted to reach my heart or in this case my soul. "Bobby, I don't care what you believe in, but you have to believe in something." Mom didn't preach a dogma. Believing didn't require sacraments, prayers, services, or commandments. While she believed in a God and a church, her faith was a spirituality born of attachment to a stronger metaphysical force or cause. Something more than me. Such a faith, she explained, would sustain me during troublesome times and comfort her.

To enjoy work it was important that the jobsite was respected and treated reverently. Prepping a job by laying out tools, donning a uniform, reviewing a safety checklist before taking a truck out of the depot, completing a sequence of steps at each rail stop, or arriving thirty minutes early to set up a classroom were all examples of workers paying homage to where they applied their trades. Below is one Indiana aluminum factory worker's detailed, careful, step-by-step, reverential preparation of her workspace and job. She knows the job intimately and treats each action respectfully so as not to defile the worksite. Her job has a cycle of life quality. It ends where it begins.

Talk to previous team leader to get briefed.
Log in to computer and read emails.
Printout schedules and mark them up.
Have safety huddle with craneman and line them up.
Have diesel driver move transfer cars.
Tell craneman what to put on cars.
Walk the chain to get coil numbers to put in computer.
Go into time system.
Put coils into computer.
Get truck numbers.
Sign crane repair, maintenance, etc. in and out.
Get on conference call.
Communicate with the warehouse.
Communicate with the craneman.
Brief team leaders relieving me.

The doing of labor was often described in ministerial terms. While the site of that activity was the marketplace or a public agency, it was no less life shaping or life giving in ways reminiscent of what faith traditions offered believers. Workers revealed how their workspaces allowed them to "repetitively repair and maintain" what needed care. It was "putting things back together," "cleaning up," "a way to live properly," and "making things better." Going to work was essential "to living a good life." To be clear, workers were not substituting work for a religious life. For some, making a living honored God, but for none of those who held religious convictions was their labor as a replacement for ecclesiastical activities. Fewer still expressed a belief in a providence that determined how and for what purpose they had to labor. Work was essential, but a "gospel of work" didn't materialize, and work's material necessity never ceased. However, when at work the transcendental objectives of religious practice were often mirrored by the labor performed. Bus drivers not only moved travelers from one point to the next; they helped customers figure out how to get from here to there. A grocery store clerk walked a shopper to the baking goods aisle. Yes, these folks were literally doing their job, but that activity included being responsive to another human being's need. Work was no less than the site of creation. The essay that proclaimed, "Work is the beginning of life" was strikingly close to the opening biblical verse in Genesis, "In the beginning . . . "

The sense of pleasure and reverence ascribed to being at work could also be appreciated when it was missing. Dejectedly, some workers pointed out, work is "overrated," "not fun," or "not fun anymore." It was a consolation to still have a job but going to a worksite every day that no longer made them feel good was a heavy burden. "Work is like going to hell each day." Sometimes, in deep disappointment, my students would lament, "[Work is] the place my soul dies daily." Workers acknowledged that there were occasions when their job was "soul crushing." You didn't have to believe in a soul to understand the pain that these workers were sharing.

Work could be "dull," "a pain in the ass," and very often "suck." But it could also be "invigorating," "enjoyable," and even "fun." On the best of days, the worksite was a "happy place." For some, "work isn't work when it's fun." While my students attributed these characteristics to the work they did, they also were commenting on the places they worked. If working for a living was pleasurable, it was because it was done in a setting conducive to pleasure. Perhaps a home, an office, school, retail store, a factory, a construction site, a hospital, or a church.

As an Ideal-Typical Place

In class conversations, each employer was judged by my students according to a strict and rigorous standard of behavior. They were unionized employers and were expected to abide by the labor agreement. Pay and working conditions were supposed to be better than in nonunion establishments. Depending on conditions then the employer could be admired or reviled. Work was too often "managed by idiots." But no matter in how bad a light the employer was characterized, the jobsite retained its ideal form. Workers consistently held to a dualistic idea about where they worked. A worker could say, for example, "I hate being at Amazon" and condemn the oppressive working conditions and labor process. Workers demanded that work happen in a "fair and respectable environment." The same worker could also explain "I do important work at Amazon" and describe with admiration how they move products from shelves to doorsteps.

In the first statement about Amazon, the employee is negatively commenting on how the employer treats workers. It is a condemnation of the labor relations and human resource practices of the firm. In the second statement about Amazon, the employee is positively commenting on the workspace as a site of production. These seemingly contradictory attitudes reveal that the workplace itself came to embody a dualistic character. Workers without exception expressed an understanding of their "fit" for the job. For those who viewed their workplace positively, work was "where I belong." Many, however, held a split view about their job. The actual job was a good fit for many workers, but the employer had made the workplace intolerable. Work could be "more of the same nonsense," "another day of problems," "just work" or "a real shithole." My dad was loath to find anything redeeming about the coke ovens, but in the same breath, he spoke in awe of the structures. He and other mill workers claimed the mills were both the hottest and coldest places in the world. And never at the right times. Where a person worked could have many different features, but it allowed a person to earn a living, and under the best conditions fulfilled a personal need to do meaningful work. What was made of the space was a consequence of the power the worker had in relation to the employer. Few, consequently, denigrated the actual spaces they worked in. It may have been the owner's name on the building, or stenciled on the side of the truck, but workers too felt a claim to the space.

My father and his steelworker buddies also held these concurrent beliefs. Republic Steel was all about pushing out steel, and the mill was a "hellhole." Yet, working in the mills was also how families were nourished, relationships deepened, communities sustained, and America built. Going to that "hellhole" meant doing something essential. And when the blast furnaces were obliterated into dust particles workers felt a deep loss. Something precious had been taken away from them. More to the emotional point, a place they had a daily love-hate relationship with had been erased. Yes, mill work was nasty, but it's where a high school graduate could proudly say, "I made that, I made that."

My students' answers to "what work is" revealed that every workstation was imbued with an organic spirit that warranted respect. A coal mine three hundred feet below the surface, a "chicken hawk" crane cab a thousand feet in the air, a "hot, nasty, dirty" room to mill rubber into tires, a school room with thirty high school teenagers, or too many hotel rooms filled with heavy mattresses was each still a place to do good work. As one essay said, "Work is where I create value." People needed to do meaningful work to be fully actualized as human beings. In describing "what work is," workers illustrated workspaces that were untainted in their essence by employer greed and disregard for employee welfare. The employer, on the other hand, was indeterminate. Some were good, some were tolerable, too many were bad, and some were outright abusive. None were sacred. The jobsite, however, was a location or should have been a site, for creative labor.

It was striking that no matter the pay and working conditions, my students retained respect for the work itself and where they labored. I realized that workers held two conceptual ideas of their worksite. One was the actual place of employment. That job was defined by multiple characteristics; most were a mix of good and bad. The other mental construct workers held was an idealized view of their employment. This job was defined by what workers needed the work to be and the potential it represented. For example, teachers pointed out that they loved educating children and being at school (the idealized job) but that the school principal didn't treat teachers well (the actual job). Nursing home attendants expressed deep compassion for the work they do with seniors and looked forward to being at work (the idealized job) but felt overworked and underpaid by the assisted living center they worked at (the actual job). In reality, workers did one job that embodied their aspirations and experiences. Work was rarely a fixed entity, neither all satisfactory nor all ruinous.

It was never the space that was innately good or bad, although it could be unsafe. If the workplace was judged harshly, it was because the employer had defiled the area. Nearly without exception my students coveted their workspace for its familiarity and predictability. Even workers who worked low-wage retail jobs expressed regard for their workspaces. Workers held back little scorn for abusive bosses or bad working conditions but reserved a sense of sacredness for the worksite itself. They could condemn an actual unpleasant jobsite but still revere the idea of that workspace. Work is, as one put it, "where I plan for the future."

It seemed as if workers' clear-eyed realization of their actual workspaces, which embodied an uneven power relationship between them and the owners, did not preclude an ontological view of the jobsite that was unsullied by class relations. But the two contrasting perceptions highlighted the gap between reality and desire that heightened worker awareness of their class-based position. In the end, my students came to terms with the contradiction by steadfastly asserting that work is "what you make of it."

As a Dangerous Place

A sense of place was also conveyed as workers regularly distinguished between their workspace and the articles essential to the design of their work. Workers readily referred to the tools of their trade. According to my students, "[Work is] where I wielded a hammer," "the place I cut cloth," "an opportunity to weld pipe" and "teaching kids how to write." Each student worked with something that mediated their contact with materials, supplies, natural resources, and people. A teacher used a pen, paper, white board, books, and computers to educate children. Carpenters used tape measures, janitors mops and buckets. They also all had a set of procedures to follow, a way to do things properly. In the union construction trades, workers spend multiple years in an apprenticeship school learning the craft. Workers had to acquire some level of training and on-the-job experience to become an elevator operator, painter, housekeeper, or nurse. It's typical that teachers serve a three-to-four-year probationary period, and it's common thought that they need at least ten years to master their skills. Union collective bargaining agreements have "seniority" clauses precisely because a more experienced worker is a more valuable employee, and the provision prevents managerial favoritism.

As previously noted, work is realized as a space where knowledge is shared and acquired. It is a practical classroom that needs to be conducive to human interaction. No matter the equipment used or whether work is done in a kitchen, factory, hospital, post office, department store or firehouse, it must always happen in "a place that is safe." Work, according to essays, is where "you get the job done safely." In fact, as much as the pay, it was the working conditions that determined the quality of the job. The importance of safety strongly influenced my students' understanding and use of space. Worksites were often "loud, chaotic, stressful, busy and physical." Space to a worker is not randomly arranged. Enlightenment Philosopher David Hume observed that through "the disposition of visible and tangible objects, we receive the idea of space."[39] Where you labor is determined by what you do, the things occupying the jobsite and the tools you use. Location—along with what fills a location's space, including other people—shapes how people work. It also forms the body of the worker. Lifting, bending, standing, reaching, and carrying redesign the body. One's hands, back, shoulders, skin, hair, voice, and facial expressions are all implicated in the rules of the workplace. Repeatedly shooting a nail gun, slotting thousands of pieces of mail, sorting endless packages, giving countless injections, or using colored chalk every day to draw images for children, for example, affect the body; before long the workplace and the worker's body image become inseparable. The work site is very purposeful, and because it can be "hazardous," "unforgiving," and "filled with unknowns," it must be "well equipped with tools" and "efficient." The space has to be functional. If not, the consequences could be deadly. "Work is where if not careful, I can die."

Workers know that injury is a common threat. According to the Bureau of Labor Statistics private industry employers reported 2.8 million nonfatal workplace injuries and illnesses in 2019.[40] Injury was never something that workers treated as inevitable, and they invested heavily in working safely. But they acknowledged that some physical harm was always possible and to some degree tolerable. Dying on the job, however, was an altogether different matter. In 2019 there were 5,333 fatal work injuries recorded in the country, a 2 percent increase from the year before. At first read, the numbers don't seem too harsh. But then consider that in 2019 "a worker died every 99 minutes from a work-related injury."[41] Then one year later COVID-19 terrorized workplaces. In the first year of the pandemic, more than 3,600 US health care workers perished.[42] Meatpacking plants alone were estimated to be associated with 6 to 8 percent of all COVID-19 cases and 4,300 to 5,200 deaths (3 to 4 percent of the total).[43]

Keep in mind what we learned about how workers conceptualized time. If time was mostly defined by the work schedule, then workers were constantly facing an hourglass of draining sand. Risk was embedded in the work. Every student had a cause for bodily decay and possible premature death: nurses faced violent patients, construction workers suffered from muscular-skeletal problems, warehouse workers toiled in overheated and poorly ventilated buildings, grocery store workers risked infectious disease, coal miners were subject to poisoning by respirable dust, and truck drivers experienced nerve damage. Carnage to the body is visible to everyone, but the dangers of work are also skin deep. Verbal abuse from bosses, customers, patients, students, and other employees creates emotional trauma that workers can't easily shake off after the workday has ended. Threats to workplace safety are ubiquitous but often a daily reality for female, gender nonbinary, and nonwhite workers. Racial and sexual harassment and discrimination is a pernicious form of psychic assault that exacts a severe toll on the well-being of workers. A Black female student employed by the post office experienced her largely negative work surroundings as a "ghetto."

The threat of a toxic workplace does not subside when the employee leaves the jobsite. The harm follows the worker home. In their stunning book, *Deaths of Despair and the Future of Capitalism*, authors Anne Case and Angus Deaton found that for mostly white Americans without a four-year college degree, "Something is making life worse."[44] They document a disturbing decline in life expectancy for many of my students. Since 2000, higher rates of suicide, opioid overdoses, and alcohol-related illnesses, or what the authors refer to as "deaths of despair," are prematurely killing 38 percent of the US working-age population. In their words, working-class Americans "are drinking themselves to death, or poisoning themselves with drugs, or shooting or hanging themselves." Maybe it's because, as one student said, "Work is a place I feel unappreciated." Therefore, when my students say, "[Work is] where I always need to be safe," or when they insist that their workplace be a "safe environment," they are expressing an awareness that more than any other activity it is their honest paid labor that most threatens their health. Without exception, workers of all races, genders, nationalities, ages, and occupations expressed vulnerability to injury, illness, mental stress, and physical risk. Work can't be "an OSHA violation waiting to happen."[45] It must be a "safe zone for all workers." Bottom line: work is "good when you work under safe conditions."

As a Place that Obscures

Yet while the fruits of workers' skills were embedded in the physical world surrounding them, they were largely invisible in the landscape. Think about what workers you regularly encounter. We see, for example, cashiers, clerks, sales agents, and wait staff. If you have young kids, you have a relationship with teachers but likely have no idea about the name of the school janitor. You may acknowledge, in passing, police officers. Perhaps, on occasion you speak with a call center worker (again name is optional) or recognize the transit employee on your commute. If there is a need, you interact with a doctor and nurse. When you need a haircut or hair coloring, a barber or hairstylist appears. But who sees the farmworker? The seamstress? The electrician? The teamster? The carpenter? The autoworker? The factory mechanic? The coal miner? The furniture maker? The book printer? Maybe, by coincidence, you glimpse and even say hello to the delivery van driver, but has anyone ever seen the warehouse worker? How do you make sense of this invisibleness and one worker's contrary claim that "work is where we are defined"?

Renowned sociologist Erving Goffman advanced a theory of face-to-face human interactions that constructed a sense of a presented self. In his seminal work *The Presentation of Self in Everyday Life* the workplace is featured as a central location in which individuals present a version of themselves for others to know. My students' essays reflect that they use the worksite as a dominant space for developing and presenting something essential about their identity. The workspace provides "a kind of shell" for workers to participate in an oral tradition of sharing personal and family stories, to abide by a code of conduct and enforce norms of behavior.[46] It is where they consider each other part of a "crew," "team," and "family."

Despite the identity formation at work, our working class is mostly hidden. We are utterly dependent on the labor of scores of workers who remain abstractions. Even when in plain sight they are invisible to the end users and the passersby. Employers, on the other hand, never go without being recognized. If you went solely by what your eyes recorded, the world's naming rights would belong to Wall Street, the Fortune 500, and Main Street. Workers never see their names emblazoned on buildings or etched into highway signs. Their authorship of all that is made is covered in layers of company branding. Firm reputations lionize the ownership and ignore the people who do the work. But despite the employer's packaging, workers don't disappear. They use their workspace to craft a record of their existence.

Nonetheless, denying the worker's presence in the production process frustrated my students. They granted the boss had a legitimate role to play in job creation and wealth generation. But the credit and rewards ascribed to the owner was disproportional to the contribution they made. Many workers described work as "making somebody else rich" or "a way to keep us poor." Workers understand that the outsized earnings of financial capitalists, CEOs of Fortune 400 companies, and even their local employers are purely a consequence of the property ownership rules in society. Owners of the physical and financial capital enshrines their roles in the commodities produced and services rendered. My students provide the labor and are paid a wage or salary. Once the transaction is complete and frankly even before it's initiated, entitlement to the things produced belong to the employer. Even though workers commit life and limb to the worksite, it belongs to the owner. Workers are the asset that propels the workplace to produce, but it's not theirs to possess. My students go to work and get paid for doing it; that's all. Fair deal, right? Well, to most workers it depends on the distribution of the wealth created. If their labor is properly compensated, then the deal is at least acceptable.

But other workers pushed backed against the possibility that the arrangement could ever be just. If the workplace was a site for creative human activity, how could it be separate from the workers? Work revealed to the worker that the space they produced in was also the space they produced. My students critically investigated and unpacked the property relationship. The mill, the office, the restaurant, the hotel, the warehouse, and the mine belonged to others. Tools, machines, computers, phones, and buses were the possessions of folks who didn't use these things. Workers had no property rights of disposition. What did the owners of private capital do? It was simple. Owners and investors made money from the spaces and the objects workers occupied and used. Public employees didn't directly confront the profit motive, but they too were subject to market incentive and forces, gross economic inequities, and anti-state ideologies. Teachers wrestled with years of stagnant state funding of schools because political leaders were opposed to raising taxes on the wealthy. Elementary and Secondary teachers are far better educated than the average private market manager but in 2021 suffered a 23.5 percent earning penalty, up from 6.1 percent in 1996.[47] Why? Because large property holders, corporate leaders, and Wall Street investors don't want to pay higher taxes on the wealth that workers produce. Schools, fire departments, public health departments, and childcare centers—to name just a few—are products of the free enterprise system's dominant influence. No matter the workplace, the social relations of production define the limits of power and control over labor.

Given a chance to think about their labor, workers from diverse occupations were forthright and noted that work is their "labor, period." And what objectively happens "is the sale of [their] labor." My students recognized without ever saying so what Marx revealed about the labor process under capitalism: "The product of labor is labor which has been congealed in an object, which has become material."[48] In this way, the worker is subsumed in the labor process. Even the workplace can hide the worker. They become subsumed in the architecture and production landscape. Construction projects overwhelm the human being "hard hats" scattered across the site. Large factories pulsate with giant machines seemingly indifferent to human actors. Hospitals are teeming with people, but it's the constantly beeping equipment that attracts the eyes and ears. The best way to teach a child is to have a teacher stand before them, but remote learning substitutes an electronic device for the flesh and blood instructor. Yes, we can easily lose site of the workers. But poet Jim Daniels knows they are there, somewhere. In his poem "Still Lives in Detroit: #2, Parking Lot, Ford Sterling Plant," Daniels describes a barren, trash-strewn parking lot outside of a factory. A brown bag, empty pallets, a lottery ticket, and a few cars are visible. A worker should be present, but the narrator is troubled by what isn't seen.

> There's a man in this picture.
> No one can find him.[49]

There was still another profoundly evocative way that workers conceptualized their work that extended their workspace beyond its actual footings. Reminiscent of my dad's habit of proudly pointing out the stencil markings on pipe made in his mill, my students could identify and take pride in the labor of an inanimate object. But when discussing "what work is" they could also see themselves, with a little nudge, in their surroundings. An electrician recognized that without his labor the lights would not turn on. A bus driver was aware that no one rides a bus unless someone drives it. Tires don't get on cars without tiremakers. Taking a drink of water from a faucet required a plumber. Nothing but nothing appears or happens without first a teacher showing how it is done. And on and on.

It's very basic and yet sublime; work is "the way the world gets made." In a later chapter we'll examine the "way," but here we focus on the "made" part. Because the roads, bridges, restaurants, hospitals, schools, homes, parks, airports, curriculums, intellectual disciplines, vaccines, clothes, packages, and meals are a product of human labor it is clear to my students that they are responsible for the spaces they inhabit. Their work activity is the actual movement of their creative power in the world. There simply is no physical place or thing without someone's labor being mixed with the natural world.

In what Marx called the "working up of objects" to satisfy material need, workers manipulate equipment and spend long hours in workspaces producing a world of things they need, including food, clothes, homes, roads, schools, and books.[50] It is a worker interacting with nature with their body as well as their mind that brings something into existence. Every time workers act on their environment they can reproduce or remodel existing conditions. But regardless of the work, what evolves is the collective development of workers' power projected into reality. It is work that "makes the world go around." Every day "the worker puts his life into the object" and he or she dissipates into the physical environment.[51] However, those everyday objects are not separated from the rest of the world. They do not stand independent and alone. Human beings interact with them and draw the objects into their consciousness. In using what's been made for sustenance, pleasure, or contemplation we develop an understanding of the material existence work has created. Therefore, both worker and work are always present in the spaces we occupy. Work is not only forever; it is everywhere. Where then are the workers?

With each hour of work, there is more stuff to buy and fewer workers to see. Packages just arrive, the lights go on, shirts show up on racks, bridges are erected, cars and trains move, food gets stocked on shelves, and a great cup of coffee gets brewed. And with very limited exposure where all that happens is hidden and workers themselves are not seen or heard. In this way the property relations of work obscure the activity of the workers. And when the people doing the work aren't known, the labor they do becomes an abstraction. Once they are shrouded in commodities, consumption, and corporate branding, it becomes too easy for consumers to take the workers, the work, and the worksite for granted. The price on the product is more tangible than the worker's wage. How the good makes us feel once purchased, consumed, or owned is more powerful than how the work feels to the worker's body, mind, and spirit. Workspaces concurrently produce the laborer, the outcome of labor, the profits from labor and enough mystery and distance to allow consumers of labor to see no real relationship with the workers. Such a disconnect is yet another form of alienation that grows out of the work process. The result is that we end up as a society more invested in consumption than in understanding and appreciating what work is.

CHAPTER 3

Work's Impact

I KNOW MY MOM worked from my beginning. Maybe not immediately after my birth, but shortly thereafter. In truth, I don't recall a time when she didn't have a job. Like my dad, and every other person with only labor power to exchange, she worked out of financial necessity, not solely for extrinsic purposes (as we'll explore in the next chapter) but material survival was unquestionably a primary driver for my mom to seek and hold a job. Motivations for why people do their jobs can be fascinating or pedestrian, but what my students impressed on me is that no matter the reasons, there is an impact. Work always does something. Things are changed. More directly, "work is creating a change." What did not previously exist, now does. Our labors come with a cost, a price to be paid, a return on investment, a reward, a sacrifice, a gift. "Work is stressful, fun, difficult, interesting, and challenging." My students' essays showed that the effect of work was on the individual, other workers, and the community. From each worker came a volume of labor and to each worker intended and unintended fortune. How they understood that exchange depended on a plethora of employment and life dynamics.

In a brief period before my mother died, she wrote in a journal. Mom's health was bad, and she was coping with several physical and emotional problems. She was a smoker who tried repeatedly to quit. Years of nicotine consumption had badly damaged her heart and lungs. I asked her to keep the journal in part because I thought it would be therapeutic. But I also asked because ever since I had written *Steelworker Alley*, I wanted to know more about my mom's work. I knew a fair amount, but in retrospect I wish I had explored her informal (as a mom at home) and formal (as a worker at home and away) work experiences more closely. She decided to write as a favor to me, but it didn't come easy. When my mom passed, I collected her journal. She had made few entries and revealed little about anything at all. I had hoped to find something evocative about her having had to work since she was very young. To my disappointment, not a word about work appeared on the pages. But we had talked numerous times about her life, and on those occasions working was always a topic she vividly expounded on. One comment laid bare a hard and undeniable reality about working in America. Mom had left me an unjudgmental but inscrutable and fatalistic statement about the consequences of having had to work for a living since she was a teenager: "I didn't have a choice; it's just what comes from not having much."

When asked what work is, my students were no less provocative and unfiltered in explaining the impact or consequences of their labor. They were also poignant about how work made them feel. I noticed their impact responses reflected one of three prevailing and interdependent sentiments: work produces meaning, work exacts a cost, and work creates and enhances life. Each conceptualization embodies both extrinsic (personal and social material things) and intrinsic (feelings, emotions, values) effects. The impacts are personal, familial, and communal. Embedded in working for a living is a sequence of human activity that follows a cycle from birth to death. The conversations I had with workers about work's impact were meant to shine a light on the activity that most defines us as human beings yet is taken for granted. When I interviewed my father and other steelworkers, they expressed some mild confusion as to why I would want to speak with them about their jobs. Dad and Mom just "did" work. They never gave it any thought. But there is a moral imperative for us to think about employment and its effects. Essayist Bob Black would prefer a world without compelled wage labor, in which nobody ever has to work for anybody. He perfectly summarizes what this chapter sets out to accomplish: "We are so close to the world of work, that we often can't see what it does to us."[1]

Work Produces Meaning

Workers find meaning in their work. Their labor is a source of meaning either because it fulfills a higher-order aspirational or basic need of being human. Regardless of what kind of meaning worker's find, work is physically, emotionally, and psychologically demanding. And based on opinion polling about work satisfaction, it's very hard for most people. The subsequent production costs incurred on both people's lives and the environment ultimately wears down and ends life. Yet the same labor that kills also brings forth new life. Work is "meaningful" was a common message communicated in divergent forms from my students. It triggered two obvious queries from me: "In what way is it meaningful?" and "What meaning is derived from work?" The answers at first appeared contradictory, but once I explored them, they became complementary.

First, workers found their jobs "rewarding" because a job gets you what you need. A common essay was "No work, no money, no food." Simple as that. Here, meaningful is not understood in the customary sense as based on an emotional reflection on the self or job characteristics. It didn't matter if the work made you happy, benefited society, or satisfied some sense of personal identity. Work was "just a job." Something you had to do because the available alternatives to securing a decent life were worse. Working out of necessity exposed workers to feeling bereft of any sense of personal agency. As one student graphically described it, work feels like being "a worm on a big hook." Time and energy expanded to secure wages. You might feel good about the ministerial aspect of cleaning hotel rooms but you also do it because you don't get decent health care in America without a job. And even with a job, too many workers have inadequate or no employer-provided medical insurance.

According to a 2019 study, 45 percent of workers receive no healthcare insurance coverage from their employer.[2] Toiling at a low wage is not a career choice but something workers are forced to do because of our private-market approach to healthcare. In the United States good health is a commercial product an individual or an employer must purchase. Workers know that it doesn't have to be this way. Healthcare could be a human right, like in Canada and most European nations. Pointing this out in no way suggests that workers view the need to acquire medical coverage through employment as a bad thing. It is just that when my students say that work is "how I afford healthcare," "get retirement," "support my family," "pay my bills," or "how we make a living," they are recognizing a phenomenological truth about American capitalism: without paid work, you can't buy what you absolutely need to live a decent life. And not any labor will suffice.

Workers have to get hired in order to have some form of labor that can be valued and exchanged for earnings. Simply being able-bodied and appropriately skilled doesn't secure a person work. Quality employment is typically secured "only with the greatest effort and with the most irregular interruptions."[3] Most, if not all, of the workers I have taught over the past quarter century have experienced some length of unemployment. None thought, correctly in my opinion, that they did anything to deserve a layoff. One day their labor was valued and bought them a mortgage and car. "Work is how I afford to live." The next day, the same labor—or according to Marx the worker's "labor power"—no longer had any real utility for the employer. One student recognized the conditional nature of his craft's market worth and referred to work as "a nontangible commodity." Creating an opportunity to convert a person's capacity to do physical, emotional, or intellectual labor into something that could be exchanged for money and generate profit (i.e., labor power) was the mechanism that brought employees and employers into a relationship. But if the employer's moment to produce suitable profit had passed or never materialized, then there was no labor power to acquire. Consequently, the quality that once made the worker's labor essential and a marketable commodity magically evaporated. It was now worthless. "If his capacity for labour remains unsold, the labourer derives no benefit from it."[4] At a future time however, their labor could once again be worth purchasing.

My students held multiple jobs in their lives. Some at the same time. Everyone in my class understood that access to work depended on multiple factors, such as an improving economy, acquiring different marketable skills, dumb luck, or resorting to doing any work available out of desperation. This process by which someone finds a job working as an electrician or a chauffeur or not working at all is not a big mystery. Job availability and destruction all happen before the worker's eyes. The process is brutal and dehumanizing and therefore pragmatically meaningful. Work in this instance is rewarding because the worker literally feels rewarded for her or his sweat equity. The pay and benefits are not a king's bounty, but they provide for a measure of economic security. Work, whether the person likes doing it or not, is to many workers a "means to earn financial well-being." It is a basic "input to achieve an output." The utilitarian function of work is incredibly meaningful in a society where workers have no constitutional right to food, clothing, medical care, education, or a job, and where the welfare safety net is threadbare. A female student offered the following entreaty about why, in America, work was pitilessly meaningful: "Work is the reason I have a home." Everything that constitutes the American dream is a tangible outcome of work. It's self-evident that an uncontested objective of work is consumption.

Many of my students were succinct in expressing an appreciation for work. One word often did the trick: work is "money." That's it. There is no deeper meaning or larger purpose. In the poem "My Father Teaches Me to Dream," Jan Beatty offers an impassive and stark perspective on work's impact, which evoked my mother's journal entry. Beatty's poem describes how a laborer gets up, takes the bus to work, works, takes the bus home, goes to sleep, and does it all over again in a seemingly endless cycle. "There's no handouts in this life," Beatty writes:

All this other stuff you're looking for—
It ain't there.
Work is work.[5]

From this perspective it appears that work's meaning is to solely provide forms of "compensatory consumption." Work is done or tolerated because it affords a person the means to purchase things that serve to justify the burdens of an otherwise unsatisfactory and meaningless job. However, the relationship of workers to the basic stuff they must buy through their labor seems to subject them to the pernicious control of their consumption choices. Somehow, as Marx wryly pointed out, work has been converted into the handmaiden of the goods and services it produces: "Commodities, in short, appear as the purchasers of persons."[6] There is, however, an alternative application of "meaningfulness" that my students used. While less sensatory, it still strongly animated how workers felt about work. The language style used here by workers is inspiring, uplifting, liberating, and inward focused. In this form, "work is essential for happiness," and the belief coexists in workers along with the visceral urgency to do "what pays my bills." Scholars define "meaningful work" as the work that employees believe serves an important purpose. The term "meaningfulness" typically captures the degree of significance employees believe their work possesses. Meaningfulness is associated with work-related benefits, including material gain and increased job satisfaction.[7] My students were adamant that they worked "for happiness" as well as "for money." The juxtaposition of desires was familiar and at least more than a century old.

In 1912 approximately ten thousand textile workers in Lawrence, Massachusetts, engaged in a titanic struggle against the giant American Woolen Company. A largely female immigrant workforce went on strike for two months and against terrific odds won substantial improvements in pay and working conditions. The workers marched in picket lines and carried banners stating, "We want bread, and roses, too." Workers were demanding both living wages and humane treatment. The material and social needs of the workers fueled the strike, and it became known as the "Bread and Roses Strike."[8] As strikers rallied, they sang the following:

As we come marching, marching, we battle too for men,
For they are women's children, and we mother them again.
Our lives shall not be sweated from birth until life closes;
Hearts starve as well as bodies; give us bread, but give us roses![9]

My students did not rise and sing in class, but they were clear that their work similarly impacted their material and social-emotional well-being.

They were also insistent that work should do both. When it did, work could be "a daily pleasure."

By *happiness* workers meant the satisfaction of their material needs and finding a measure of positive feelings in the work they perform. The two were not incompatible. First, without work and the things that only money can buy, it's difficult to be happy. As one exasperated worker said, "[Work] makes me wish I was rich." But secondly, work is a source of pleasurable feelings. Being at work helped my students feel good about themselves. Work made workers "feel accomplished" and "empowered." Philosopher Martin Heidegger claimed, "You are your projects." And my students stressed that having work always mattered to being a useful person.[10] Whatever the duality of the work experience, it was "required, unless you're rich."

My students were parents, spouses, lovers, brothers, and sisters. They had friends and belonged to groups and clubs, but it was their work that allowed them to feel that they were "worth something." Many stressed how much they enjoyed the comradery of others, the chance to do something useful and be respected by others. To be a self-providing agent and not reduced to financial dependency was a comforting feeling. Workers' lives were "dignified" by the quality and honor of their labor. Work itself, by itself, was ennobling. "Work is good," was a repeated refrain. My students had a positive orientation toward work that superseded their present job. With rarely an exception, work served as a medium for living a life of purpose. By purpose I don't necessarily mean something visionary or spiritual. I mean that, in the nitty-gritty of a life, it was holding a job—no matter the pay or task—that adorned the worker with dignity. Al Gini, emeritus professor of business ethics in the Quinlan School of Business at Loyola University Chicago, has written that "nothing else in our lives can give us the sense of objective identity that work can."[11] Not every worker in my classes has been equally thrilled about their jobs, but everyone noted that life without even a "bad" job would be intolerable and demeaning. It was simple really: work itself is good. Even when the job is crappy.

In classroom conversations, workers quickly identified the elements that constituted a good job. They always included fair wages, good benefits, stable schedules, safe working conditions, a respectful workplace culture, and union representation. Students came from varied occupational backgrounds, and their skills, compensation, and working conditions were different. Not surprisingly, there was a relationship between job quality and worker satisfaction. Students were clear that it was easier to feel happy about a higher quality job than a "shitty job." Everyone had experienced both kinds. Work could be "hot," "cold," "noisy," and "dangerous." Depending on the circumstances—usually an antagonistic supervisor—work could leave a person "feeling unappreciated." If the job provided little direction or had few positive aspects, it could also leave a worker feeling "confused." In the dramatic words of one student, when the employment relationship is hostile, "work is virtually turned into torture." Like the mythical Sisyphus endlessly pushing a rock uphill, the worker is condemned to perform the same futile daily rituals, working without fulfilment or purpose. Albert Camus suggested that an eternity of meaningless labor is a "hideous punishment."[12] Under these conditions "work is a brutal exchange based on necessity." However, job characteristics didn't completely predict a job's capacity to make workers feel good or even "happy."

Workers derived meaning from doing work that "is rewarding" not only because of what it purchased—"work is hot and my source of income"—but also because of the impact on how it made them feel. According to one student, "[Work is what] makes me feel good about myself." Workers acknowledged that they often felt pride in their work. They also cited pride as a job ingredient, as in "work is always done with pride." A job was more than a functional task; it was a way to be useful and do useful things. Folks needed to have their packages delivered, their vaccines given, their highways safe to drive on, their children taught, their fires extinguished, their records kept, their hospital rooms cleaned, and their calls taken. The calculation was straightforward; work made people "important" because they were "needed." Work did not have to be grand; it just needed to be a service to others. Not all work is inspiring. A few of my students felt "called" to their jobs, but the majority didn't go that far. Most jobs, for them, were more perspiration than avocation. Yet, to be doing work that is even slightly helpful or useful to anyone, could be "satisfying." Management professor Barry Schwartz summed up the idea nicely: "You can be a salesperson, or a toll collector, but if you see your goal as solving people's problem, then each day presents 100 opportunities to improve someone's life, and your satisfaction increases dramatically."[13]

Workers did put a premium on the freedom to use their judgement at work. Work that permits a person to "apply knowledge without interference (i.e., from a supervisor)" was seen as rewarding. Essays often expressed the instrumental value of having a voice in the work process. Here's one that angrily stated what happens when worker agency is absent: "Work is for mules." And another groused that without a sense of individual efficacy, "work is a damn shame." When a worker contributes to the appropriate method of doing a job, it satisfies their intrinsic need to be more than an automaton. Problem solving and "doing more than what you're told" is the kind of work that workers praised. "Doing more" was not a reference to the amount of work but to the ability to do more than follow someone else's orders, to use discretion and choose to act. Workers bristled at being compelled to abide by a proscribed course of activity that diminished the role of the individual and undermined craft principles. For instance, several teachers despised having a curriculum imposed on their class by school administrators. Many curriculums came with scripted lesson plans. Teachers called it "teaching by the numbers," and they stressed that it violated their professionalism as well as degraded the profession. Union carpenters scoffed at work being done by nonapprenticed workers who had no training in the craft. Prefabbed or modular homes required skilled labor, but building a house piece-by-piece, nail-by-nail, site-by-site was valued far more by the carpenters who had completed four years of apprentice training.

Work that enabled a person to feel good because it allowed them to realize a part of themselves in the object produced or service provided was more a "privilege" than a chore. The workers are always there from the smallest pin manufactured to the largest cable installed. Work is intrinsically meaningful when workers can see themselves manifest in the world as creators of a better society. Whether it is waiting tables, picking up trash, making steel, caring for a disabled child, or directing traffic, work is always "helping people." It is apparent to me that much of what workers intrinsically value about work stemmed from relationships. Amy Wrzesniewski, professor of organizational behavior at the Yale School of Management, described the need for a positive set of work social relations in the following way: "Most jobs involve some level of contact with or interdependence with other people, whether those are co-workers, whether those are clients or customers. It's often these relationships and these interdependencies with other people on the job that are the sources of the greatest joys and the greatest frustrations."[14]

The work my students did was not a solitary activity. Their work was part of an interdependent web touching multiple lives. "Work is maintaining and creating social relationships." Cabbies knew other cabbies and countless fares. Firefighters had the "B.O.B or brotherhood of the barrel."[15] Waiters worked with other waiters, hosts, and kitchen staff, and served too many patrons to count. Teachers taught with, met with, and planned with other teachers and fostered relationships with students and parents. Nobody's work was detached from the lives of others. Workers could, however, be made to feel alone and isolated from customers, citizens, and other workers. My students did describe feeling "lonely" at work for numerous reasons. A misplaced belief in a mythical "rugged individualism," manipulative employer labor-management practices, schooling, socialization, cultural representations, capitalism, remote workstations, and government rules governing work all hide the social relationships. But still, through the deceptive mechanisms used to convince workers that they are solitary agents, workers know that work connects folks. In a variety of phrases, I heard workers proclaim that "work is creating value for yourself or others." Work often made "new friendships" possible. Over a prolonged period, those interlocking relationships could morph into something greater than an iterative daily activity. Yes, work is necessary, but it is also "a way we can find ourselves."

Think of the implications. "Hard labor, dirty hands" can assemble from many parts a person and community. Through work the individual can bring the divergent strands of human activity together. Finding personal joy, social relationships, and civic commitment through honest labor is a path to realize a stable, coherent identity. Not just for the individual but for her society. In the context of all the essays I have read, the following has generated the most thoughtful and enduring personal reflection: "Work is a unified self-worth." To be honest, when I first read these words, I was uncertain about what the worker meant. The essay had an evocative quality that I revisited repeatedly. Linking the terms "work," "unified," and "self-worth" by the verb "is"—meaning "to be"—brought the full potential of labor into focus. After turning the essay around in my brain for a good while, I believe that the writer had something like this in mind. Work—a necessary and productive activity—brings into harmony the individual's desperate human need for "bread," "roses," society, and individual value. It is the individual's labor that merges the private and public spheres of his or her life. Through work the person is unified—made whole. Only with work is the person able to claim a measurable degree of liberty from want, dependence, servitude, and external control. "Work is freedom and stability." In being a complete person, the worker then recognizes their self-worth, enabling them to realize and live consistent with their species' essence. To my students there was no greater impact from the waged labor they provided than the ability to be valued as a person of worth. They were a respected self, family member, coworker, friend, and citizen.

Make no mistake, labor sold as a commodity was seen as objectively alienating. Even under ideal working conditions the idea that labor was a commodity was dehumanizing. Karl Polanyi claimed that treating labor as a commodity is "fictitious." He argued that "labor is only another name for a human activity which goes with life itself." It cannot be "produced for sale . . . nor be detached from the rest of life, stored or mobilized."[16] Labor commodified could also be subjectively abusive. When my students described work as grueling or dangerous, they were not romanticizing their labor in a fashion that obscured the reality of class exploitation. Workers didn't treat their employment relations as part of the natural order. They knew it was a convention of the political system that established the rules that governed production. In a capitalist political economy "work is exploitation." In class discussions about state "right-to-work" laws, students claimed the system was "rigged" against their interests. "They were rightly critical of the expansion of state legislation, like right-to-work measures, designed to weaken and diminish the capacity of unions to act."[17] Workers were aware of the enormous differences in wealth between them and those at the apex of the socioeconomic pyramid. They scoffed at any legitimate justification for such extreme inequality. How much wealth taken from the workers' labors was enough? Worker attitudes recalled the warnings that eighteenth-century philosopher Jean-Jacques Rousseau wrote in the *Social Contract* about wealth disparities: "In respect of riches, no citizen shall ever be wealthy enough to buy another, and none poor enough to be forced to sell himself."[18] Nonetheless, at the same time they drew from their work a deep significance about themselves and the world they inhabited and built. Perhaps it's contrary from what theories and studies about work meaningfulness suggest, but work's impact is complex, profound, and integrated.

Work for many was "a way of life" that brought a sense of "pride," "accomplishment," and "happiness." Personal fulfillment wasn't self-centeredness; it was dependent on how your work touched other lives. In other words, they viewed the work they did as "an opportunity to serve." My students' work generated positive feelings and helped them to feel good about their lives because it was their "contribution to the human project." That project, however, was a demanding master.

Work Exacts a Cost

Millions of American and British viewers were avid fans of the PBS series *Downton Abbey*. In episode eight of the fourth season one character is offered the job of managing a pig farm. After being warned that the position was extremely strenuous, the person offered the job sarcastically comments on the effect of working for a living: "Work's like old age, m'lady. The worst thing in the world except for the alternative."[19] One of my students said as much minus the metaphor; work is "better than not working." And from the perspective of surviving a standard Monday through Friday workweek, work was described as "more fun on Fridays." Most students put it matter-of-factly that work is "not an option." Worker after worker in one breath expressed an intrinsic appreciation for their labor and in the next shared how laborious it can be doing work of any kind. Work is "stressful," "mentally draining," "frustrating," and "exhausting." It can be so all-consuming that some workers regrettably admitted that their jobs devoured their existence. "Work is like

I don't have a life." My students were compelled to enter the labor force and once there hoped to stick around. But whether the job was secure or unstable, my students agreed. As one said, "Work is taking up most of my life." Or to put it more grotesquely, "work is what we exchange to live." For people with few material assets beyond their own labor, the job—any job—was a "requirement of life." Here was a worry about "missing out" on something in order "to pay . . . bills" and "put food on the table." Remember, these were workers mostly earning at or slightly above median incomes, who if they put in fewer hours at work, would suffer an appreciable financial loss. Now, the trade-off between more nonwork time and increased compensation is complex, personal, and idiosyncratic. For hourly workers who believe they are earning enough, they can pass on working more hours. However, if the earnings are too low then they need as many hours as possible.

Salaried employees, like K-12 teachers, always feel—at least for nine months—that there is very little separation from work and a personal life. A study lead by my colleague YoungAh Park found that teachers worked forty-five or more hours per week and that 16 percent invested over fifty-five hours in school-related work. The study further found that the more parents expected teachers to respond to their communications after schoolwork hours had ended, the more stress teachers experienced. These work-related contacts were also positively related to participants' average level of insomnia and an assortment of physical symptoms.[20] In both the hourly and salaried cases, my students emphasized that they really loved their work. But it was a balancing act. Or as one student cleverly put the tricky problem, work is "trying to make passion profitable."

Under the best circumstances, my students viewed working for a living as a "daily grind" and a "necessary evil." Workers' essays shared, in part, Mark Twain's belief that "work is a necessary evil to be avoided." But importantly, my students always left off "to be avoided." The word *necessary* is understandable but why *evil*? And why not *to be avoided*? And how could a job be both rewarding and evil? My students explained that it wasn't the actual work that was evil. It was the rules of the political-economic system that coerced workers into jobs they needed to survive that was evil. In America you can work full-time at a minimum wage job and still be poor. Take home health aides. In 2021 there were approximately 2.4 million aides caring for seniors and disabled individuals in private residences and group facilities. It's hard to imagine a more service-minded and critically important profession. Over 80 percent of home health aides were employed by establishments under private ownership.[21] Therefore, the work of taking care of our dramatically increasing elderly population and most vulnerable citizens is largely driven by the profit motive. Our capacity to help ourselves to live dignified lives as we age or encounter disability is dependent on creating a labor force whose labor power can generate high enough profits for investors and owners. Thus, labor costs are something to depress. Is it any surprise that one in five of these workers earns poverty wages after typically working more than forty hours a week?[22] As a result, my students developed a barely subdued confrontational view of their employers—even toward friendly bosses. To many workers the employment relationship is foremost about "producing profit for the ruling class."

Private entities aren't the only ones that are invested in degraded job opportunities. In the early summer of 2021, twenty-three states with Republican governors rescinded an extra $300 in federal unemployment payments to pull workers into poorly paid jobs. The free market was offering these jobs at below the rate that workers were willing to accept. Thus, at the behest of low-wage employers, government swung into action by degrading a person's economic standing to force them to accept jobs that were poorly paid. My students accurately and bitterly referred to these kinds of rules about employment as being "employer-centric." Employers of course could have bid for the labor, and the companies paying appropriately would have secured the labor and talent they needed. So much for the free enterprise system. And this does seem evil.

In noting egregious employment practices, my students derisively spoke about Amazon's treatment of employees. Under the twisted vison of its multibillionaire owner, Jeff Bezos, work was never meant to be satisfying or a means to a decent life. The company's employment model was to hire and dispose of workers as quickly as possible. In 2019 the firm hired over 700,000 hourly workers, but at the end of the year it had only grown its entire workforce by 150,000. Even allowing for seasonal spikes in employment, Amazon's turnover was approximately 150 percent a year. Working at an Amazon fulfillment center "picking" product off shelves stocked by robots was not a system meant to develop a stable workforce that over time would prosper as the company's profits increased. The approach instead was to create an employment system that shuffled bodies in and out at an alarming rate. Work was high pressure, fast paced, and readily available. But none of these workers should plan on a steady schedule, a fair paycheck, and expectations of a job over any reasonable length of time, not even a year, at least for most folks. Bezos saw a decent middle-class paying job with a modicum of tenure as "a march to mediocrity."[23] His acquisition and exploitation of labor power makes Henry Ford look like a union sympathizer.

Ford modernized, mechanized, and popularized the Tayloristic system of mass production, which was predicated on the belief that workers naturally shirk from labor. Based on the pioneering studies of Frederick Winslow Taylor, workers were supposed to be tightly directed and closely micromanaged by company engineers and managers. Taylor dismissively held that "hardly a competent workman can be found who does not devote a considerable amount of time to studying just how slowly he can work and still convince his employer that he is going at a good pace."[24] Job tasks were redesigned to direct workers to follow prescribed orders. Every minute was accounted for, every worker movement measured for efficiency. Thinking on the job was minimized.

In 1913 the labor process included the fast-paced moving of car parts brought to a stationary worker doing only one menial task, over and over; in 2021 it featured apps and technology that tracked worker "time off task." Bezos was as ruthless in his pursuit of efficiency and profit as the "father of the assembly line," the "eight-hour shift," and "$5 a day." But in 1926 the automaker became the first large employer to institute a forty-hour work week. It was good for business, but it represented a reduction of the workweek from six to five days. And the five dollars a day offered in 1914 was a doubling of the average manufacturing rate. The pay increase worked mostly as a bonus to drive up workers' productivity, but it was mainly devised to stabilize the workforce.[25] In 1913 the Model T assembly line was introduced. The assembly process rapidly increased efficiencies, driving down production costs and customer prices, and stimulated demand for the vehicles.

There was a problem, however. The goal of the moving assembly line was to apply Taylor's engineering insights to convert relatively skilled craftwork and reduce it to simple, rote tasks. Workers who had once taken pride in their labor were now controlled and pushed by a mundane mechanical invention. Money was better and jobs were plentiful, but large numbers of workers stayed away from the Highland Park plant, home of the Model T. Absenteeism was common, and so many workers quit that, like Amazon, Ford "found itself with a crippling labor turnover rate of 370 percent." Unlike Bezos Ford decided that higher wages and more stable work would attract more reliable workers. "It was an absolute, total success," according to Ford Motor corporate historian Robert Kreipke.[26] The higher wages also contributed to the ability of workers to afford the cars they were building, thereby expanding the commercial market for Ford's cars.

It took unionization in 1941, but over time improvements in the working conditions at Ford contributed to a job meant to endure. As unionization grew across the mass production industries, Ford's novel practices eventually became the model for long-term full employment. This was the path from work to middle class respectability. Here, under the banner of worker collective power, was how work would make possible the American dream. Amazon and Ford are useful examples of work's impact on a person. What must have been Bezos's understanding of "what work is" for him to be coldly indifferent to the labor of nearly a million people who raised his net worth to $190 billion? Now, we do have extensive quotes from Henry Ford honoring the intrinsic value of work and the worker. There is nothing of the sort from Bezos. However, in Ford's case practice most often diverged from rhetoric. It did not escape my students' awareness that both business titans were deeply hostile toward labor unions. Ford eventually recognized the United Autoworkers, and Bezos woke up on April 1, 2022, to the reality that his first Amazon facility in America had been unionized.[27] Perhaps in time, with further unionization, Amazon and the model of employment it represents will become more like Ford—a better employer.

But no matter the job, work involves "blood, sweat, tears." For good or naught, workers pay a price. Work's impact was intensely sensual. The body hurts due to work. Physical labor leaves an indelible stamp on the body. Working for a living literally transformed—deformed—and configured my students into working class bodies. Workers were in complete agreement that working for a living is "a hard life"; in fact, "hard as hell." The words *hard* and *tough*, along with similar phrases like *a rough life*, were used repeatedly to describe the impact of being a worker. Most wage workers pointed out the pain that accompanied their labor. Feeling "beat up" was a favorite way to describe the work experience. It was commonplace for workers to suffer from an assortment of muscular-skeletal problems. Many of my students relied on pain medicine and anti-inflammatories to stay on the job. Construction workers were especially challenged by physical disabilities and job injuries. Dealing with this pain has included a recognized overuse of alcohol and prescription drugs. Studies have found that 15 percent of all construction workers in the United States, or almost twice the general population of adults, have a substance abuse disorder and that construction workers are very vulnerable to opioid abuse.[28] A construction worker in my class sarcastically proclaimed, "[Work] makes me feel like being an alcoholic." Prescribed opioids have become a go-to way of coping with the pain. Nearly 75 percent of injured construction workers were prescribed a narcotic pain killer in 2016. Opioids account for 20 percent of the total spending on prescription drugs in the construction industry, a higher amount than any other industry. The rampant opioid abuse and addiction within the construction industry is associated with an increased risk of overdose and death. In fact, construction workers have the highest mortality rates for drug and prescription opioid—related overdoses.[29] Marx charged that work under capitalism "squanders human lives, and not only blood and flesh, but also nerve and brain."[30] No matter the occupation, my students knew that even under the best employment conditions the body wears out.

But what choice does a carpenter, operator, iron worker, laborer, mason, or pipefitter have? In a declarative voice one worker shouted a rhetorical question that he promptly answered himself: "You want to know what work is? No work, you don't eat." Everyone in the class understood. Construction workers make money only when they work; there are no paid sick days. But the lack of paid sick days or long-term leave is not unusual for American workers. The United States is unique among the wealthiest countries. It has no "national policy requiring employers to provide paid sick days for workers who need to miss five days of work to recover from the flu"[31] Unlike, the twenty-two leading nations ranked highly in terms of economic and human development, there are no federal legal requirements in the United States for paid sick days or leave. Astonishingly, "the United States is the only country that does not provide paid sick leave for a worker undergoing a fifty-day cancer treatment."[32]

Instead, some American workers fortunate enough to be employed by companies subject to the Family and Medical Leave Act (FMLA) are eligible for up to twelve weeks of unpaid sick leave.[33] The law does allow eligible employees to use any earned time off in lieu of lost pay. But only 56 percent of employees are eligible for leave, and nearly three-quarters of workers who utilize their FMLA do so to care for their own illness or to care for sick spouses, children, or parents.[34] However, 84 percent of those workers who receive partial or no pay report that they limit their spending during their FMLA period, and one-third borrow money or put off paying bills.[35] It's a little something, and workers use the law without burdening employers. The Center for American Progress found that 90 percent of firms reported that paid family leave had a "positive effect" or "no noticeable effect" on "productivity, performance, and profitability." And nearly 87 percent of employers report "they had no added costs due to employees using paid family leave, and 9 percent of employers reported cost savings."[36]

The FMLA, however, is a weak protection against life's mundane and sudden health burdens. And the pains aren't all physical. "Work is the root of my anxiety," said one student. And workers in some occupations have confronted frightening levels of mental stress. In a national study that I coauthored, 93 percent of nurses reported experiencing "moral distress." The condition is caused when nurses feel that the ethical course of medical action they know to follow with patients cannot be implemented "due to organizational or institutional constraints."[37] Teachers haven't used exactly the same language, but after years of COVID schooling a sense of emotional abuse is evident in what they have experienced. A RAND Corporation Report funded by the America Federation of Teachers alarmingly found that "teacher and principal stress is twice that of the general public."[38] For far too many Americans "work is depressing" and "no damn fun."

Whether the health indicator is physical, emotional, or mental, if employers don't have a policy or there isn't a union contract permitting some extended or any paid time off for illnesses, many workers continue to go to work when they are sick. How many? Some conservative estimates suggest 20 million.[39] Work uses up "energy" and is usually exhausting. One essay stressed the incremental weight and agonizing effects on the person who labors. "Work is a slow, painful death," it said. No one in my class ever took exception to the claim, "Work is slowly killing us." This essay, however, had a chilling coda. Here is the complete version: "Work is slowly killing *without us even knowing.*" My students stressed numerous times how tiring it was to be a customer service representative, an assembly-line worker, or a construction worker. They got breaks and lunch periods, but these brief respites never lessened the feeling of "being bone tired" at the end of the working day. There was only so much a person could give to a job; "I wear myself out, daily." Work could produce "a blindness to life" and make you feel that the job was "wasting your life away." Coincidentally, while reviewing these essays a colleague shared a poem with me by Pietro Pietri that dramatically expressed the extractive power of work that my students were articulating. Here are selected lines from the opening:

They never took days off
They were on the calendar
They worked
Ten days a week
And were paid for five
They worked
They worked
They worked
And they died[40]

There were those who acknowledged being exhausted by work but "feeling great if they learned something" and feeling "better on payday." Students called this realization being "good tired." Regardless, work creates "stress" on their bodies and minds. It is "a pain in the ass, sometimes" because work could be "rigid," "myopic," and consequently, "frustrating." Work could make a person feel "angry," "miserable" or "unsatisfying." Perhaps the most debilitating effect of work is when it is "dull." Imagine the physical and psychological degradation produced by a job that is a "headache every single day." For some workers, work caused them to be introspective of past and current choices. Work made folks feel that they should "spend more time at home" or should have "done more schooling."

My students noted many uniform physical and cognitive impacts of work, but the effects also varied by occupation. Hard was hard but differentially hard. For instance, workers who engaged with customers, clients, patients, or students expressed a lot of satisfaction about helping people. Teachers, nurses, and personal care workers genuinely felt concern and even affection for those they served. "Work is an act of love." But they also shared a deceptive truth about their work: emotional labor is taxing. One worker described the effect the following way: "Work is depleting." Sociologist Arlie Hochschild has written persuasively about "emotional labor," which as she conceived it, referred to the work of managing one's own emotions, which was a requirement of certain jobs. Emotional labor is work you're paid for that involves having to evoke and suppress feelings. Depending on the amount of regular contact with other people, emotional caring is a job skill required by all occupations to some degree. Flight attendants were Hochschild's canonical case. On the other hand, painters and steelworkers don't typically have to act like they're having a good time to do their job. Projecting a work-crafted emotional self is predicated on how often a worker encounters other people while working.

The US Department of Labor houses a public-facing database, O*NET, containing standardized and occupation-specific descriptors on almost one thousand occupations covering the entire US labor force. The O*NET system "describes occupations in terms of the knowledge, skills, and abilities required as well as how the work is performed in terms of tasks, work activities, and other descriptors."[41] When describing "Hosts and Hostesses, Restaurant, Lounge, and Coffee Shop" positions, it reports that 88 percent of the folks who work in these jobs and responded to a survey said they had "constant contact with others."[42] Jobs with similar person-to-person engagement included, "Fast Food and Counter Workers, Waiters and Waitresses, Ushers, Lobby Attendants, and Ticket Taker and Cashiers." Teachers are just as socially embedded. More than eight in ten elementary school teachers had "constant contact with others" and 86 percent had "Face-to-Face Discussions Every day." That's a lot of people being emotionally "on." By comparison, structural metal fabricators and fitters, boiler makers, and plumbers did not even have "constant contact with others" and "Face-to-Face Discussions" listed as a "work context" variable.[43] You don't run in to too many people in a boiler room.

In my class, teachers, nurses, retail clerks, restaurant wait staff, personal service workers, and hotel employees reported that they were expected to produce a work feeling. Teachers are a particularly interesting case. The prevalence of burnout syndrome among teachers is higher than in other professional groups. Roughly 8 percent of teachers leave the profession yearly, and an equal number move to other schools, bringing the total annual turnover rate to 16 percent. Estimates are that a third to half of teachers leave their position within five years.[44] However, teachers also have very strong work motivations and engagements in their daily educational practice. Their job demands include a healthy dose of prosocial behavior and role performance. Teachers in my class told painful and beautiful stories that underlined the severe psychological demands of their jobs. They had to work with large classes of diverse learners, students' complex and at times confounding learning needs, extraordinary time demands, requirements for regularly communicating with parents, sometimes dysfunctional interactions with principals, but always with the perceived expectation to care for others in a very positive nurturing way. Much of their success comes from how their emotional interactions with students and parents build positive relationships. But it requires a heavy quantum of emotional labor, and the cost can be severe. One study found that 9.6 percent of teachers suffered from burnout syndrome, which is "defined as a psychological syndrome that develops in response to chronic work stress."[45]

Not unlike teachers and nurses, workers in the private commercial sector must act perpetually happy toward the customer or client, and always "wear a smile." What made this labor hard, was that it was predicated on a deception. Instead of a business transaction, which it formally is, the contact is designed to make the customer feel like it's not their money that invokes personal service, but something more intimate. The objective is to have the customer walk away after a purchase and proclaim in earnest "wasn't that agent so nice and friendly!" Of course, the employee must do this repeatedly with multiple people over an eight- or ten-hour shift. Every day. And each time, customers need to experience a warm, fuzzy feeling. Selling pants or insurance or checking temperatures or safely getting passengers off a plane or teaching a kid how to play the piano—the actual job description—isn't enough. The work must be accompanied by an emotional dividend for the customer. Hochschild referred to the practice this way: "A situation where the way a person manages his or her emotions is regulated by a work-related entity in order to shape the state of mind of another individual, such as a customer."[46]

Workers' emotional labor creates a bizarre dynamic where workers detach their personal feelings from the work they do. One of my students expressed this impact in a very nonclinical fashion: work is "dealing occasionally with jerks with money." Working for money under capitalism is necessary, but my students understood that only working for money is debilitating. It led too often to the following conclusion: "work is sucking the joy from [one's] soul." Coping with difficult work relationships and having to constantly suppress your honest feelings are two points on a continuum of how work is hard. My students made certain I was aware of a more extreme juncture. Work is "what will likely kill me eventually." Yes, "work is life, life is work till death." The threat of death by work is not illusory.

While worksites filled with potentially sick people became more suspect during a pandemic, work itself has a deleterious impact on human health. The World Health Organization has emphasized that "health and employment are inextricably linked" and "health inequities attributable to employment can be reduced by promoting safe, healthy and secure work across all sectors of employment."[47] For the past thirty years the American Federation of Labor-Congress of Industrial Organizations (AFL-CIO) has produced a report on US workplace deaths. Their 2021 study revealed that 5,333 workers were killed on the job that year. The overall job fatality rate had substantially improved from 9 per 100,000 workers in 1992 to 3.5 per 100,000. But while employers reported nearly 3.5 million work-related injuries and illnesses, the study contends that the "true toll of work-related injuries and illnesses is 7.0 million to 10.5 million each year." Risk of injury and death is heightened by the very low probability that a third-party regulator is monitoring the worksite. In 2020 the Occupational Safety and Health Administration (OSHA) had only one safety inspector for every 82,881 workers, and the agency's budget amounted to $3.97 "to protect each worker."[48] At this paltry level of capacity, employers are effectively free to ignore workers' health without fear of penalty. According to one study "it would take the agency [OSHA] a whopping 165 years to inspect each workplace under its jurisdiction just once."[49] Lack of oversight not only puts the worker's health at risk but it increases their financial vulnerability. A paltry 22 percent of workplace injuries and illnesses are covered by the workers' compensation system, which in 2007 cost the US economy an estimated $249.6 billion.[50] Fortunately, my students were nearly all unionized, and they had a variety of safety protocols to rely on. But that did not fully inoculate them from the punitive nature of work. Nor did it depress the necessity to keep working, or as workers withdraw from the labor force "by wear and tear and death," to continually find "an equal amount of fresh labour-power."[51]

Injury, physical deterioration, cuts, bruises, breaks, hospitalizations, surgeries, and daily pain were common. Nurses and teachers, as well as electricians and landscapers, got hurt while they worked. The damage to the body wasn't all from the standard occupational hazards. Nurses experienced a lot of violence on the job from patients. The AFL-CIO report showed a 52 percent increase in workplace violence in the healthcare industry.[52] My nursing students knew the risks of victimization very well. In a study I coauthored, 90 percent of surveyed Illinois nurses experience at least one episode of workplace violence in a twelve-month period with 50 percent of nurses experiencing six or more episodes of workplace violence in a year.[53] The cost of job injuries and illnesses is not only in broken bodies and shortened lives. The financial penalty of lost workdays on the economy is estimated between $250 billion to $330 billion a year. To avoid losing the means to "support . . . family" due to work's inevitable toll on the body, workers resort to different strategies. Some self-medicate, others rely on prescription pain killers. Some use cannabis. And many mentioned relying on coffee to do their jobs. As one said, "[Work is] why I drink so much coffee every day."

Work Creates and Enhances Life

In my students' experiences work had near unlimited properties. It could inspire, be fun, build character, give meaning to life, depress, hurt, and destroy. But at the same time, work is also life-giving. In Marx's view the primary function of labor was "the production of life."[54] Because people work, community happens. Through the daily collective efforts of millions of folks, towns rise, people are fed, goods are produced and moved, kids learn, and the sick get better. Before work, nothing. After work, everything. Work "is the fuel for the economy"; it "energized." Importantly, the work folks did was both responsible for and "a contribution to society." Work is how "we get involved in life" and how "everything happens."

Work embeds a person in a social network that included fellow workers, colleagues, friends, and acquaintances. Workspaces were governed by shared norms of conduct, rules of interaction, and formal and informal relationships. Putting in a "good eight" was predicated on everyone agreeing to a set of values. At work, my students observed, "you learned how to get along" and "be a responsible person." In fact, it was through and at work that a person molded a definition of self and others. Workers found out who they were as individuals and constructed an identity based primarily on what they did for a living. Years of conversations with diverse workers has showed me the multidimensionality of their personalities. But one feature is defining: work is inseparable from who workers are and how they think.

When people work, they "come alive." Work is, said one student, "why I am a proud father." As a female student asserted, "[Work is] how I raise the kids." Being a parent didn't require having a job. Being a proud parent did.

Why? For some, it was because work "made [them] productive every day." Parenting was a demanding role and undoubtedly contributed to a personal sense of accountability. Nonetheless, for my parent and nonparent students, working "made [them] responsible." The effect was universal. Work's capacity to provide internal affirmation of a person's worth transcended race, gender, age, nationality, and language. As noted, while class registration data was collected, in order to encourage honest disclosure student essays did not contain personal demographic information. However, the essays reveal an overwhelming appreciation of work that belies any significant racialized, gendered, or ascribed identity responses.

The feelings workers had about their characters were deeply intertwined with their roles as workers. It was through their labor that my students could "be part of building something." In numerous comments and conversations, my students emphasized how their work literally brought life into being. I don't mean figuratively. It was by providing a service or making a product that a person had a hand in creating society and, further, of becoming a fully recognized self. Work impacts both the worker and recipient of that work. It gives birth to both the worker and the world the workers made. Our labor is "what gives us life" and "what keeps us living." Workers talked about their jobs the way poet Robert Frost joyfully celebrated doing work for "heaven and the future's sakes."[55]

The result of work is that we get things we materially need and an identity in life. My students described an unsentimental understanding of work that got the bills paid. Some workers didn't need six words, saying that work is "work." Or work "ain't nothing but a job." And yet, they also illustrated an awareness of labor that represented a manifestation of their authentic being. Here are two consequences of labor coexisting in time and space. But they are not the same. Workers grasp protectively, sometimes lovingly, and always respectfully at the chance to work; but they never claimed to be their work. Work is "necessary," "fundamental," "a passion," "a pathway," and a "pain in the ass." It is an unquestionable source of stability in the precariousness of human existence and a way to be "somebody." But the force of that work did not erase the boundary between what people did for a living and the self.

Consider the following evocative and popular student response to the exercise: "Work is why I wake up." When students discussed the answer, they pointed out a dual meaning. The pressing uncertainty and fear of material dependency motivated them to get up and go to the construction site, the hospital, the hotel, the school, the factory, and the store. But they also wake up each day because, no matter how hard their job was, it enabled them to feel like a dignified, whole human being. In our class conversations I often hear in my mind the lyrics from Bruce Springsteen's song "Reason to Believe." The opening stanza reflects for me the against-all-odds faithful commitment working-class folks have to making good out of nothing each day.

> Seen a man standin' over a dead dog lyin' by the highway in a ditch
> He's lookin' down kinda puzzled pokin' that dog with a stick
> Got his car door flung open he's standin' out on highway 31
> Like if he stood there long enough that dog'd get up and run
> Struck me kinda funny seem kinda funny sir to me
> Still at the end of every hard earned day people find some reason to believe.[56]

Economic conditions compel people to work to do better than merely survive. No matter how much time my students spent on the job, they insisted it was just work—a rough means to an essential end. At the same time, all the labor they performed often amounted to its own reward. An authentic personal identity emerged. In the encyclical words of Pope John Paul II, "Work bears a particular mark of man and of humanity, the mark of a person operating within a community of persons."[57] It is a necessary and noble end. As one student said, "Work is great and shitty on occasion."

Work is, therefore, both a means of material and identity production. It is "a necessary evil" and "something [people] love." My students described how they were known to others by their work and how what they did for a living primarily configured their place in the world. The experience of work provided substance to a psychological space that craved attention. Numerous workers shared that they were "fulfilled" through work. So many of my students said this that I wondered what was missing. To be fulfilled is to add something that was absent. Understanding this need for fulfillment requires first appreciating how hypervalued work is in our society. Oren Cass, the author of *The Once and Future Worker*, explained that "we've created this idea that the meaning of life should be found in work." Through education, popular culture, media, and law, work is portrayed as a civic altar where we should place unquestioning faith. But of course unlike faith in a god, work is tangible and controlled by the "mercurial hands of the market." Nonetheless, my students' expressions of work's impact portrayed a commitment to "worship a god with firing power."[58] Notwithstanding the vulnerability of fulfilling a person's intrinsic needs through employment, work was a potent guide to self-identity because the statements "I did" or "I do" were more definitive to consciousness than "I feel."

What innate psychological needs did my students attempt to satisfy through their work? There were four that seemed most important to experiencing purpose through their work: competence, autonomy, responsibleness, and relatedness.[59] First, workers wanted to be in possession of a talent or skill they were good at and that was valued. Second, they wanted to claim some authorship and control over what they did for a living. Third, my students stressed the importance of doing their job as a way to be accountable to others. Finally, workers prized the relational nature of their jobs. One of my students summed it up this way: "[Work] completes me." Upon reflection I realized the above mental constructs produced a composite state of mind that was quietly expressed by many workers in my classes. Work for those who have it and feel secure in their employment relations was a "peace of mind."

Yes, work's impact is good, bad, and ugly. It buys bread, causes pain, and makes a person feel useful. Marx saw the individual by nature as a worker: "What they are, therefore, coincides with their production, both with what they produce and with how they produce."[60] It seems experientially true that "the work [people] do is fateful." Personality as well as body, nature, and society are made by and influence the work a person does. Labor acts on and thereby shapes human consciousness. If workers are denied genuine control over their own labor and work under demeaning conditions, they will likely have their being "mutilated by the needs of the production process."[61] However, if work is done under respectful conditions that allow workers to be creative, then they are less likely to be alienated from their own productive activity. The most colorful expression of work's agonies and enhancement is the double entendre I heard from a construction worker: "[Work is] the shit that fertilizes my life." Workers know and feel the full impact of what work does.

CHAPTER 4

The Purpose of Work

MY FATHER NEVER WANTED to be a steelworker. "I wanted to play a trumpet in a jazz band," he told me. As a young man, the "Kings of Swing" like Glen Miller, Tommy Dorsey, and Benny Goodman inspired my dad to pursue a life of musicianship. The famous clarinetist Artie Shaw was one of his favorite big band leaders from the 1940–50s. Mom and Dad recalled dancing to Shaw's swing band in the spacious and beautiful ballroom at Idora Park in Youngstown, Ohio. The park ballroom had the largest dance floor between Chicago and New York City. It attracted the biggest orchestra names from around the country. The "Jumpin' Jive" section of an area paper captured a review of one of Shaw's local performances: "Well, we were entitled to a real session of 'jive and jump' last Sunday evening at Idora's mammoth barn! The 1939 king of swing Artie Shaw was there with his excellent band. Close to 2,500 'jitterbugs' jammed their way into the pavilion for a look at Artie and his 'swing hounds.'... And they weren't disappointed one bit.... The band sounded at its best—and the hot men were really solid."[1]

The opportunities to fire up dreams of playing music before "cats" were plentiful in the area. Other first-class establishments like the Elms, Krakusky Hall, Craig Beach, the DAV Ballroom, "Million-Dollar-Mansion," and Stambaugh Auditorium featured the likes of Miller, Goodman, Tommy and Jimmy Dorsey, Stan Kenton, Lawrence Welk, and Guy Lombardo. Along with Shaw, the band leader my dad most admired and enjoyed seeing play was Charlie Spivak. Celebrated as the "Man Who Plays the Sweetest Trumpet in the World," Spivak was voted the second most popular swing band stylist.[2] In Spivak my dad got a glimpse of the kind of work he would be happy to spend his life doing. Only he never got the chance. As a high school senior, my father was working in a hose factory. At eighteen he went to work at the Lansingville Plant of the Republic Steel Company. Dad never really had the option of working as a horn player. Never even played it for fun. He didn't take a job to make himself happy or to fulfill a dream. He worked because it was financially helpful to his parents and three sisters. But dad also worked for others he never knew and for reasons that were too obvious to talk much about. As one essay declared, "work is people joining together for common cause"; it said, "[Work is] how I create my life journey." In this chapter, work's complex purpose is explored.

To someone with a high school degree, the mill offered good money. It was in a fashion the family business. His father and uncle were steelworkers at other mills. Dad doesn't remember any adult encouraging him to be anything but a mill worker. And once he was working to earn a wage, there was no escaping his path. Mom didn't fare any better. She aspired as a young girl to become a flight attendant. Mom thought traveling the world would be inspiring. Instead, she worked as a beautician, factory hand, and in a support-staff position for a mental health hospital and clinic. Unlike dad, though, she not only enjoyed the jobs but she expressed satisfaction doing the work. The jobs no doubt gave her an opportunity to apply her very curious intellect and comfort with problem solving. But I also know she just liked getting out of the house. Mom did the unpaid reproductive labor at home. She never regretted being a mom and wife, but we spoke about how much more she wanted out of life, and these other jobs outside the house required doing some kind of useful paid labor. So why didn't she do more? Her mother died when my mom was very young, and she was left, along with her older sister, to take care of the household for her steel working father and brother. Family income was perennially tight, and after high school her part-time jobs contributed to the household budget. Mom's father and brother were harsh, ungenerous men, and they never recognized her desire for self-definition. But it's also true there was little wealth to go around, and her older sister Katherine, or "Kay" as my mother referred to her, got what consideration could be spared. After her mom's death, Kay got out of the primary responsibility of caring for her father and brother. However, she didn't move any further above her working-class station than my mother. Kay worked a decade as an assembler at a local General Electric Lamp Plant. Under these conditions, college and world travel were out of the question.

I've reflected a lot on the absence of a genuine career choice in my mother's life. She stopped dreaming about being a flight attendant and later in life became a responsible and productive office manager. She didn't lament what she didn't have, but still I wonder. Did mom harbor remorse and some self-blame for not doing more? One student's essay triggered a painful reflection about my mother's life of labor. While students were given the option to include their names on their essays, nearly none did. But Cindia "Lynn" Fields was a very special exception. She is a Sargent at the Southwestern Correctional Center for men in East Saint Louis, Illinois, and President of Local 3654 of the American Federation of State, County, and Municipal Employees, Council 31. Lynn, as she is commonly known by coworkers and union brothers and sisters, has worked in corrections for over twenty years. She holds the distinction of being the first African American female to head a union bargaining unit at an all-male public Illinois institution. When she thought about the writing prompt, she drew inspiration from some cautionary advice she constantly heard from her grandmother when growing up.

Lynn's parents were teenagers when she was born, and she was raised by her grandmother. Her grandmother wanted Lynn and a twin sister to not fall victim to bad choices, as teenagers, that would limit their life options. Work, her grandma pointed out, would be dreadful if Lynn wasn't able to do something she enjoyed because of life events that forestalled pursuit of her dreams. Lynn had a close example of what grandma had in mind. Her dad was imprisoned as a seventeen-year-old for robbery. Once released, he caught a break. His godfather offered to get him a full-time "union job," if he could stay out of trouble. Every night, for two years following his prison stint, Lynn's dad cleaned union halls—often accompanied by Lynn—in the East Saint Louis area. After recreating some stability in his life, his godfather made good on his promise. Lynn's dad took a position with the Illinois Power company (now Ameren) and became a member of the Laborers International Union of North America, Local 100. Lynn made clear to me that the "union saved [her] life," because "it saved [her] father's life." Her dad passed away in 2009, and her mom holds onto some of his personal belongings, including a wallet. Inside a worn sleeve is her dad's first union card with his name still clearly legible—Lynn Antonio Maggard. My student Lynn—who chooses to use her father's name—wrote a provocative essay which chillingly described what my mother may have believed deep down but never said out loud: "Work is a debt paid for abandoned goals."[3]

Dad and Mom's stories are very common. It is rare among the generations of manual hourly wage workers to find workers who, when they were kids or in high school, intended to grow up to be janitors, hotel housekeepers, crane operators, electricians, or like my father, a millwright, or my mom, a health records office manager. Despite the American myth that individuals are the free agents of their lives, workers don't believe that. They take it as part of the natural order based on experience that work "is a necessity to live comfortably" rather than a social convention under capitalism. I was enlightened by the essays I read and very surprised by the essays I didn't read. Only one student wrote that "work is a choice." It was the second shortest essay turned in. The workers I've taught didn't consult the *Harvard Business Review, Forbes*, or job advice blogs focused on making career choices. Being wary of the "5 Signs You're About To Make a Bad Career Decision" rarely entered the thinking of workers in search of a decent way to make a living.[4]

I have been asking students for two decades to raise their hands if, when they were younger, they dreamed about doing the job they were currently doing. Less than a tenth of 1 percent have thrust their hands into the air. Even most teachers hadn't imagined themselves one day working as teachers. In truth, it was never my ambition. But all of us, me included, wanted more than an income out of our work. While workers in my class never imagined what kind of work they would do, they mostly expected to be waged laborers. Paid employment is an "opportunity to display your creativity," or it could be a signifier of the loss of control; "work is a reminder of my unintentional lifestyle." However, being a worker for a lifetime wasn't the only way to live for at least two reasons "necessary to the production of social wealth." First, not everybody with any sizeable wealth or income is a wage or salaried worker. Obviously, no one in the Walton family, heirs to the Walmart fortune, needed to become wage workers. In 2015 six Waltons were on the Forbes 400 list and were collectively worth $136.1 billion, "making them the richest family in the United States." How rich? Their wealth is equivalent to the wealth of 43 percent of American families combined.[5] Second, millions of people working for wages to generate profit for a small number of owners isn't an inherently natural phenomena in society. We work the way we do because modern capitalism has hegemonically organized our productive activity. Work in America is "not God given." It's "how somebody else gets rich." Or as my mom believed and one student declared, "work is the rich robbing the poor, unnoticed."

While not in any legitimate way choosing their occupation, the vast majority of my students expected or hoped to have a long career doing what they were currently doing. Only they rarely called it a career. A career to them appeared to be more like what I had. From their perspective, at some point in my life, I decided I wanted to be a college professor. Here was our first point of departure. Except for a very small number of my students, none intended to put up sheet rock or take care of disabled seniors for a living. My students recognized that I made an intentional choice to follow a plan to arrive at an employment objective. I then pursued a determinate life goal predicated on a series of incremental steps leading to my professional status. People like me with careers went to college and followed a prescribed course of activity that was required of someone with a particular career. Point of difference number two. My students ended up with years on a job primarily by doing it one day at time without any preconceived notions of what it would all add up to. Workers had been doing their jobs for varying lengths of time, and many expected to have long tenures, but few thought of their work as a professional journey. Sometimes they used the word career to describe their job, but what they meant was that they held the job for a comparatively long time. It was typically just a job—"I'm a tire builder"—a job, like repairing railroad cars, which they could do until they retired if they were lucky. But working a job they found and didn't aspire to didn't mean work's purpose was one-dimensional. The purpose of working was intricately woven into the diverse ways that work was meaningful to human beings in forming an identity and life. My students worked because they needed money to live decently. And because they liked "pizza and dark beers." If they had a family, no matter the job, they also worked to provide for them. Work enabled a worker to "bring up a child into maturity." At the same time, they worked because they needed to do something useful. "Work is the thing that gives me purpose," one said. As we will see in this chapter my students worked for personal fulfillment and happiness. They worked for selfish as well as selfless reasons.

Individuals, day after day, sell their labor power for more than "just a job:" they want to have a sense of purpose in their work beyond paying bills. Laboring only for a buck had little appeal to my students. Work reduced to mere pecuniary reasons was "an unfortunate necessity." They desired work that was not purely driven by necessity or obsession with financial gain. When a job is tethered to only a monetary exchange it limits a person's drive for creative fulfillment. Under such conditions "work is a pyramid of money hungry people." Hungry here connotes two contradictory meanings: an absence of a basic good that causes pain for the person without it and an excess of a thing that reflects a distorted sense of what makes us human. Instead of serving only a transactional function, however, the workers writing essays in my class kept returning to the idea that work is a "way to make my mark" in society.

While income is an important element of a good job, workers have consistently noted that the "intrinsic" benefits of work are most essential. When asked in surveys to rank the importance of aspects of their jobs—pay, security, free time, chances for advancement, and the opportunity to do "important work [that] gives a feeling of accomplishment"—respondents on average ranked important work highest and pay third.[6] Work's purpose is to provide a "way to [personal] achievement" and "to feel accomplished in life." Few students of work would agree today with Frederick Winslow Taylor, the father of "scientific management," who boldly and derogatorily asserted in 1911, "What workers want most from their employers, beyond anything else, is high wages." My students knew what Taylor was up to: getting the workers to "trade knowledge for pay." Yes, income and benefits are important because a life without paid work is brutal to the individual's wellbeing. But employees have always sought meaning and satisfaction from their jobs. When Johnny Paycheck (could there be a better name for a guy singing about a job?) sang "Take This Job and Shove It," his reasons included how a worker was being treated. "Well that foreman, he's a regular dog, the line boss, he's a fool."[7] Studs Terkel prosaically described this purposeful duality: "Working is about the search for daily meaning as well as daily bread, for recognition as well as cash, for astonishment rather than torpor; in short, for a sort of life rather than a Monday through Friday sort of dying."[8]

The workers in my classes offered diverse reasons for doing their jobs. While their responses can be categorized as extrinsic and intrinsic purposes for working, the specific nuances of what folks said calls on us to broaden these frameworks to better portray the richness described by workers themselves. Investigating "what work is" to workers unearths why Maya Angelou said, "Work, [is] something made greater by ourselves and in turn makes us greater." Or as a student proclaimed, "[It's] what betters my life." Camus famously pointed out that if workers simply resigned themselves to getting nothing more out of life than struggle and toil, then they could find happiness in meaningless labor.[9] However, workers had high extrinsic and intrinsic expectations for employment. Spending decades in a factory was supposed to enable a person to "provide and survive." Few saw work as a mere "distraction" from pursuing other more satisfying life activities. Contrarily, many claimed their labor was "what makes life happen." In searching for a conceptualization that denoted work's purpose, I found Professor Anthony L. Burrow's definition on the mark. "Purpose," he says, "is a forward-looking directionality, an intention to do something in the world."[10] Much of why my students worked was future oriented and about living out a plan for their lives. As will be obvious in the essays, to have a purpose also involved working for someone you loved. Purpose, according to Burrow, is different from having goals. In my students' rendering, however, I have included immediate and mundane achievements, as they clearly represented reasons big and small why they were working.

In a *New York Times* essay, Jonathan Malesic situated work at the "heart of America's vision of human flourishing." His use of the term "flourishing" is an evocative choice to describe the potency of what our work can produce. In the *Nicomachean Ethics* Aristotle uses the Greek word *eudaimonia* to refer to a worthwhile life based on the pursuit of excellence and living in accordance with virtue. It's commonly thought the term meant *happiness*. However, most scholarly interpreters of Aristotle believe that *eudaimonia* is best defined as *flourishing* to connote a fuller development of human potential. Malesic asserted the uncontroversial point that work provides us with the "right to count in society and enjoy its benefits."[11] To a great extent what worker essays expressed about the purpose of work was how it enabled individuals to re-produce their lives one grind at a time. Work not only produced the material contours of a civic life, but it enabled individuals to inhabit and develop their lives. Their labor not only produced and sustained the natural world, it also continuously formed a person's human nature. What is clear from my class conversations is that workers expected their labors to help them do well in life in multiple forms. "Work is what I do to live well." Workers continue to want "flowers" as well as "bread." For themselves, their families, and society.

Work to Provide

No term was mentioned more than *provide* in answer to why workers la-bored.[12] They worked to be able to exchange labor for never enough wages to buy the material things necessary to live a decent life. The sequence of actions began with getting a job. "Work is the beginning, providing is the end." Work's purpose was not endemic to the labor activity itself—it was for "money" to "pay the bills" and was "crucial for a healthy lifestyle." On an even more basic level work's purpose was what you did to "survive." In *The Theory of Moral Sentiments* Adam Smith argued that it wasn't our nature that compelled us to work hard: "We submitted to labour, in order to avoid the greater shame and pain of poverty."[13] It's how workers purchased "a liveli-hood" for themselves and their family. Workers understood the relationship between the expenditure of their labor power and the quality of their home, car, dinner table, kid's education, and healthcare. "Work is how I bought my first house." They expected to have a boss for most of their lives. At best, they thought they would have some say over who the boss would be, but my students never doubted they would be bossed. Nor under typical condi-tions did they really consent to a loss of freedom that being bossed entailed. Ironically, as we will see shortly, workers also embraced the need to work in order to live as free men and women.

The reason to work "was to make ends meet," even if it meant, as a reluctant student quipped, doing "things I do not like" for an income. "Making money to provide" required "making goods for a wage." What choice did a person really have? My mother said she worked because "four boys needed to eat." A student agreed with my mom: "Work is what puts food on my table." It was a daily need, a constant purpose to find "a good sense of security." Work was the source of "stability" and the path to "self-sufficiency." It could do even more. "Work is what pays for your vacations" and "how I get nice things." Marx noted that as workers provide for their own subsistence, they "are indirectly producing their actual material life."[14] Work, in other words, is "life's building blocks." To the students in my class, work "keeps the world turning." Workers acknowledged that their commitment to years of productive labor also originated from an absurd motivation; to stop working. They worked so that "retiring with dignity" would be possible. What a paradox this is. They work forever so that they can never have to work. "Work is a means to my retirement." One of my students, Todd Behny, an Indiana manufacturing worker and United Steelworker Local 809 member, poignantly described keeping up with the quest to end a life of labor in his poem, "The Grind."

> Alarms screaming for the 3rd time.
> Daylight creeping through the blinds.
> Just 5 more minutes. I'll be fine.
> Feet touch the floor and the body shudders, fighting back.
> The aroma of beans brewing in the pot, to get me on track.
> Wipe the steam from the mirror as I give thanks for 40 years
> Of work, for a few more lines, a little less hair.
> Shoes on, keys and lunch in hand. Kiss the wife and say—
> 'See you tomorrow? Same place and time?
> As I head out to join the race,
> Me already a few laps behind. Just another normal day.
> In the grind.

The pressing realities of having to work, however, did not preclude workers from seeking personal "growth" or seeking to "maintain a particular lifestyle" through their jobs. One worker understood personal development as an interdependent relationship: to do work "is to grow, growth is work." Here, the objective—establishing work's purpose—profoundly exceeded the mere need to reproduce the next day. The bar was set extremely high for an economic exchange of labor power for wages. Work was the mechanism for "attaining confidence in myself" and "essential for reaching my goals." It was a "way to live my best life" and to construct "a quality way to live." And not just any activity would suffice. Alternatives to working for a living existed that required little ethical regard. But work is not only a "way of life"; it's "an honest way to live" or "making an honest living." Imagine the implications. The "daily grind," for all its hardship, was the workers' vehicle to the best life possible. A life purely of intellectual introspection and leisure was never possible.

Work would also be the best means the workers in my class had for living a life that corresponded to that of an authentic human being. "Work is a way to live properly." Through work, a person develops their innate human powers and realizes a full life. The purpose of work was to feel a sense of "accomplishment, pride, satisfaction." My students desired to be useful. They saw work as an opportunity to develop their human potential by taking on "challenges that were rewarding." However, from rubber factories to schoolhouses, too few jobs gave workers the chance to expand their skills. In national surveys only a third to a slightly more than 50 percent of non–upper class respondents state that it's "very true" that they hold jobs that require them to "learn new things" and have supervisors that are helpful.[15] More problematically, just a quarter to 43 percent of lower-, working-, and middle-class workers say it's "very true" they have jobs where they can "develop their abilities."[16]

My students disparaged employers who were indifferent to the commitment of workers to "getting something done" that was high quality. Students in my class used some of the darkest humor to describe the Rubrik's cube-like messes that supervisors could cause at work. The "shit show" nature of some workplaces left exasperated workers with an unsatisfying "dilligaf" attitude. Yeah, that's how I first heard it. Give up? It stands for "Do I look like I give a fuck?" and it expresses a worker's exasperation at their employer's disregard for the quality of the work. Workers routinely pointed out that the only genuine thing that employers wanted from them was their ability to generate more profit. But if the boss is indifferent, why should anyone else be upset? Nothing seemed to outrage workers more than employers who cared only for bottom line measures of production. They were infuriated by managers who didn't manage and supervisors who didn't provide the supports needed to do the job right. Now, they were equally critical of other workers for not "showing up to do [their] job[s]." Union or not union, management had the responsibility of staffing and overseeing the job. But in some situations, out of necessity "the workers were running the mill." The workers too often seemed more invested in making capitalism work than the capitalists.

Work to Build Society

Workers' desire to improve themselves necessarily leads to another larger purpose for working. Workers understood how much they needed a safe, healthy, and vibrant public community, which they expressed in essays like this one: "Work is necessary to a functioning society." None of my students were rich enough to wall themselves off from the more extreme risks of civil society. They, more than the very wealthy, needed well-funded public safety departments, health services, transportation, schools, parks, and social services. My students saw improvements in their lives because of union wages and benefits, professional development, apprenticeship programs, and enforcement of legal rights on the job. While having labor power to sell situated them into the economic structure of society, without a collective identity and purpose it guaranteed nothing. Each protective measure was evidence of how their solidarity lifted people into and fueled the construction of a middle-class society. Workers never needed to be reminded of the reason they worked; it was to "be useful to society," to "make life better," and to be "important to everybody." Many workers interpreted the societal benefit of work through a galvanizing patriotic lens: "Work is the foundation that America stands on," and "doing your part for the American way." One student saw a more universal purpose. Along with education and recreation, this student said, "work is one of three pillars of society."

Their focus on community building was reminiscent of what Hannah Arendt believed about work: it makes a world in which humans can live. Students spoke of a labor that, despite its repetitive functionality and banality, was as Hannah Arendt described "born of a great urgency and motivated by a more powerful drive than anything else, because life itself depends on it."[17] Marx offered a naturalistic universal conception of labor: "[It] is a condition of human existence which is independent of all forms of society; it is an eternal natural necessity which mediates . . . human life itself."[18] My students made the things that gave the world a useable form. Arendt put the purpose of work this way: "Viewed as part of the world, the products of work—and not the products of labor—guarantee the permanence and durability without which a world would not be possible at all."[19] Work produces an objective world that constitutes a shared human reality. According to Arendt work constitutes the very structure of human experience by constructing a world that we all inhabit, and to which, in our own way, we contribute through our own work. The objects of our work, she points out, provide a common ground for entering a community. Workers from diverse occupations repeatedly shared this idea of lifting all life. Work is what "gives . . . purpose in society" and is "how we prosper in today's world." It is a mechanism for having a positive role in the community and contributing to a "good life."

Workers view work, no matter the pay and occupation, as a net contribution to social well-being. It is work that makes "societal advancement" possible. And consequently, as one student said, "[Work] makes me feel needed," and creates "my self-worth." In fact, work is the "basis of self-worth." Notice the relationship. Workers have the power to be productive, and when they have the means to do good work it adds value to social capital. The collective labor of the working class is more than a mechanism for setting prices and determining wages. It is additive to the common good and the source of "how value is created." Very often my students said that work "empowered" them. It could be physically, intellectually, and emotionally draining, but their labor exercised a human power to be productive. Nurses and teachers articulated a desire to contribute to human and societal betterment, but so did workers who made artificial limbs, milled crank shafts, and cleaned school hallways. Essays revealed that creating the good society was not only the effect of work but also a purpose workers intentionally held. A Chicago bus driver contended that work had a moral imperative. It ought "to be satisfying emotionally and financially." After hearing workers explain how their labors make the world a bit more livable, I reached for the poem "Bill Hastings." Written in first person, it reveals an electrician lecturing a presumably condescending "college boy" about how labor can matter to the well-being of a young girl. In breathtaking style, the narrator describes a series of tasks that a power line worker performs to turn the heat back on and illuminate the dark during a dreadfully cold night. When the job is done, something like Aristotle's notion of "beauty" (e.g., harmony, symmetry, order, clarity, unity, and wholeness) is achieved.[20] Or as one worker wrote, "Work is what keeps the lights on."

> Finally you slam the SMD fuse home.
> Bang! The whole valley lights up below you
> where before was unbreathing darkness.
> In one of those houses a little girl
> stops shivering. Now that's beautiful,
> And it's because of you.[21]

I was moved by how students conceived of their labor as a moral imperative. What is work? Nothing less than "an obligation for a good life." Teachers, nurses, firefighters, building trade workers and factory workers went further. They all agreed that work is "saving lives." Their efforts of course were shamefully unappreciated. After more than a year of pandemic-induced economic sheltering, in 2020 the average salaries of S&P 500 CEOs increased by more than $700,000 over the previous year. Recall that in April 2020 a record 41 million layoffs occurred. An incompetent and immoral White House's failure to take seriously a global public health crisis devastated the lives of working people. But not so the capitalist heads of S&P 500 companies. On top of the sizeable income-tax breaks they and their firms were gifted in 2017, they received, on average, $15.5 million in total compensation. While working people bore the brunt of the pandemic, on average, for every one dollar a worker earned, an S&P 500 chieftain earned $299.[22] In Illinois, where the majority of my students resided, the CEO-to-worker pay ratio was a hefty 196:1, and an average S&P CEO earned $13,123,543. I did some math. If I assumed that every student in my biggest single class (roughly one hundred) in 2020 earned an average $50,000 (a very generous and certainly wrong assumption), they would be collectively paid two-thirds less than one Illinois S&P 500 chief executive. That's a whole lot of surplus value generated by workers "providing a service" and "making a product." In the words of a very self-aware student, work is "mostly profitable to nonlaborers." In case the meaning is obscure here, let me interpret: work produces disproportional benefits for people who don't work. And workers know it. They also know when they are being asked to sell their labor and souls cheaply. Struggling to find employees to work for very little pay during the Delta variant Coronavirus surge, Walmart announced to much fanfare that it was raising pay for 565,000 employees by at least one dollar an hour.[23] What did that generosity do for average wages? Brought them all the way up to $16.40—about five dollars less than what school bus drivers were earning in parts of Illinois. Oh yeah. Minimum pay would rise to $12. Students scoffed in disgust at the idea that this was how work would "provide." The true value workers create was magnified by the realization of how little the superrich were paying in taxes on the enormous wealth they siphoned out of the production process. Charles P. Rettig, the IRS commissioner, estimated that the country was losing roughly $1 trillion—that's $1,000,000,000,000—in unpaid taxes every year. Who is not paying? You know darn well who. Natasha Sarin, a Treasury Department official, spit it out plainly enough: "Ordinary workers are fully compliant with their tax obligations. The companies and wealthy executives that employ them are not."[24]

It's not just the obscene differences in compensation between employers and workers that is offensive. What happens to a worker's commitment to the greater good when the people and employers they serve intentionally put them at risk? We've seen how my students experienced work as a dangerous place, but disregard for employee health threatens their other-directed motivation. Seeing work as a form of citizenship is extremely difficult when it raises the specter of individual survival. Thousands of face-to-face and essential workers stayed on the job during multiple waves of the coronavirus pandemic. Immigrant meatpackers helped to feed the country while giant employers like Tyson, Smithfield, and Iowa Beef left workers to process meat without proper personal protective equipment and mitigation measures. Workers' symptomatic conditions were ignored, and ill employees were ordered to come into the plant. The result was illness and death. A lot of illness and death. Tyson plants alone had more than eleven thousand workers infected.[25]

The meat companies' disregard for employee safety may also have taken a heinous turn. The United Food and Commercial Workers (UFCW) International Union, which represents over 250,000 workers in meatpacking and food processing plants and whose local members were well represented in many of my classes over the years, reported 128 meatpacking workers died from COVID-19 and 19,800 were infected or exposed. The union filed a lawsuit alleging that employees were ordered to report to work, even if sick, while supervisors wagered money on the number of workers who would be infected by the virus.[26]

Hospital nurses in Chicago who wrote essays for my class were obviously influenced by ministering to the ill while a deadly virus raged. As of August 21, 2021, 1,200 nurses had died from the virus nationwide. One report found that more than 3,600 US health care workers perished in the first year of the pandemic alone.[27] A few hundred of those deaths were staff at long-term care facilities. I personally know the exposure and fear that nursing home employees felt early in the pandemic. A good friend who worked for a large local provider shared that the company couldn't get ahold of enough face coverings for their staff. Demand for masks was super high, and supply was minimal. In response, my wife, Lynn, took to her sewing machine and became a one-person manufacturing powerhouse. She made over two hundred masks for her friends and coworkers. The firm was enormously grateful and sent her a letter of appreciation. She got another thank-you note from the village mayor. Women like Lynn stepped up all over the country and provided hours of volunteer work to help keep people safe.[28] The profit motive wasn't necessary to induce good and meaningful work. Work was a "challenging opportunity to help people."

Emergency room and intensive care unit nurses were pushed to the emotional and physical edge by the surging demands of sick and particularly unvaccinated patients. Nurses wrestled with the moral dilemma of how to provide quality care when their hospitals were badly understaffed and many fellow citizens refused to be vaccinated. How do nurses square the reality that their commitment to the life of the sick exceeds a patients' self-regard for their own health, a disregard that reveals an indifference to the nurses' Hippocratic oath? Anger, dismay, and abandonment follow. "Work is putting me at risk of dying," said one student. When the ambulance pulls up to the hospital, work becomes "a betrayal of trust." The most profound essays on using work to help others were those that, in their simplicity, communicated work as a craft with a standard of care. Unfortunately, too many healthcare employees lamented that "work is impossible."

Teachers also struggled to do work that many described as a calling. They were confronted by abusive voices fueled by irresponsible political officials demanding that they risk their lives to teach the ABCs in a classroom. To experienced educators the ugly characterizations of their profession during the pandemic were echoes of past cultural diatribes against public schools. The public health crisis universally exposed longstanding vulnerabilities, stresses, and dangers of working for a living, but teachers bore a familiar and extraordinary denunciation. Conservative parent groups, corporate champions of for-profit schools, and right-wing politicians have at different times allied to try and dismantle a system of free, universal, and taxpayer-funded liberal arts and science education.[29] On every occasion teachers and teacher unions have been targeted for vilification. Teachers have always had to navigate a climate driven more by fear, hysteria, and rank political opportunism than by the incredible meaningful work that lies at the heart of what public schools contribute to the development of young people and the stability of our constitutional republic and civil society. Steering through the hostilities has often meant engaging in a "fight for the soul of public education."[30] In response to contemporary attacks on teachers and public schools, in 2018 and 2019 roughly 645,000 educators participated in work stoppages.

Teaching is arguably the one foundational profession. If no one learns, no one builds, heals, serves, eats, or protects. But teachers did not want to be anyone's heroes. Sadly, many became martyrs. As of August 11, 2021, 290 active teachers had died of COVID-19.[31] A 2020 surveyed sponsored by the American Federation of Teachers (AFT) and the New York Life Foundation found that more than 26 percent of teachers knew of a member of their school community (including direct family members of students, teachers, or staff) who had died from the coronavirus.[32] Despite in many cases having to work under multiple and changing formats and in some cases being demonized by parents and elected officials and left unprotected by some school boards, teachers didn't run for the exits. Roughly 6 percent of educators (including superintendents and principals) voluntarily left the profession after 2020, a level commensurate with prepandemic separations.[33] The number may yet rise, but as the 2021 school year began educators remained driven to do work that changes lives. "They are frustrated, they are tired, but they are committed to the work," according to L. Earl Franks, Executive Director of the National Association of Elementary School Principals.[34] Remarkably, when teaching during a pandemic, educators approached their work a lot like they did at any other time. One student's essay said, "[Work] is what happens between me and the students." The cacophony of loud voices outside the school building and inside board meetings is "just noise."

Aside from disappointments about how they were treated and the broad income disparities between employers and employees, my students did their jobs faithfully in search of more than commodities. Workers' pursuit of non-commercial or financial objectives was common but perhaps very surprising to the end user or consumer of that labor. Freud for example, concluded that "as a path to happiness, work is not highly prized by men." He contended that "they do not strive after it as they do after other possibilities of satisfaction," and more problematically, that most people have a "natural human aversion to work."[35] Freud never met my students. A job was never only about pleasure or in many cases ever pleasurable at all, but it wasn't something to be avoided. Work needed to be "something you like[d] to do." Life was better with nicer things, and the ability to fulfill desires off the job—time permitting—was important. "Work is good for your bank account." But it wasn't the be-all and end-all of employment. Workers sought out "work with a why."[36] They wanted to have everything their work could pay for, but that didn't mean that labor was exclusively about becoming a contented consumer. Students rejected the idea that they had transferred their pursuit of personal fulfillment into the stuff they owned. Happiness may have been directly felt at the point of a purchase, but their subjectivity was constructed through their point of production. Work was supposed to be a "process of evolution" whereby as a person grows in a job the individual is defined more through doing than having. They advocated for the idea that "money is never sufficient reason for work."[37] Options not to work were too ugly to consider, but workers described the purpose of work as fulfilling a dual function.

Work is both a rational response to the basic necessities of existence within a capitalist economy and the principal means by which individual identity and uniqueness are formed. It is a powerful means to "making a name for [one]self." The absence of work was punishing, my students reported, but a job without meaning was a never-ending kind of dying. As one said, "[It is] why I get up every morning sadly." Workers neve scoffed at being employed but decried having jobs that merely furnished them with nothing more than the means to pay bills. It was common to get essays that read, "Work is not my life." Contrarily, workers shared knowingly with each other that their jobs enabled them to "feel hope" about today and tomorrow. They attested, like James Baldwin, that a "good job not only has to pay well; it also has to offer hope."[38] While "hope" is not a work outcome ever surveyed, there have been efforts to define or measure a "good" or "quality job." The Organization for Economic Cooperation and Development uses a framework for measuring and assessing job quality that impacts worker well-being that features three categories: "earnings quality," "labor market security" (i.e., the risk of unemployment), and "quality of the working environment" (i.e., noneconomic aspects of a job).[39] Cornell University Law School developed the US Private Sector Job Quality Index (JQI) to assess job quality in the United States by "measuring desirable higher-wage/higher-hour jobs versus lower-wage/lower-hour jobs."[40] Based on years of student essays, here's my own more detailed list of what customarily should legitimately constitute a good/quality job:

Earnings
Employer-provided benefits
Working time/schedule
Intensity/duration
Voice at work
Autonomy: control over work
Job stability and security of work
Work/family balance
Fair and equitable treatment
Workplace safety
Diversity in the substance of work
Body-brain balance
Skill level/training
Opportunities for advancement
Moderate stress level
Good managerial practices
Satisfaction/personal fulfillment
Happiness

Regardless how job quality is measured, the record here in the United States is not encouraging. The problem likely starts with how people with very lofty jobs think about jobs for everybody else. For example, Michael Boskin, chairman of President George H. W. Bush's Council of Economic Advisors from 1989 to 1993, reportedly pronounced (then denied having done so) that "potato chips, computer chips, what's the difference? A hundred dollars of one or a hundred dollars of the other is still a hundred dollars."[41] Turns out it actually does make a sizeable difference. According to the JQI, job quality has been falling for decades. When looking for a reason why labor-force participation rates were not higher in the United States during a pre-pandemic white hot economy, *Forbes* offered a straightforward answer: "Workers don't re-enter the workforce because many of the jobs themselves are rotten."[42]

A report by the Russell-Sage Foundation titled "Declining Job Quality in the United States," revealed a forty-year decline in job quality.[43] A Gallup study found that quality further deteriorated in 2020: "40% of U.S. workers have experienced worsening job quality since the start of the COVID-19 pandemic."[44] *Forbes* went on to quote a JQI white paper to demonstrate the weakness in the country's job-creation capacity based primarily on compensation levels: "The success of superstar companies like Google or Apple or Pfizer should not blind us to the fact that today Leisure & Hospitality is our largest sector with 14.7 million non-management employees. It's a sector that pays such workers $16.58 an hour and the average worker works just 25.8 hours a week—resulting in an average weekly income of $428. (Benefits like health insurance in the sector are small to nonexistent.)"[45]

While CEO indifference contributes to work's degradation, it doesn't end there. The federal government has been a willful agent in undermining work and betraying the workers. A painful example is the auto industry. In 2008 Congress passed an auto industry bailout for General Motors and Chrysler. As a condition of the federal loan, the firms had to lower—yes, that's not a typo—the average wages and benefits paid to GM's and Chrysler's unionized employees so that the average per-hour per-person amount was equivalent to what employees of the nonunion companies, Nissan, Toyota, or Honda Motors were paid.[46] For the US nameplates this would largely impact future assembly-plant hirers. Can you guess where this is headed? While the difference among assembly workers was not extravagant, foreign owned firms with plants in the United States were offering a lower total compensation package. In a historic use of government power, thousands of autoworkers had their compensation lowered, and the effect rippled across the working class. Bad as it was, that's not the end of it. An additional requirement forced the US firms to downgrade work rules to match the foreign companies. By 2013 the industry did see a very healthy rebound, but was it still offering middle-class paying jobs? Consider for a moment that the average auto industry—wide wage in the 1970s was roughly 150 percent of the average private-sector wage. Auto manufacturing jobs were once a solid middle-class job. But by 2013 the average factory worker made 7.7 percent below the median wage for all occupations. Including auto parts employees who made up three out of four industry hires, roughly 1.5 million manufacturing workers (25 percent) made $11.91 or less.[47]

While too few jobs qualify as high-quality, fewer are likely to make people happy. Many, if not most, of my students did like their jobs. Some went as far as to note, "[Work is] what makes me happy," and "[Work] produces happiness." The daily act of making steel, checking train tickets, reading x-rays, and helping a special education student could cease feeling like work "when you're having fun." But most students did not claim that their jobs made them happy or even expected them to. Instead, they sought a nonexploitive way to develop and use their human capacities to stitch together a healthy community. The objective was less personal joy than to be "engaged mentally" in a "rewarding" activity that they "should be proud of." Their work was the intersection where "pride meets determination." It should create a "foundation for a successful life." Unfortunately, a large number of workers are denied the "honest eight" activity that is "essential to a fulfilling life." A 2016 survey found that a bare majority (51 percent) of employed Americans felt that their job gave them a sense of identity. A hefty 47 percent said their job was just how they made a living, or as a few of my students said, work is "just work." Among those who have a high school diploma and work at middle-class-paying hourly-wage jobs, a segment of the population that also describes the majority of students in my classes over the past quarter century, only 38 percent say they get a sense of identity from their jobs.[48]

Finding a level of satisfaction and fulfilment in work was instrumental to forming a respectable community. Workers viewed their human labor as contributing to an evolving ecosystem. Their labors aimed at something beyond themselves. One student who belonged to the sheet metal workers union said affirmatively, "Work is a way to touch people's lives." They were a part of and mixed their labor with the natural world. By doing work they transformed the objective natural conditions in a way that conformed to human needs. Each of my students labored in conditions not completely of their own choosing, but their essays revealed that they did not conceive of themselves as merely creatures of a preordained environment. In addition to producing and consuming the inanimate things they could not live without, like food, clothing, and shelter, humanizing the environment was paramount to a healthy social order. Workers shared how their work was produced and developed with the help of others. "Production by a solitary individual," according to Marx, is "preposterous." The common good is produced by the workers, and the aggregate wealth they create amounts to the "universality of the needs, powers, enjoyments and productive forces of individuals."[49] Work is a social activity, and in my students' understanding "a main component of society."

Work to Be Free

The proportion of workers in my classes whose labor was tightly wound up with how they thought of themselves and related to others was significant.

Implicit in the pursuit of intrinsically meaningful work that they described is the personal freedom it enables. To work and have some control or mastery over your socially necessary labor is to achieve a degree of liberation from the coercive actions of other humans. My students likely didn't choose the way they earned a living or to be someone's employee, but there is a personal liberty that can be derived from labor. "Work is freedom to choose a life path."

Freedom, for my students, was twofold. First, by holding a middle-class-paying job workers were able "to live a dignified life." The English philosopher John Locke noticed the subjugation of one man to another began when a person "preferred being" another person's property, "subject to starving."[50] Social theorist Jean-Jacques Rousseau warned against the objectionable control of one person over another caused by extreme wealth inequality: "No citizen should ever be wealthy enough to buy another, and none poor enough to be forced to sell himself."[51] This is freedom from the viciousness of being tossed out of the labor market. Second, by default employees have less power than managers at work. When the balance of power is extreme, workers get exploited. But my students were in unionized jobs, and that meant they felt less vulnerable. To be clear, they did not feel completely invulnerable. Bad things happen to union workers, as well as nonunion. I was horrified to learn from students in my class of a union plant in Indiana where workers were forced to clock sixteen-hour shifts and work Fridays and Saturdays three weekends a month. All of this was part of the collective bargaining agreement. The general difference was, nonetheless, that in union jobs the workers had a countervailing force with the legal right and means to use power on behalf of the worker against the employer. The positive difference a union makes when it asserts its power to protect the freedom, dignity, and welfare a worker experiences from working is profound.

Union representation can be the thin line between a relatively independent life and one of insecurity and dependance. Nothing dismantles a feeling of liberty and security more than fear of death or a lost limb. In a report my colleague Frank Manzo and I did examining the outcomes of thirty-four thousand Occupational Safety and Health Administration (OSHA) inspections of construction worksites, we found that union worksites averaged 34 percent fewer safety violations. They also were 19 percent less likely to have any OSHA violations. In Illinois union worksites had 52 percent fewer violations.[52] Unions were also associated with 6.8 percent lower COVID-19 infection rates among nursing home staff.[53] While demonstrating how much better the exchange of labor power is for union members, Frank and I have also chronicled the continuous decline of union membership.[54] Without union representation there is a decreased probability that workers will have the autonomy to find meaning in their work that extends beyond material necessity. If "*el trabajo es prosperidad*" (work is prosperity), then prosperity is only possible, as a student insisted, by embracing work's social character and by "standing together to push us forward." Working collectively was the only effective way to ensure that work could bring the "freedom to live as you please."

Personal freedom was never the objective of capitalist production. Its objective is instead to surrender to the logic of the marketplace where everything must be purchased—freedom included. Capitalism needs and orchestrates a dependency on a flow of goods, services, and labor, from dog food to cardiac surgery. As Mike Konczal notes, freedom defined in market terms will always give the "bosses an advantage because under market dependency, workers need to work in order to survive, in order to have the resources to continue living."[55] My students understood the implications. "*El trabajo es la base fundamental de sobre vivir*" (work is the fundamental basis of survival). Contrarily, the employer chooses if they want to hire new employees, how many employees they want to hire, when to hire them, and who they want those employees to be. But the individual worker always needs the job, and the person hired doesn't have to be *you*. The power asymmetry is profound, which is why work and the rules under which labor is secured are political acts. Work is "the currency of the people's power." It belongs to those who only have their labor power to sale. To my students work is the essential asset that reduces the power imbalance between them and the holders and overseers of vast amounts of profit-making private property.

Capital for the owners and income for the workers is the basis of the employment relationship. Nevertheless, without labor power to sell, a worker has a tenuous hold on any claim of self-determination. Isaiah Berlin famously laid out his distinction between "negative" and "positive" liberty. The absence of obstacles or constraints characterized negative liberty, while positive liberty was the capacity to affirmatively act to take control of one's life. Berlin explained the positive side this way: "I wish, above all, to be conscious of myself as a thinking, willing, active being, bearing responsibility for my choices and able to explain them by references to my own ideas and purposes."[56] Freedom in both senses meant having the ability to achieve full human potential and live virtuously. It also required a consciousness of the needs of others, for without social cooperation individuals would be constantly interfering with one another's aspirations. Workers experienced their labor as mediated by workplace relations. Getting a job done well might depend on someone else— a worker they likely knew—doing their job effectively. My students insisted that to assert autonomy from within their situation as a waged laborer (i.e., someone who is someone else's employee), "work is essential to progress." It is, as one worker asserted, "a stepping stone to future freedoms."

Work to Be Fulfilled

The purpose for working is not one-dimensional or dichotomous, and it didn't neatly fit with how work meaningfulness theorists conceptualized work orientation. An individual worker worked for different reasons. Scholars have proposed that individuals tend to see their work primarily as a job, a career, or a calling.[57] But working for "bread" and a chance to put the "impress of mind and skill on the material world" led my students to multiple and simultaneous orientations toward work.[58] I learned this because they rarely followed directions. When I asked them to write a six-word answer about what work is, many students composed multiple essays. Not only did they write more than one; they wrote different kinds. Here is a prime example. Work is:

> ... providing for my family.
> ... a way to always keep learning.
> ... the path to a better world.

Students were focused on the material benefits of their work ("providing for my family"). How could they not be? But not to the exclusion of diverse forms of personal fulfillment. For some, like teachers, nurses, and construction workers who had completed apprenticeship programs, work was part of a career trajectory ("keep learning") that brought some hope for higher levels of self-esteem and social standing. But financial ends remained a strong reason for clocking in. How could it not? At the same time these same workers expressed something like a "secular calling" for their work. Work is an end in itself that contributes to the greater good ("a better world") and makes life more plentiful. But still, they needed to be paid. And it would be good if they could advance in their trade.

Another student juxtaposed the following purposes: "making an honest living," "making a name for" themself, and "being part of a team." This student not only placed a value on intrinsic and extrinsic gains but stressed the importance of "self-realization," as well as social connection. In this example, the worker seemed to embody the secular sense of a calling as a "meaningful beckoning toward activities that are morally, socially, and personally significant."[59] I previously mentioned that much of what I heard was a secular "calling." With rare exception, workers did not define work by using the word calling or a synonym. I don't believe my students believed that they had to do the work they were doing to fulfill their unique purpose in life. Some even rejected the idea that any job had a teleological quality; "work is not the intended purpose of humanity." Few offered, even if they had an idea, what the ultimate purpose of life was. But nearly all of my students felt their work was connected to their identity and contributed to the "fulfillment of life." They held significant beliefs about the value of work, the motivation for working, their orientation toward work, and the good they intended for their work. Work for many was the visible embodiment of their moral integrity: "work is a representation of my values." It is a lifelong "action that builds character." In conversations with students, I realized they were explaining work's ability to develop within them ethical qualities which Aristotle called an "excellence." Working enabled the individual to develop virtuous characteristics and as a result "cause his [or her] own work to be done well."[60] In the words of a reflective student who articulated the holistic purpose of labor in a person's life, "At the end of the day start with your work."

While the majority of my students claimed a belief in God and held a reverential feeling about where they worked, not many were active in any religious congregation or referenced spiritual texts as inspiring their work. But their holistic purpose for working was encapsulated in a historic clerical writing. Pope John Paul II's famous Encyclical, "Labor Exercens" (On Human Work), declared that "THROUGH WORK man must earn his daily bread." He went on to claim that "man is made to be in the visible universe an image and likeness of God himself, and he is placed in it in order to subdue the earth. From the beginning therefore he is called to work."[61] In the words of one theologian, *Laborem Exercens* declared that work "contributes to the building up of God's creation, builds up the individual, and generates a wage."[62] To the pontiff, it didn't seem to really matter whether a person personally felt a particular call. Maybe just "working hard for the money," as Donna Summers belted out, was close enough to doing God's work.[63] And no one was delusional about the economic compulsion to hold a job. Any job. One student said, "[Work is] putting a roof over my head." It's necessary, not glamorous. In 1891 another papal letter, *Rerum Novarum*, recognized work's necessity in its basic phenomenological form: "In the sweat of thy face thou shalt eat bread."[64] And drink; "work is good, beer is better." However, students also said, "[Work is what] makes me happy," "fills me with pride," and "enables me to thrive." Why work? Because work is "good for your body and brain." For most students work took care of themselves and others; for some, it was also a way of "honoring God."

My dad took a job in a steel mill to help his family afford to live. He never expected to be personally fulfilled by the work. In reminiscing about the distant past, my father recollects that playing the trumpet would have more likely achieved an intrinsically rewarding purpose. Was he called to the band stage and just got misdirected? Was dad's going through the Stop 5 Entrance Gate at Republic Steel for the first time and never ceasing for the next thirty-seven years evidence that horn playing wasn't his calling? Was being a steelworker a posteriori proof that being a millwright was? My mother wanted to be a flight attendant. She was a strong, caring person who would have done that job well. Instead, she did the best she could and earned a living in other ways. A common and dangerous American myth is that everyone has options when it comes to finding a buyer for your labor power. Millions of people take on the singular identity of their paid labor because the political-economic system compels a hard division of labor. Marx suggested however that under a different set of societal conditions there would be "no painters, but at most people who engage in painting."[65] In such a society I imagine my father could have worked in a mill but not been just a millworker. Mom could have assisted with medical records but not been a medical records specialist. Maybe then there would have been time and opportunity to play a horn or help people fly safely around the world. Like my parents, few students in my class had ever done work they aspired to do. Nonetheless, without feeling called to a job, workers found all sorts of personal meaning in their labor.

Professor Amy Wrzesniewski and her colleagues at the Yale School of Management document in their research how workers engage in "job crafting" to infuse their work with meaning. The process involves "redefining your job to incorporate your motives, strengths, and passions."[66] In my conversations with workers they noted countless ways that they personalized their work and went the "extra mile" for a customer, student, patient, or another worker. Those incidental and idiosyncratic acts of kindness aside, few of my students had the freedom to genuinely craft out their jobs. Employers were not turning the "reins over to employees, empowering them to become 'job entrepreneurs.'"[67] It's true that workers attempted to apply their knowledge and skills in the way they thought best. They preferred more control over their job than less. Work was meant to enable a person to have a "sense of accomplishment." But these acts happened not as reimagined tasks or relationships but within the formal job they were hired to perform. Workers asserted their being on the job as a way to reintegrate their productive activity into their identity. It is an attempt to subvert the arid necessity of work that Marx observed where a worker only feels "himself outside his work, and in his work feels outside himself."[68] If my students had their way, employment would be a liberating, conscious activity that determined how we should share the planet. "Work is our way to live life."

Yes, for nearly every worker what they did for an income made it possible to "enjoy life outside of work." On one hand, the purpose of my students' work was merely instrumental and obligatory. Their labor had been reduced to an abstraction, hollowed out by capitalist social relations and objectively realized as a cost of production. At the same time workers hoped, strived, and organized for what they defined as "fulfilling and rewarding" jobs. They described work as a way to take care of the people they love, realize their value as human beings, liberate themselves from the control of others, and construct a community. One essay writer connected the relationship between work and its transformative purpose: "Work is life changing." Workers were aware they were compelled to work ("work is survival") and likewise knew that their labor was the activity that most defined them as human. There was no paradox. Both premises were valid and acted on. In work, a unification occurred. "Work is an extension of one's being."

Mom understood and accepted—at times resentfully—the limits of her upbringing that restricted her options to be a person that travels to new worlds. Nonetheless, she found joy making women look beautiful and satisfaction in managing patients' medical records. In doing this work, she had a purpose that transcended the role of wife and parent. Dad never once held a trumpet in his hands. Still, he did have that one moment along the railroad tracks when he wanted his sons to know what he had made. As train cars rambled by, his purpose was known.

CHAPTER 5

The Subject of Work

GROWING UP I WAS only dimly aware of how my parents were personally impacted by work or the purposes their work served. I saw my mom alone and unhappy a lot when my dad worked the night and graveyard shifts. I also felt her pride in wielding a pair of scissors and commanding a room of women with hair needing to be dressed. She had gone to beautician school and passed a licensing test. She was good at what she did, and she had a large, loyal following of women. There were plenty of inconvenient times she got panicked calls from a woman who had a formal affair to attend and had suffered a hair emergency. Mom always invited them over to the house, no matter the hour, for a literally face-saving fix. Later in life she got hired as a records manager at Parkview Counseling Center in Youngstown where she worked for about thirteen years. She provided support for several doctors, and the work made her feel needed. It turned out to be the last job she held.

Dad hired on with the Republic Steel Company, and following a series of corporate mergers, retired from the LTV Corporation, with thirty-seven unbroken years of service except for two years of duty in the Korean War. He knew only one employer but had done several jobs. Unlike my mom, my dad never told me what he felt about his work. My father was a classic stoic. He said very little and accepted what he couldn't change. Never complained. Work made him tired, and he hurt physically. I only know that because my mom told me. I never saw him joyfully or dejectedly heading out to work. He had really close friends in the mill and enjoyed their comradery. The mill was a place to socialize with the "guys," talking high school football and "about your kids." But he rarely frequented the many bars across from the mill gates. He bowled a lot with his mill buddies at the Struthers Holiday Bowl, located up the street from where we lived. Mom had her own bowling coterie of working women, and she brought home a number of individual and team trophies. All that work did to my parents was hard to realize in real time. Retrospection and investigation have provided a much fuller picture. However, it didn't require the passage of too many years for me to understand on whose behalf my parents worked. It was as clear as the sound of heavy pipe banging on train cars and the voices of women coming from the basement conversation. They worked for me. They worked for my brothers. They worked for each other. They worked for their friends and neighbors. They worked for the community. They worked for themselves. If you step back and see the bigger picture you realize that it's good that there are many subjects of our labor. I particularly celebrated this essay: "Work is how we connect the world." It is, according to another student, "unifying."

The subjects my parents labored for were very much like the ones my students identified as motivating their work. In my years of conversations with workers, who you worked for resonated as the truest element of work. Work could provide, frustrate, empower, disappoint, drain life, decay limbs, shape the environment, develop the person and society, create life, and kill. It all mattered, but it was who you worked for that exposed the most meaningful aspect of our labors. The subject of that labor could reverberate across generations. Rudy Ballines is an Indiana steelworker who, while in my class, was serving as a union steward. His parents were among the 4.5 million Mexicans who came to the United States between 1942 and 1964 to work primarily in agricultural fields as part of the Bracero Program.[1] The program was a contract labor agreement that allowed millions of Mexican men to come to the United States to work on short-term, primarily agricultural labor contracts. It is widely seen by historians as a form of labor control by large agricultural businesses over submissive farmworkers. When Rudy talks about what work is, he is inspired by his mother's time in the fields. In his original poem, "Mama and the Grape Vines," Rudy shared with the class for whom his mom and now he works.

> Fighting off thirst, bee stings!
> Heat and hunger.
> Working from dawn to dusk,
> Even longer.
> Grape vines,
> Cured blade cuts,
> Could not complain.
> Mama ill, pregnant,
> Working thru the pain.
> Mexican like Cesar

It was 1962.
Kept on working,
Not knowing about the UFW.
Pesticides everywhere.
Mama pregnant
No gear
No protection.
Baby coming,
No defects, no detection?
No time off for strikes
Or a farmers union fight.
Yet ... I was left
With a reminder,
Of the effects of mama's plight.
Have to use my voice!
No time to be shy
No time to be meek.
For an angel had kissed
And left a mark on my cheek.
A sign of strength!
A future, as a union griever.
A dream of continuing,
My mama's work
Of making you a union believer.

To appreciate Rudy's present work inspiration and intimate connection to his mother's life of labor, first consider how Anglo employers and citizens thought of Braceros. Here is an extended excerpt from an expose written by Pauline R. Kibbe about the experience of Latin Americans in Texas:

Generally speaking, the Latin-American migratory worker going into west Texas is regarded as a necessary evil, nothing more nor less than an unavoidable adjunct to the harvest season. Judging by the treatment that has been accorded him in that section of the state, one might assume that he is not a human being at all, but a species of farm implement that comes mysteriously and spontaneously into being coincident with the maturing of cotton, that requires no upkeep or special consideration during the period of its usefulness, needs no protection from the elements, and when the crop has been harvested, vanishes into the limbo of forgotten things-until the next harvest season rolls around. He has no past, no future, only a brief and anonymous present.[2]

It was common for signs saying "NO DOGS, NEGROES, MEXICANS" to be posted on establishment doors wherever Braceros were employed. Work for a Bracero was brutal and remains harsh for any contemporary agricultural worker. Nonetheless, Rudy's mom persevered. And she did so while pregnant with Rudy. She worked for her unborn child. How could she have endured it otherwise? In Rudy's lovely homage to his mom's sacrifice and the thousands of conversations with my students, I realized that what truly animated a person's work experience was the person or people who were the recipients of the labor. For whom we work is the focus of this final chapter.

For Family

There is no better way to understand what work is than to name and appreciate who we work for. Either long days for modest pay or not enough hours with too little compensation, workers grasp onto the lifeline that work provides. Joanne B. Ciulla, professor and director of the Institute for Ethical Leadership at Rutgers University, boldly posed a question rarely asked in our society: "What's so good about work?"[3] Yes, the conditions of a capitalist economy compel people to work—it is a necessity—and it often brings personal developmental benefits: "It offers instant discipline, identity and worth. It structures our time and imposes a rhythm on our lives. It gets us organized into various kinds of communities and social groups." She adds that "work works for us."[4] But even allowing for the intrinsic reasons people work, its material necessity places a genuine burden on our lives. And yet, workers log away most of their lives trying to avoid, as a Spanish-speaking student said, the "*vivir, sin trabajo no hay comida*" (no work, no food) reality. A big proportion of my students acknowledged that work is "my family's opportunity."

Spouses, children, parents, even grandparents motivated people to go to work. Typically, roughly a third of each of my classes had students who were married. The majority of those folks had kids. For students with family, they worked to provide for someone at home who was not working or to add to the earnings of a partner. In describing what work is, the word "work" was very often paired with "family" in retrospective, contemporary, and prospective terms. Working for a living was dedicated to family even when there wasn't any. In talking about what a person wanted to get out of work, a student said, "a good life someday with family." Here, working today was preparation for someday getting married and having children.

My students were enduring work today for a person they hadn't yet met, fallen in love with, or taken vows to cherish in sickness and in health. They were working at this moment for a someone who didn't even exist. At least to their knowledge. And their present labor was also an investment in a child not yet conceived or known to them. Work was done as a crucial precondition "to raise a family." Single workers in every occupation were working in the present to eventually start families. But what they continuously shared was that family was only possible in the present and future through work. The idea of family is synonymous with achieving the American dream and becoming middle class. Work bound them to people they loved and would love. Sigmund Freud noted that "no other technique for the conduct of life attaches the individual so firmly to reality as laying emphasis on Work; for his work at least gives him a secure place in a portion of reality, in the human community."[5]

Idealized notions of family were diverse, but every conception included having a good job. As workers correlated working with building a family, they were not expressing any concern for a proper work-life balance. It's not that they were uninterested in a healthy balance. Those who had families expressed deep concerns about the time they spent engaged with the job. A student flipped the customary capitalist value exchange of work. Instead of an employer paying for an employee's labor, "work is the price . . . for family." The "price" was measured in lost opportunities to be with people my students love while working to care for people they love. According to a national survey, balancing work and family life makes parenting more difficult.[6] In the United States the share of two-parent households where both adults work full time is 46 percent, close to its all-time high. Only 26 percent of households had a single parent working full-time and the others not employed. The research shows that two-working-parent households were better-off economically than those without. But the better financial security came with a cost.

A hefty 56 percent of all working parents said it was difficult to find "equilibrium between the two poles of obligation." A previous report found that nearly four out of ten working mothers and fathers say holding a job makes it harder to be a good parent.[7] The necessity of work is a real threat to sustaining a healthy family environment for middle- and working-class wage earners. Getting a job is more than a practical means to an end. It imparts a duty on the wife, husband, partner, parent, guardian, or caretaker. "Work is my obligation as a father." However, prior to worrying about a work-life balance, workers need to secure work in order to have a family. Among workers who have or hope someday to have kids, they wrote that work is "to give opportunities I didn't have." Work was a generational transfer. It was according to Ariel Lopez, a student and female operating engineer "about setting up generational wealth." The average hourly worker wasn't leaving behind a plentiful inheritance. In fact, children in the top 5 percent of household incomes are nearly twice as likely to receive an inheritance than kids growing up in the households of my middle-income workers.[8] For children who did receive inheritances, the difference in amounts were like the earnings gaps among households. In the bottom 90 percent of the income distribution, the value of an inheritance was between $90,000 and $158,000. The average inheritance of those in the top 5 percent of the income distribution was "about $424,000, or roughly three times the size of the inheritance received by those in the bottom 90 percent."[9]

Instead of a wealth transfer, my students were planning to use their weekly or bimonthly paychecks to give their kids a chance for a richer, fuller life. Work is a "steppingstone" for the children to climb. Who do we work for? "Work is *four* kids." Not abstractly just "kids" but specifically the number of children a worker raises. It's a phenomenological answer. The opportunities that work generates for the family ranged from the mundane to the life transforming. In every situation, work brought food, clothing, shelter, and maybe a pet or two. Some cases included lots of books in the house, summer camps, music lessons, and family vacations. In others, the opportunities were college tuition, study abroad, good health care, a quality K-12 school, and most important of all, the freedom to be a kid. My students with children worked principally for their kids. One said, "Work is fulfilling my needs as a father." Work is "providing what the family needs," meaning basic material goods. Work is also their "kid's ticket being punched." Here workers are clearly associating their labor with making a future life for their current or wished-for offspring.

Work is giving your kids a fighting chance for a good life. Not any life. But a life that exceeds the opportunities that my students have experienced. It's about making possible something better than what the parent-worker can achieve for themselves. My dad told me he never wanted his boys to follow him into the mill. He worked too hard to just continue a legacy of Bruno factory workers. It was bittersweet to hear his words, and for the longest time I felt bad that he didn't value his work. But I now realize my focus was on the wrong thing. It wasn't the work itself or its impact or the varied reasons he labored in the mill that truly mattered. To my dad, his work was how my brothers and I would realize a better life. Not by replicating his work but by overcoming it. What mattered for dad was the subject of his work.

Repeatedly, my students made clear that the point of their work was who it was meant for. Family as the subject of labor resonated across all occupations, races, genders, languages, sexual orientations, and ages. Work was "*importante para mi familia*" (important for my family). It "gives [families] many opportunities" and "takes care of family." Work is "what we do for . . . family." As we labor, we "raise a family." Work becomes a "family's livelihood."

The list of what work makes possible was varied, but it was "always important to . . . family." For one worker the practical distinction between the activity of paid labor and the beneficiary of that labor—family—collapsed. "Work is family." The equation seems oblique. How can work be family? Workers hoped and expected to work a long time. In constructing the means to allow their children to prosper, a worker would use work to "leave good memories to [their] family." Digging out a new sewer line, painting a water tower, driving a subway car, cleaning a hallway, or operating a shearing machine was about "securing an inheritance for the children."

As noted, the dollar amount might be modest, but the opportunity for the child to live more fully because of the parent's work was the real payoff. The work of one generation left something else incalculable behind. A name. As one said, "Work is my origin." Another student expressed the reciprocal relationship between an enduring identity and productive labor: "[Work is] only as a good as my name." In his poem, "Cement," Hayan Charara inspired class conversation with his poignant ode to what part of work is meant to outlive the worker's labor but is too often lost. A son recalls his construction worker father who poured the foundation of parking lots, sidewalks, and buildings. Teenagers carved the family names of the workers into the wet concrete. But many years later the convenience stores closed, and the cement cracked. Now, no one's father is working, and one boy wonders about the names.

> My father doesn't work anymore.
> When I ask about the names,
> He says he forgets.
> It was a long time ago.
> I was eight years old,
> Too young to realize that my name
> Was a gift, that I could
> Rub my fingers over each letter, and
> This much was enough.[10]

What is work? "Getting out of bed every day." Why? "To provide greater opportunities." Now comes the inspiration to work. For whom? "Family," meaning spouse, kids, loved ones. When I read this following essay out loud in class, I got choked up, and my students sat motionless: "[Work is] my kids doing better than me." The message was instantly understood. Immediately recognized. Universally embraced. Essays that articulated an unbroken line between parents and children and offered a covenant between one generation of working-class people to sacrifice on behalf of the betterment of the next generation was illustrative of the immigrant experience in America.

Union crane operators hauling a thousand pounds of metal during twelve-hour shifts made good money. Good if you're just counting the pay. Brutal if you measure the exhaustion and danger of being one button push away from dropping the metal where it doesn't belong. But still, a woman in my class has been doing the job for seven years. Why? She has a daughter who wants to work in Japan doing anime. Therefore, her mom carries metal for the mill furnaces. Each load is a down payment on her daughter's inheritance. That's what dad was trying to tell me. Like the workers in my class, he sacrificed, did a tough job, risked his health, and never complained. My mother faithfully reproduced her family through labor at home and sold her labor power outside of it.

Understanding now that their work was for their sons, I think back to my confusion upon seeing my dad leave the house at odd hours. What if he had not returned? I often recite the poem, "The Gates" to my students to express the weight of what a worker like my father carries for the people they love. Three kids wait anxiously in the car with their mom for their father to walk out of a steel mill after an evening shift. As each minute passes they worry that their dad won't come out. Perhaps the mill, "belching smoke and fire and steel like a monster," ate him? They had heard stories of terrible fortunes; "the dinosaur mill devouring its workers." Thankfully, the dad arrives, and none too soon. "And we too escaped, A family rescuing nightly its father."[11] My dad always walked out of the mill. He was never eaten. Knowing now for whom he and mom fought the "dinosaur" accentuates the meaning of their labor and the value of my inheritance. My students remind me of my parents.

For Myself

Workers of course worked for themselves: "[Work is] for me." Work served as a power source for a multidimensional individual: "Work is fuel for the mind, body, soul." Labor was a "motivation to be a great person." One said, "[Work is how] I build myself to be better." The self was a primary object of labor, and the individual worker was meant to benefit from productive activity. While work was necessary to everyone in similar ways for both physical and emotional welfare, the labor a person did was personal. It always involved an impermanent and interdependent "I." The work is "how I grow." A person's labor wore the body and mind down, but contrarily, it was the primary means to enable a robust sense of self that was critical to individual well-being. "*El trabajo me hace sentir saludable*" (work makes me feel healthy), said one student. Sometimes work was described as "what I enjoy doing," other times as "things I do I don't like." Nevertheless, work was the "way to live [one's] best life."

My students were not naïve about labor's necessity and hardships. But despite the human costs of a life of toil, work had the potential to make people "feel great and amazing about" themselves. The body may ache, the mind may feel annoyance, and the pay may be only tolerable. But still as one student put it, "*l trabajo me hace sentir genial*" (work makes me feel great). Students are not saying the details of their jobs are ideal or even good. They are, however, sharing a genuine feeling about how work gives them an identity. Work is "a part of who I am." Being a worker is not the only way for students to define who they are, but it makes a sizeable contribution to a very favorable and honorable version of the self. At a minimum, "work is what keeps you honest."

Work even probes into and uncovers an essential self. One worker said it marvelously for all the others: "*El trabajo me hacen sentir fuerte y te ace sentir onesto*" (work makes me feel strong and makes you feel like you). What my students were expressing about their work is how it personalizes them. Their identity is shaped and made knowable through the work they do. If there is an essential self, it is work that gives it form and from which it is realized. Work is the concept of "you in a nutshell." Another student understood it as a "direct reflection of you." Working for your own preservation and development is the path to awareness of a basic truth my students held: that you are you. Unlike the Greeks, who regarded work as a curse to be conducted with a heavy heart, my students found a meaningful sense of the concept "I" to embrace in their labors. As stated in the Christian Book of Mathew, the work that folks do reflects who they are: "You will know them by their fruits."[12] Work wasn't the end goal of life, nor necessarily a good thing itself. But work could help a person find a piece of their genuine selves. It was, therefore, an ontological tool; "work is how I can become me."

Workers associated who they are with the work they do. An identity as *homo faber*—"person as maker"—is neither hegemonic nor delusional. Marx's contention that work is meant to develop a person's nature and create individual identity was commonly reflected in my students' ruminations. Marx saw that under capitalism work would never be fully liberating, but his view of work's essential nature was that it was "the individual's self-realization, which in no way means that it becomes mere fun, mere amusement. . . . Really free working . . . is at the same time precisely the most damned seriousness, the most intensive exertion."[13] The work experiences of my students support both labor's ability to define a genuine "I" and the "damned seriousness" of its character. Culinary workers, as well as janitors, millwrights and nurses, hotel clerks and teachers all found that to be "visible, to be appreciated," or "to exist" is to work. The collection of work activities over a lifetime amounts to nothing less than "achievements that define who" someone is. Work forms the individual consistent with his or her compact to live life honorably. It is as a student beautifully put it "life's integrity signature."

The daily activity of producing goods and services for pay amounts to a different body of life outcomes depending on the vantage point of the viewer—employer or worker. One perspective leads to a physical body of work for each worker measured by units of production and hours. To a great extent counting production outputs is an employer's objective. They tell the story of labor through a profit and earnings narrative. To the employer, the worker is objectively and foremost a special force of production that creates capital but is calculated as a cost on the balance sheet. Workers are summed up as an expenditure item in a budget and financial statement. From this vantage point the workers have been reduced to wage labor and robbed of their full dimensionality as thinking, feeling, desiring individuals with a consciousness of their own identity. Employers may act abusively, but they are not inherently being evil when they see things through a cost-benefit lens. It's rational for them to behave this way in a capitalist economy. The job after all is available not because it contributes to a social good or personal fulfillment. Employment exists because there is a market for another worker's labor power. Working may allow an individual to do something that will make them happy, but it's not primarily a business concern of the employer. Again, this work relationship doesn't make the boss a bad person. The employment relationship is a mixed bag of personal, social, and class dynamics. With few exceptions, however, from the employer's vantage point the workers as human beings are flattened.

There is a second worker-oriented perspective of what a cumulative body of work represents. The person's labor is contributing one brick, bus ride, student, and patient at a time to an assertion of individuality. It is the development of a person's active will to exist as she would choose within a social framework. Marx famously stated that "men make their own history, but they do not make it just as they please: they do not make it under circumstances chosen by themselves, but under circumstances directly encountered."[14] Workers are pursuing a meaningful life within the severe restrictions of the law favorable to the dominant economic interests which circumscribe what rights belong to workers. Sometimes the laws are less onerous depending on who holds political power, but the balance of workplace power always favors the employer. Nonetheless, work is never just worker exploitation. Workers use their work to form their sense of self and to find a place in the world.

As a "collection of achievements" work "defines who I am." Workers agitate, strategize, and organize against having to do abusive work. Necessity compels folks to do a lot of unfulfilling labor. But my students are not looking to end work: just the necessity part. They desire a life that is unencumbered by the kind of work that only fulfills the need to "make ends meet." On this point they would find agreement with Marx: "The realm of freedom actually begins only where labor which is determined by necessity and mundane considerations ceases."[15] Through work the individual asserts their presence in the world and stakes a claim to being an authentic person. The students in my class were either born under circumstances or were pushed by social forces that required them to "punch the clock every day." Nonetheless, being a worker meant having a craft that allowed a person an opportunity to construct their own subjectivity.

Through work people were paid cooks, bus drivers, coal miners, special education aides, and masons. To the boss and the economic system, that was all they were. But my students knew they were more than a cost of production. The work they did further defined them on their own terms. It's work that "makes [people] feel important" or "accomplished." Along with feelings of importance, my students spoke about work's ability to "make them feel empowered" and noble. A number of workers wrote that work is empowering. As one said, "[It's] what makes me a proud mother." It wasn't the power to revolutionize capitalism, but it enabled individuals to act more like a sovereign agent over their lives.

As I read one essay after another filled with similes for being accomplished and empowered, the philosopher Friedrich Nietzsche's concept of "will to power" seemed an apt way to understand how work is functioning.[16] Nietzsche described a basic human drive for mastery over others, oneself, or the environment. There were forms of mastery that provided benefits and others that were destructive. The desire is neither good nor bad. It seems that one prominent way that an individual's basic drive for power would be pursued is the engagement of the individual with the natural world through work processes. With the aid of technology, science, engineers, and other workers, an individual laborer interacts with the environment. The more skilled they become in their work the more power they have over it. Developing their work skills also gave them greater agency in shaping their own identities and living conditions. As opposed to being forced to accept a permanent slot in life, "work is something to help you grow."

Let's look at two occupations to see how this mastery develops. In the unionized building trades, there are two worker designations representing levels of training, knowledge, skill, and experience. While in training, for example, novice carpenters are called "apprentices" for four years. Once they've completed their course of study, they become "journeymen." The gendered language bias is antiquated and unfortunate, but it signifies that the worker is a "master carpenter." Teachers have their own probationary, development period. Depending on state laws, teachers of pre-K through twelfth grade work an "untenured" three to four years before they can become "tenured." During the untenured phase instructors are more intensely and more often evaluated. If they don't demonstrate the capacity to learn the craft, they can be fairly easily released. Once tenured, however, there is a presumption of competency. Some tenured teachers will go on to be called "master teachers" and even mentor junior, untenured faculty. I think Nietzsche would call a worker's use and development of productive activity a "will to power."

A life without work to the workers in my classes was unimaginable and unwanted. Not because folks were confused or had bought into a false consciousness that kept them in a subservient position to people who controlled the means of capital. Ideological chains have likely been fashioned, but that hasn't denigrated the role of work in my students' lives. Workers know they were not created for the purpose of selling their labor power. That feature was a seemingly unavoidable consequence of class relations within a capitalist society for millions of people. But even under the rules of the labor market, work still had the means to define the positive qualities of an individual. One student said, "Work is how I become somebody," which is more than a statement about becoming a consumer. It speaks to a person being their own maker; it allows for self-definition.

Not everyone in my class held a "skilled" job, as society defines it, but all my students wanted to do a job well and, most importantly, with considerable craftsmanship. Let me say that again. Every job from room attendant to teacher consisted of what Richard Sennet described as an elaborate and "intimate connection between hand and head."[17] Work gives "people an anchor in material reality" and creates an identity to be proud of as manifested in the thing made itself.[18] The world is the composition of nature worked up and labor objectified. It embodies what the worker has produced and "thus he can look at his image in a world he has created."[19] And each person's work then is the nexus and prerequisite for the formation and development of community. Going to work enabled the person to use their "talents to better [their] community." I believe that philosophers would see in the work that people do an attempt to construct an authentic life. In that lifelong pursuit, *work is* becomes *my life's expression*.

Work has the capacity to shape the self in an additional fashion. It can politicize the individual. Yes, workers have to find jobs. Necessity is a driving force. But in part because of that necessity, along with labor's capacity to influence the self, union workers use their work, their workplaces, and work relations to digest what is happening to them in the world. Work has not served as a distraction or suppressant of political engagement. Despite long, hard hours of labor, union membership increased a worker's political awareness and participation. Many students were conversant in political topics, familiar with candidate records, and aware of union endorsements. Some enrolled in classes on politics, attended rallies, sent text messages to representatives, made phone calls to the White House, signed postcards to support prolabor laws, worked campaigns, and eagerly voiced opinions on legislation and elections. Their work inspired them to action and turned them into citizen actors.

Work alone did not lead to political engagement. The problem of individuals having to labor excessively for their daily sustenance has been cited by political theorists and philosophers, as well as political leaders as a threat to democracy. Without the provisions of a stable life, only the wealthy would participate in political action. I often share with my students the following excerpts from Theodore Roosevelt's extraordinary 1910 "New Nationalism" speech, which draws the tight connection between class status and citizenship. Roosevelt warns that a person's meager material conditions will stunt their ability to be political actors. The first situation predicts the latter.

> No man can be a good citizen unless he has a wage more than sufficient to cover the bare cost of living, and hours of labor short enough so that after his day's work is done he will have time and energy to bear his share in the management of the community, to help in carrying the general load. We keep countless men from being good citizens by the conditions of life with which we surround them. The right to regulate the use of wealth in the public interest is universally admitted. Let us admit also the right to regulate the terms and conditions of labor, which is the chief element of wealth, directly in the interest of the common good. The fundamental thing to do for every man is to give him a chance to reach a place in which he will make the greatest possible contribution to the public welfare.[20]

Union members can be conflicted over how much their union should engage in politics but work in a union shop could be a potent politicizing experience. It certainly had that effect for many of the workers in my class. The insecurity of employment, dismissive treatment of employers, gaping economic inequality, antiworker and antiunion legislation, and increased economic vulnerability created fertile terrain for a heightened worker political consciousness. Individuals did not come into the factory, school, or fire station fully formed beings. They went to work for a lot of reasons, and when they got there they became someone with a strong political character. Political beliefs were not homogeneous, and many were irrational and self-defeating. In many of my classes I measured political ideology. On average, the workers were slightly left of center. They were strongly left on economic issues and moderate on cultural issues.

Service and retail workers, teachers, nurses, transportation, and other public employees were more liberal across the board, while manufacturing and building trade workers held more conservative social views. But they all wanted to see much stronger protections for unions and felt cheated by capitalism. And for good reasons. In the time they had been employed the number of right-to-work states had only grown and, in 2022, numbered twenty-seven. America was more a company nation than a workers' rights country.[21] Wages had been stagnant for more than forty years despite productivity gains, while corporate profits soared, and CEO compensation escalated without pause. All of this coincided with and was brought about because unionization rates had fallen to 1920 levels. Loss of union density did not come naturally. US employers have always fiercely opposed organized labor. Well-financed antiunion groups, like the US Chamber of Commerce, the Business Roundtable, National Right to Work Committee, American Legislative Exchange Council, the State Policy Network, and right-wing foundations funded by billionaires like the Koch Brothers, Ken Griffin, and the DeVos Family have viewed organized workers as an existential threat to their control over the economy.

In 2006 *Business Week* called what happened during the previous three decades "one of the most successful antiunion wars ever" waged. The resistance is multidimensional but since the 1970s there has been a tremendous growth in the size, scope, and sophistication of the union avoidance industry. One study found that over three-quarters of employers hired consultants when confronted by organizing campaigns. In the 1980s consultants advised employers that corporate political influence was so ascendant in Washington that they now enjoyed an opportunity to get rid of the union threat once and for all. One consultant wrote in the *Wall Street Journal* that the "current [Reagan] government and business climate presents a unique opportunity for companies . . . to develop and implement long-term plans for conducting business in a union-free environment."[22] Capital heard the message and acted with impunity against their own workers. A 2019 analysis found that US employers were charged with violating federal law in 41.5 percent of all union election campaigns. In nearly a third (29.2 percent) of all elections, employers were charged with coercing, threatening, or retaliating against workers for supporting a union. That same analysis of unfair labor practice charges showed that employers were accused of illegally firing workers in 20–30 percent of union elections.[23] To my students capital was indifferent to work's capacity to construct livable communities and enable a participatory democracy. As a consequence, "work is a burden because of capitalistic greed." Maybe the employers' opposition to respecting the will of their employees emanated from how they understand their own existence. Appearing before a Senate committee in 2003 the president of the Business Roundtable, John Castellani, sought to correct any illusions about how and for what purpose a corporation functioned. "There is a misperception that corporations are democracies. In fact, they are not."[24] It all added up to a weaker hold on the promise that a job was the ladder to middle-class prosperity. Students bemoaned the degradation of work's promise. Work is "not what it used to be." Work is "a shadow of what was promised." As one student said, "[It is] where my soul goes to die."

My students acknowledged a terrible fear that the people they worked for and the people they believed themselves to be no longer mattered. It wasn't enough for them to exchange their labor for their family's future and personal fulfillment. What if their kids wouldn't do better than they did? What if social mobility was a cruel lie meant to squeeze the life out of a worker? What if work to the employer and politicians was only done for and about profit? What if "work is the exploitation of the lower-class?" Workers kept working, but every time the job felt more like it was locking them into an ascribed slot in a caste system, it confronted their ability and faith to use work to "take care of family." In response, they became more political in divergent ways.

A strong majority of union workers (but not most white members) voted for Barack Obama, 40 percent of them (but very few black union members) voted twice for Donald Trump, and I suspect most manufacturing and building trades workers wanted Democratic Socialist Bernie Sanders to be president. Conversely, in 2016 and in 2020 millions of nonunion workers without a college degree rallied behind Trump who campaigned in favor of right-to-work laws and against raising the minimum wage. Come 2020 and nearly every union president thought Joe Biden might just become the most prounion president in their lifetime. Questions about work and its relationship to citizenship are largely absent from political theory and political science curriculums. The oversight is inexplicable given the centrality of employment to consciousness, self-examination, and identity; "work is the subject of much discussion within." Work is largely segregated into a private relationship between individual and employer. Except for policy efforts to enforce Civil Rights, the protection of minors, weak minimum-wage and hour standards, and very spotty health and safety rules, work is treated as a "series of individual contracts" instead of as a "social structure" and "site for the exercise of political power."[25] Understanding working-class political ideologies and electoral behavior is a fascinating subject with numerous rabbit holes to get lost in. The point is workers go to work and their work experiences contribute to their political thinking and identity. Work forms the experiences that, in Professor Week's analysis, "will represent the most impactful relations of power that people encounter on a daily basis." And in a moment of poignant reflection students acknowledged that "work is the only power some people have." If you worked for a living, being political was inevitable and essential. As one student wrote, work is "awesome with democracy" and by implication coercive without it.

For Others

Being political meant that my students' work and subsequent activism was meant for more than just their own benefit. As conceived through a worldview shaped in part by working for a living, they worked on behalf of others. "Work is collective effort toward achieving desired outcomes." In their minds, work was done for the greater good, even if the "good" was contested. Workers in my classes were politically engaged, and some were enraged. They didn't, however, move in a unified direction. Except in one fashion.

As work lost its firm hold on its ability to care for others, many of my union students found another subject to work for: the union. Work is, my students said, "better with a union." Work is "solidarity with other workers." Speaking on behalf of other workers, one student stated "[work is] why we need to be union." Work is "where a union belongs." Work is "making the union stronger." Work is "better when its organized." Work is "made possible by [a] union's members." Work is "more valuable when [workers are] united." Work is "a bitch, without a union." Working with others to improve the working experience under a shared set of values, practices, and conditions generates an understanding that the union is itself a good that produces benefits in excess of what individuals can attain.

The recognition by union members that the union itself is a subject of labor is a fundamental principal embedded in the asymmetrical class power relations at work. Take for example union electricians who work on outside telephone utilities for several Illinois counties. They are members of International Brotherhood of Electrical Workers, Local 9, and their bargaining agreement with an employers' association has the following remarkable language: "The Employer and the Union, pursuant to the expressed findings of the Congress of the United States, recognize that the *individual worker* [italics added], operating individually *without group assistance* [italics added], is commonly helpless to exercise actual liberty of contact, to protect his/her freedom of labor so to obtain acceptable terms and conditions of Employment."[26] Accordingly, the contract goes on to state that the individual employees of the employers are represented by Local 9. Group representation and solidarity are necessary because, as individuals, the workers have little to no agency—they are "helpless"—in determining the conditions under which they exchange their labor.

If the union is sufficiently responsive to worker needs, it becomes a subject that individual workers are committed to bettering and supporting. Essays that asserted "work is undervalued by management" explain why a labor organization that stands up for and represents workers becomes a subject of their labor. Some union members, like those in the building trades, associate their work opportunities with the union hiring hall that assigned them to the job. They know they are paid by the contractor, but the job assignment came from the union. When the impacts of union-negotiated work provisions and the contract benefits are closely aligned with the worker's social relations then the union becomes a legitimate subject of work. Therefore, if, as one student wrote, "work is being in a team," then a unionized nurse taking care of an ill person in a hospital is applying her trade for the patient, as well as for the union.

Family and individual well-being were subjects of labor, but who you worked for extended beyond self and blood. Student fealty to their unions was not without reservation. They praised where praise was earned and criticized when they felt let down. But no matter the race, gender, age, or political affiliation, workers associated better working conditions and consequently, a higher quality of life with signing a union card. It's not just my classes of union members who experience work this way. Research by Patrick Flavin and Gregory Shufeldt find that "union members are more satisfied with their lives than those who are not members and that the substantive effect of union membership on life satisfaction is large and rivals other common predictors of quality of life."[27] While they did not describe unions as bearers of a historical cause, they could point out how the labor movement was an agent of historical change. Yes, they proudly proclaimed, the folks who brought

America the middle class were in unions. Labor history is not without the sins of racism and misogyny, and unions did not operate as Marx's revolutionary force. Nonetheless, my students adhered to what crusading labor lawyer Clarence Darrow stated about organized labor: "With all their faults, trade unions have done more for humanity than any other organization of men that ever existed. They have done more for decency, for honesty, for education, for the betterment of the race, for the developing of character in men, than any other association of men."[28]

Focusing on the subject for whom we work revealed a peculiar response from the student essays. Or more accurately, the lack of a response. Workers were cognizant that they were employed, for example, by a school, hospital, construction company, hotel, restaurant, or logistic firm. Surprisingly, though, out of thousands of essays no worker said that. The closest any essay came was the following: "Work is for the brand." Just one. Why would workers getting their paychecks with the name of their employer on it, working in some cases with their company's name or logo on their clothes, not directly indicate that they labored for the owner? I would have expected many to do it almost reflexively. But no one did.

Conversations about why they never mentioned their employer triggered mostly disregard for the idea that workers sacrificed their time, bodies, and minds for a business or public agency. Workers may have loved their jobs, took deep meaning from doing it and thought approvingly of their employer. But it was still a transaction—labor for money. "Work is for the profit of the corporation." My father and the workers taking my classes had little reason to think employers had any regard for their labor beyond its capacity to generate pecuniary surplus. In the 1980s the CEO of United States Steel Corporation, David Roderick, discarded any illusion of what motivated capitalist production and blithely said the industry was "no longer in the business of making steel." While steel companies had heavily invested in oil and petrochemicals, they also had thousands of workers and billions invested in industrial production. What then did my steel-working father make for nearly four decades? Had it ever been about a real connection to a physical asset whose use was foundational to building the twentieth century? Was work, as the English designer William Morris claimed, meant to find "hope of pleasure in our daily creative skills?"[29] Not to Roderick. The industry was, all along, "in the business of making profits."[30] No one should have been surprised by his declaration. In truth, the legal rules underpinning American capitalism had been settled for a long time. In what would become an infamous, influential, and unmodified legal interpretation, the Michigan Supreme Court declared in 1919 that "A business corporation is organized and carried on primarily for the profit of the stockholders."[31] Employees be damned.

Some of today's employers, for example Starbucks, rhetorically espouse a commitment to worker satisfaction—"we are better side-by-side."[32] But despite their public relations, in reality "they're focusing on profits."[33] The relationship was not of friends, family, volunteers, or mutual admirers. One day you are joyously embraced at work and the next you are unemployed. There was an obligation to give a full day's work for a full day's pay, but from the workers' perspective the subject of labor was never the private profit-seeking firm or public body. Workers bitterly objected to being treated merely as a means of corporate gain instead of as equal rational beings. The employer was never the subject of labor because their employees held a Kantian view of the moral integrity of individuals. Immanuel Kant wrote, "Act in such a way that you treat humanity, whether in your own person or in the person of any other, never merely as a means to an end, but always at the same time as an end."[34] My students understood the instrumental chain of reciprocal actions that, for instance, got your car repaired but never accepted that they were *only* tools of profit seeking. Workers were dignified subjects of their own labor. They were not objects to be simply priced and valued like commodities.

You worked for students, patients, consumers, taxpayers, citizens, neighbors, yourself, family, and the country. While reflecting on the work my students did, an odd notion occurred to me: workers mostly work for strangers. Certainly, teachers know the children they teach and nurses working in local doctors' offices know their patients. But except in exceptional and superficial situations, workers use their labor for people they don't know. The customer has no idea who built the car they purchased. The food we eat was grown, harvested, and slaughtered by people who are alien to us. Alienation is a hallmark of our labor. Despite the absence of any personal connection with the end user, workers recognize where their labor goes: it goes to somebody or lots of people who will likely never know the creator of what they are enjoying. For the most part, no one is going to say "thank you" for the bridge you built. And yet workers keep doing it anyway. Even when, perhaps, they would be justified in withholding their work.

Sometimes the labor we do puts us at genuine risk from one another. I was reminded of this while reading a student essay of an airline employee. An increase in air travelers in the summer of 2021 transformed Arlie Hochschild's classic case of emotional laborers—flight attendants—into casualties of a political war. Demented behavior from passengers angry about having to abide by company mask mandates led to roughly four thousand "unruly passenger incidents." The Federal Aviation Administration described the number as "a rapid and significant increase."[35] To add insult to injury, flight attendants also felt badly exposed by their airline employers. Abuse of flight attendants reminded me of how teachers felt demonized by parents and politicians during multiple surges of the COVID pandemic. Grocery store clerks and restaurant employees bitterly complained of hostile treatment by customers over mask rules. What does it foretell about our country's mindset and socialization when the benefactors of labor turn abusive toward the producers? It seems a dearth of societal-level appreciation for who is doing the work is another ugly truth, along with racial, gender, and class inequality, about the nation that COVID has revealed.

I suspect in part because of how workers are treated while doing their jobs that the employment relationship functioned as a kind of shell under which workers produced. At times it seemed to the workers that the particular employer didn't matter. As long as there was one, and it acted and paid fairly. Work was too fundamental a personal life activity to be done on behalf of a hiring institution. Instead, workers saw work as serving yet another larger subject.

For Society

Work is "the backbone of ... society." It is work that "supplies America" and "what moves America forward." When we work, we activate "the process of running a society." My students often reflected on the difficult issues that divided American citizens. Race, gender, immigration, abortion, gun control, sexual identity, COVID-19—the list was and always seemed endless. But work, as a concept, process, and practice had special qualities that functioned differently than all the other identity concepts. Nearly everyone needed to work for themselves, and importantly, for someone they loved. Working was "the lifeline" to stability, prosperity, and happiness. People went to work out of necessity and to become more fully human. No one rationally chose to live as a beast of burden.

However, work is also "fundamental in everyone's growth" and a process of "bettering ourselves." People wanted to do work that was meaningful. It was through work that individuals were constantly becoming something more than they had been before. My students' essays revealed that they believed that a true self could be realized through work. There is much that shapes our sense of self, but worker essays stressed that the process of working was the great common denominator in our lives. It is through work that we are interconnected and can feel like "part of something" and have a "lasting outcome for everyone." Work, therefore, is "the unity of people." It is the "foundation of society" and the force that moves history forward. Millions of daily labors propelled the engines that "allow for society to progress." What students were pointing out is that intentional and conscious work is the one basic activity that builds society and makes communal relationships possible. Workers labored with others and consequently many of their essays revealed they related to work as a social activity. Work was never a solitary function. It was instead a recognition: "What I individually produce, I produce individually for society, conscious of myself as a social being."[36]

Workers also recognized that their own efforts to construct a decent life had a cumulative effect on the body politic. Through each individual's labor, work was "making work better for all." In multiple ways work is realized as one's "contribution to society." Doing work "keeps you useful to society" and in turn society is possible. The cumulative decisions and labors of millions of people brought the material world and society into existence. Work was both a self-referential and universal activity. When folks work, they satisfy their own individual needs, but they also make possible the fulfillment of other workers' needs. The relationship is interdependent, and each instance of work contributes to forming a greater universe of human activity, which codeterminately embodies and makes possible acts of productive labor. Consider the structure of the following essay: "Work is society's duty to give back." Notice the student begins with the premise that society—not the individual's private life—is the product of work. Society—made possible and constituted by the personal labors of millions—subsequently provides opportunities and sustenance for individual agency.

A favorite example I use with my students to illustrate this point is the coffee aroma that typically accompanies our classroom. I ask students to guess how many workers were involved in getting a good tasting cup of coffee into their hands. Some reply just a few or a couple of hundred but many correctly say "thousands."[37] A hot cup of coffee gets served because farmworkers harvested the beans, then someone processed (e.g., depulped, fermented, washed, dried, milled, and sorted) the beans and another packaged the product, and a truck driver drove the coffee to a café where a barista served it up with a smile to a paying customer who likely did some work to provide the store employee with a wage. I've left out lots of labor, but the point is one person's labor, even if it is intended only for personal gain, made another's possible and everyone derived some benefit. Adam Smith would have agreed with the principle.

The woollen coat, for example, which covers the day-labourer, as coarse and rough as it may appear, is the produce of the joint labour of a great multitude of workmen. The shepherd, the sorter of the wool, the wool-comber or carder, the dyer, the scribbler, the spinner, the weaver, the fuller, the dresser, with many others, must all join their different arts in order to complete even this homely production.[38]

Unjustly however, Smith's unbenevolent lyrical troika of butchers, brewers, and bakers may have provided our dinner, but they were not the ones suitably compensated.[39] The farm and business owners first and foremost are rewarded for American's caffeine addiction while baristas are left dependent on tips, which is why in the US Starbucks' employees were furiously unionizing.[40]

The interlocking nature of incommensurable acts of production was nicely described by the nineteenth-century German philosopher Georg Wilhelm Friedrich Hegel: "The labour of the individual for his own needs is just as much a satisfaction of the needs of others as of his own, and the satisfaction of his own needs he only obtains through the labour of others."[41] Marx more plainly explained this social relationship: "My work for your need."[42] Work is part of the fabric of society and society is made up of everyone's quilting. Embodied within each pounded nail, delivered package, cut stone, and bandaged wound is the larger world that workers built. And oh yeah, nobody did a darn thing without a teacher. "The whole becomes, as a whole, his own work."[43] One student working in manufacturing put it this way: "Work is what makes us whole and appreciated." No one could dispute that "work is vital for the world." My students were describing a view of work that aligned with Marx and Arendt who both believed "that the human condition of labor is life itself."[44] This realization was dramatically demonstrated to me while writing my 2008 book, *Justified by Work: Identity and the Meaning of Faith in Chicago's Working-Class Churches*.[45] I interviewed religious congregants and clerical leaders about the relationship between being working class, doing work, and their theological beliefs and practices. One conversation stands out for infusing work with the power and legitimacy to make the world possible.

In the years following the book's publication I have shared with my students the occasion I spoke with a pastor from the southeast side of Chicago. At one point in our meeting he brought a surprising halt to the discussion by reaching across the circular table we were sitting at and grabbing both my wrists. I was rather stunned and proceeded to drop the pen I was using to take notes. To that point it had been a pleasant standard interview. The pastor then pulled my arms upwards and towards him and calmly but assertively said, "Professor, do you see these hands?" He meant my hands.

Before I could respond he repeated the question, this time making clear he was intending to answer it.

His reply is unforgettable. "These hands, professor, are the only ones God has in the world." In numerous essays workers drew attention to the symbolic concept of a person's hands: "Work is dirty hands, clean money." Once releasing my wrists, the pastor further elaborated that it is the hands of workers that give form to the world. If you believe in God, as he did, then you believe that the Almighty works through the painters, truck drivers, and teachers within his congregation. Ultimately, however, it didn't matter whether I believed in a deity or not. As the pastor explained, workers mixed their bodies and minds with the natural resources available and gave life to what sustains the community. Work was the source of all life, and in using their power to create, the workers were "miniatures of God."[46] A student working as an operating engineer suggested to me that the pastor may have been drawing from a biblical passage. After our class he pulled up Psalm 82, on his cell phone and read verse 6: "I said, 'You are "gods"; you are all sons of the Most High.'"[47]

The pastor's startling yet inspired tutorial sent me back to review John Locke's words on property ownership. The seventeenth-century British political theorist had offered a rationale for private property that seemed relevant to the pastor's idea that the constructed world was the product of labor. In Locke's famous *2nd Treatise on Government*, he lays out a provocative theory that a worker is entitled to his labor and the product of that labor. "Though the earth, and all inferior creatures, be common to all men, yet every man has a property in his own person: this nobody has any right to but himself. The labour of his body, and the work of his hands, we may say, are properly his. Whatsoever then he removes out of the state that nature hath provided, and left it in, he hath mixed his labour with, and joined to it something that is his own, and thereby makes it his property."[48] One student pretty much articulated the same thing this way: "Work is mine and not yours." This essay may appear to contradict other views of working for others, but I suspect it's not meant to deny the social nature of work. Instead, I believe the writer is simply asserting a Lockean notion of individual property rights. According to Locke,

> He that is nourished by the acorns he picked up under an oak, or the apples he gathered from the trees in the wood, has certainly appropriated them to himself. No body can deny but the nourishment is his. I ask then, when did they begin to be his? when he digested? or when he eat? or when he boiled? or when he brought them home? or when he picked them up? and it is plain, if the first gathering made them not his, nothing else could. That labour put a distinction between them and common.[49]

No one should be fleeced of the fruits of their labor or forcibly made to work without proper compensation.

The pastor's account resonated with my devout, atheist, and agnostic students alike. They saw what too often the employer, government, media, and community missed about their work. Repairing machines, manufacturing rubber, conducting the alchemy that produced colors in paint, and transporting someone on a bus from here to there brought new life into existence. "Work is necessary to continue life." My students claimed no pretensions about being philosophers, but their profound acclimation that "work is life" aligned with Albert Camus's divinatory comments about work: "Without work, all life goes rotten. But when work is soulless, life stifles and dies." A worker's labor wasn't the beginning of the world, but it was responsible for everything that came next. "Work is what makes everything happen in life."

Understanding who we work for places a compelling flesh, bone, and blood human being at the center of our working lives. Our work pays the bills, provides goods and services, and produces wealth. But that all seems to be a derivative effect of working under a set of legal rules that makes work an economic necessity. A basic truth about our work is that it's a gift to ourselves and others, the majority of whom we never know. The bequest comes with a duty: "Work is showing up and doing your part." Calling it a gift may strike some readers as a stretch. But if, as one essay writer proclaimed, "work is what gives life meaning," and as another wrote, "work is giving an opportunity to someone else," then being able to work and creating the circumstances in which a person's talents and society might thrive is indeed a gift. Without the daily labors of millions, our communities, society, and nation would cease to exist. The seventeenth-century political philosopher Thomas Hobbes argued that a country needed a powerful governing sovereign to avoid falling into chaos. His admonition that without a "leviathan" people would be so driven by unrestrained self-interest that life would be "solitary, poor, nasty, brutish and short" could amply apply to what happens to a society without sufficient, high-quality, and creative work.[50]

My students were self-interested. To live decently they had to be. Capitalism made them particularly attentive to competitive individual instincts with little or no intentional regard for promoting the public interest. But their labor was also informed by a social ethic to contribute to the common good. Economic necessity had not determined for them, as it appeared to have for large corporate CEOs, that the only subject of their creative power should be themselves. As one essay said, "Work is how we all prosper." Here, workers are making a moral claim about the relationship between labor and the social order. If you work, you and society *ought* to do well. Everyone has talents they can put to productive social use. A good job for all citizens should be the pathway to prosperity, not an inheritance or monopoly control over capital accessible to only a fortunate few. Seems to me that work has the potential to fulfill political philosopher John Rawls' principle that society's distribution of wealth be to "everyone's advantage," and consistent with "equal citizenship and equality of opportunity."[51]

My students did not do glamorous work, but most spoke approvingly of how their labor mattered for the communities they lived in. Working was pleasure and sacrifice. Worker essays and class discussions revealed that their union status contributed to the connection they made between work and the welfare of the community. Labor's strong defense of the public sphere, including democratic institutions and practices, is the biggest underappreciated contribution to the popular opinions that citizens hold about unions. One essayist from the Chicago Plumbers Union Local 130 drew inspiration from the labor movement to explain the subject of his brothers' and sisters' labor: "Work is protecting the health of the nation." My students' belief that their work is essential for advancing the development of society did not come with a radical consciousness to end or even seriously upend capitalist social relations. It did, however, include a vision of social justice that valued community and was suggestive of "an association in which the free development of each is the condition for the free development of all."[52]

Conclusion

IN LATE AUGUST 2021 roughly one thousand workers who make Oreos, Chips Ahoy!, and other popular Nabisco snacks were on strike in five states. The company, Mondalez, Inc., is very profitable. In Portland, Oregon, local union vice president, Mike Burlingham, of the Bakery, Confectionary, Tobacco Workers, and Grain Millers union insisted, "This is a good job." He explained it was the kind of job "where people plan for retirement." But this kind of work was at risk of extinction. "If the company could have their way," he warned, "that would be gone and it wouldn't be a job worth fighting for."[1] However, worker solidarity prevailed, and after a five-week strike the workers approved a new, four-year contract. It was, according to the Chicago local union president Donald Woods, a "huge" win for the union.[2] Nonetheless, it revealed an enduring reality. What work is and what it is worth to the worker is decidedly different than it is to the employer. But to both, work is unquestionably an all-encompassing hegemonic life activity.

The proposition that work is everything is scary. Can anything be so important that it is everything? "Work is death and life" doesn't leave much untouched. Is a person not a person without the opportunity to develop and utilize their creative productive capacities? Is work that one activity that civil society can't exist without? Certainly, human beings are far more than producers. The facts of our lives bare that reality out. My father was a steelworker, a friend, a husband, a son, and a brother. He was a golfer too, who enjoyed playing pickleball and listening to Dean Martin and Neil Diamond. Work was the most important thing he did, but it did not amount to a full definition of self that consisted of one who labors. Mom really felt happy when she was working, but she was sister, friend, daughter, neighbor, bowler, dancer, reader of fiction, lover of mysteries, believer in God, and fan of situation comedies on television. If she had an essence, it had to be as a servant to others. And what about my students? Work was immensely influential in explaining the facts of their existence. "Work is first in my life." Few, if any, would quarrel with the idea that the work they did best defined their lives and shaped their identity. I never asked them if they thought they had an enduring essence, but their essays strongly suggested a true self existed and its development was related to their work.

The objective reality of being a worker featured a lot of commonalities. Time was artificially divided between work and leisure. It was always experienced in relationship to work obligations. Either you were going to work, at work, coming home from work, or taking the day off from work. "Work is another day, another dollar." Time was contradictorily valued as money and relief. In both cases it was a two-sided liberation. On one side, the time worked was traded for earnings essential to live "a life free of poverty." On the other, time off the clock was freedom from the tyranny of production; a chance to "go on vacation." Time away from work was purchased with and dependent on time spent at work. In the end, students conceded that "work is worth [their] time."

Work bounded space as well as time. The workplace was where a person fulfilled personal goals and complied with capitalist rules to sell labor power. And once labor was collectively applied to the environment, then workers were surrounded by spaces that embodied them. No matter where they went, my students as workers couldn't get away from one another. It's just that their presence was buried beneath layers of deception.

Work's impact was practically encoded into the DNA of a working-class person. Pain. Exhaustion. Joy. Life. Death. Because my students worked, they suffered, and they prospered. Everyone sacrificed, and good and bad things happened because of work. Work's consequence lied on either side of the Gospel of Matthew's biblical order to be a servant to others.[3] Whether healer or sick, clothier or naked, farmer or hungry, a person's labor or lack thereof was deeply implicated. But the widest and most profound impact was the world's very existence. The conscious grasp that work has on our lives coexists, often tenuously, with other life activities, but without labor nothing is possible. "Work is the core of everything around us."

The student workers in my class labored for many common and idiosyncratic purposes. They held a job in order to eat, to put a roof over their heads and clothes on their backs, to afford medicine, "to afford child care," to not be poor, and to avoid having to resort to a life of crime. Work was a means. Who knew that the disciple Matthew was such a prophet of work? My students also worked to be inspired, to live a meaningful life, to create, to care for others, and to give life. Incredibly, they were compelled to labor for their daily bread, while working to be a better version of themselves. Work was an end in itself. They were makers of things, as well as transcendent beings. They were paying the bills and using their craft to be a bit more godlike. And for whose benefit would workers endure it all? Life is far too short, and work shortens it. Tennyson's piercing cries of a forlorn life is a warning to avoid the mounting years of constant toil:

> Hateful is the dark-blue sky,
> Vaulted o'er the dark-blue sea.
> Death is the end of life; ah, why
> Should life all labour be?[4]

Indeed, no life should be all labor—at least not the labor that must be sold to another to survive. Work should never be a "form of paid slavery." Repeating historical cycles of one smaller class of people buying or using the labor of another much larger group perpetuates a one-dimensional existence of exploitation and oppression. Being dependent on markets for labor and goods and services to survive is, according to Mike Konczal of the Roosevelt Institute, "a profound state of unfreedom."[5] Nonetheless, workers work for family, people they love. They also endure for their own personal growth. They hold as subjects of their labor other workers and community members. In a forthright act of citizenship their productive activity is done on behalf of their country. My students go to work so life continues, and consequently we all become more fully aware of our shared humanity. Yes, work is all that. So, what does it all mean? Where do we go from here?

What Needs to Be Done?

At the end of my classes I ask the students, "If work is all that you claim that it is, what needs to be done to preserve it?" Now understand I have been posing the question while workers in the United States have experienced a severe increase in income inequality, deterioration of job quality and benefits, political hostility, and near constant declines in union density. I am also challenging union workers who are still earning middle-class wages. Notably, some of my asking occurred while a pandemic pushed millions out of the labor force and millions of others onto the frontlines of a deadly virus. Some of my conversations with workers also unfolded as unions were experiencing a moment of increased popularity and power. No matter the class date, my students have been workers faced with the possibility that the grand American narrative of nearly anyone of good nature and sound mind can climb from obscurity to prosperity through the sweat of their brow.

In 2017 US Ohio Senator Sherrod Brown released a thought piece on "Restoring the Value of Work in America." The opening paragraph begins by restating the eponymous myth about America but then immediately takes note of the gap between values and experience: "The American Dream has always been based on the premise that hard work leads to prosperity, but for too many U.S. workers the connection between hard work and the middle class has been severed." It ends with an ominous statement: "Put simply, the value of work is declining for workers."[6] When roughly 1,600 Americans own as much wealth as the other 90 percent combined, the principal that "work pays" loses some credibility.[7] There is no economic reason that it shouldn't pay. Since the early 1970s, worker productivity has increased nearly six times faster than wages. The nation's household wealth in the summer of 2021 had grown to $136.9 trillion.[8] And yet wealth inequality kept expanding.[9] No surprise then that a smaller percentage (50 percent) of people today are considered middle class than those in 1971 (61 percent).[10] My students wondered if America should still be considered a middle-class nation. It's a questionable call. How do we justify only about a quarter of workers earning above $50,000, while nearly twice that number make less than $30,000?[11]

Work has become so uninviting that, despite its necessity, there has been a kind of "flight from work." A year after the pandemic began, record numbers of workers quit or changed their jobs. The US Department of Labor reported that a record high one million workers voluntarily walked away from their jobs in April 2021.[12] It was a startling number that kept growing. In August 2021, 4.3 million workers quit, and the next month the total exceeded 4.4 million. In the two decades the government had been keeping track it was the highest number of people who had ever walked away from paid employment.[13] Some economists have come to cheekily label it the "Great Resignation." I referred to it in media interviews as the "great refusal," because while some workers were permanently retiring, most were choosing to not work certain jobs under conditions they found unacceptable.[14] The "refusal" was a mass uncoordinated action—an assertion of power against capital. It was millions of workers firing their employer.

In my quarter century of teaching in the labor and employment-relation field, it was typical to hear views that suggested that an individual worker needed employment more than an employer needed an *individual* employee and therefore, only the highest valued labor, like a superstar professional athlete, could select their employer. This made sense to a worker who wrote "work is trying not to die of poverty." There is an asymmetrical relationship between employer and employee that compels a worker to "enter the labor market in search of a job."[15] In disputes over employment conditions Adam Smith observed that "many workmen could not subsist a week, few could subsist a month, and scarce any a year without employment."[16] He closes by saying, "In the long-run the workman may be as necessary to his master as his master is to him, but the necessity is not so immediate." And yet median- and lower-wage employees were giving up their jobs, in most cases, to find better ones. Workers must pay the bills, but their unhappiness with their employers triggered an unprecedented retreat from work.

One more element my students considered as they answered the "what now" question was the fact that more work is being done outside of the employment context. According to the International Labor Organization, in 2017 approximately 55 million people, or 34 percent of the workforce in the United States, worked either full- or part-time as "gig workers."[17] These workers have been treated as independent contractors and not employees. Sometimes also called freelancers, these workers are allegedly self-employed and operate independently of an employer. They are, in effect, their own business entity. The designation is tortured and not without serious criticism and legal challenge. In my view gig or app-platform workers are intentionally misclassified or allowed to function as contractors as a new form of social relations of production. By all measures, for example, a rideshare or delivery driver is in an employment relationship with an employer without the limited protections that come with being an employee. You work, you have a job (think Uber and Lyft), but since you're not an employee, you don't have access to the labor standard protections and benefits (i.e., minimum wage, workers compensation, unemployment benefits, paid time off, unionization, employer paid healthcare, and a pension) that employees have, inadequate as they are. There wasn't a prepandemic surplus of permanent, full-time, forty-hour type jobs with full benefits available, but irregular and substandard employment has expanded.

I find the conceptual idea of the precarious, app-platform-based labor force to be Orwellian in nature. Companies like Uber and Amazon's Flex division boast that they are providing opportunities for people to work and earn without the need for more employees.[18] "With Amazon Flex, you work only when you want to," and with Uber "you to decide how, where, and when you earn."[19] Yes, work is prevalent but workers (i.e., employees) aren't needed. Marx wrote that under capitalism workers would not only be separated from the products of their labor but would also be confronted by the outcomes of their work in an alien form as a market commodity. Workers would be reduced to waged employees in exchange for surrendering ownership over the products of their labor. But here the exploitation is ramped up to a level Marx could never have anticipated. The gig economy has seemingly given magical birth to a new kind of profit-generating productive activity: ghost labor. Workers not only lose control over their labor but they also forego even their marginally helpful status as employees. In turn they are corralled into a state of employment-relations limbo. Not unemployed, not legally an employee, not genuinely an independent contractor, and certainly not a capitalist. Instead of being returned to their original position as creative producers, they are compelled to continue selling their labor power surreptitiously under the fraudulent label of small-business owners.

Nonemployment labor is just one debasement of work and worker abuse. In 2019 the number of people working for contract staffing agencies rose to sixteen million, nearly double the amount in the year prior to the 2008 recession. Staffing revenue in 2022 was projected to reach a record of $212.8 billion.[20] You could get a job, working at but not for the employer, and only on an indeterminate basis. The average employment contract was slightly more than ten weeks. Take Google for instance. Their parent company, Alphabet, employs approximately 150,000 full-time employees. But that's less than half the number of part-time workers the firm hires through a third-party contractor. The employees work at and for Google but are employed by the contractor. Why? Because Google doesn't want the responsibility for the workers' health insurance, 401(k) matches, defined pension contributions, vacation time, or other earned benefits that come with being the employer of record. Shedding employees while using their labor is an effective way for the company to minimize costs while maximizing profit. It's not just a phenomenon specific to the information tech industry. Staffing employees work in "virtually all occupations in all sectors."[21] Roberto Clack, the executive director of Temp Worker Justice, a nonprofit that advocates for and supports temp workers, points out "The richest and most powerful companies in the entire economy completely depend on staffing agency workers."[22] This is not exactly how work was supposed to produce the American dream, and it's certainly not what one student had in mind when saying, "Work is the path to your dreams."

What then should workers do about work? More pointedly, since my students as well as millions of others intend to have a job for a while yet—including my daughter—what is the future of work? Marx imagined a society where people "carried out production as human beings .... our [work] products would be so many mirrors in which we saw our essential nature."[23] Is that future possible?

The subject of work's transcendence has become a topic of popular, political, and academic interest. On August 21, 2021, Illinois Governor Jay B.

Pritzker signed into law the "Illinois Future of Work Act." The act's first paragraph states the case for focusing on work: "The future of work is a critically important conversation for those currently in the workforce as well as those looking to reenter or enter it as Illinois contemplates an equitable economic recovery from the coronavirus pandemic." An additional section called for the formation of "The Illinois Future of Work Task Force," which was charged with planning for the "future of work while simultaneously addressing the state of work today."[24] Topics covered by the task force included workforce development, labor benefits, protections, and standards enforcement, new technologies reshaping work, worker classification, equity and inclusion in labor market access, low-wage work and economic inequality, transportation, logistics, and green jobs. On May 31, 2022, the task force released its report and included the following definition of a quality job:

> A Quality Job provides a family-sustaining wage and benefits package including access to healthcare and the ability for employees to take time off from their jobs when they are sick or need to care for a sick family member without having to risk financial or career stability. A quality job offers safe working conditions for all of its workers and ensures a culture and environment that treats all workers with dignity and respect, including respect for workers' right to form a union without interference, and to organize and bargain collectively for better conditions. Additionally, a quality job provides workers with predictable work schedules, creates opportunities for training and advancement, and gives workers power and voice within their roles and organizations.[25]

The definition was informed by research that I was doing along with my colleagues at the University of Illinois' Project for Middle Class Renewal (PMCR). In addition, we constructed an employment quality index (EQ-IL) that was adopted by the task force to determine the breakdown of good and bad jobs in the state. Our metric had seven components, each supported by multiple employment indicators: 1) pay, 2) benefits, 3) hours and scheduling, 4) job content, 5) working conditions, 6) social equity, and 7) training and outlook.[26] Importantly, among the report's fifty-eight recommendations, the task force called for using "a job quality measurement mechanism to award state funding."[27] We later published an employment quality study called "A Good Job, Not Any Job," which adjusted the metrics.[28]

The AFL-CIO offered its own "Commission on The Future of Work and Unions." In 2019 the federation issued the commission's forty-page report. In an opening letter to the AFL-CIO Executive Board, the now-deceased federation president Richard Trumka framed the commission's mission as follows:

"Will we let the drivers of inequality pervert technology to foster greater economic injustice and social unrest? Or will we demand that technology improves lives and raises standards and wages across the board? This report is our plan to achieve the latter. It is a recognition that technology doesn't just fall from the sky and inequality is not inevitable. It is also a reflection of the commitment and purpose that defines today's union members and workers not yet in unions, an unprecedented number of whom are embracing the idea that strong and growing worker bargaining power is our surest path to an economy that works for all of us, not just the wealthy elites. Our movement must rise to meet this moment."[29]

The private consultant industry also saw the potential and need for analysis and contemplation about work's future. McKinsey and Company featured numerous articles on technology, wages, gender equality, post-COVID workplaces, and remote working.[30] Not-for-profit public-policy research groups, like the Institute for Work and the Economy, hosted conferences with obstruse titles like "The Many Futures of Work: Possibilities and Perils."[31] Business periodicals like *Fortune*, *Forbes*, and *The Economist* also looked to put their own spin on the subject. Sarita Gupta, Stephen Lerner, and Joseph A. McCartin took a different approach to the topic. In 2018 they cowrote an essay for the *American Prospect* titled, "It's Not the 'Future of Work,' It's the Future of Workers That's in Doubt."[32] The piece flipped the lens on the question and instead focused on worker protections, industrial democracy, and worker organizing. A similar framework was taken by industrial relations academics in a 2021 publication by the Labor and Employment Relations Association. Edited by Tobias Schulze-Cleven and Todd Vachon, *Revaluing Work(ers): Toward a Democratic and Sustainable Future* argued that in revaluing work "the efforts and contributions of workers is crucial to realizing the promises of democracy and improving sustainability."[33]

The portals to considering what is happening to and will become of work in America are so numerous as to defy an obvious logical entrance. Kai Erickson referred to the multitude of work-related transformations that affect the people who are exposed to them as "like the filaments of a huge circular web, a tissue without beginning or end."[34] Admittedly, it is a lot to think and act on. My students also had definite thoughts about their futures as workers. So did I. We used our class time to discuss a future of work yet undetermined but likely to be shaped by powerful and deeply invested economic forces. The workers writing essays weren't in agreement about what needed to be done or even precisely how to do that. What they did better understand was how work had functioned in their lives. As a multiyear, multiclass project the "What Work Is" essays helped me arrive at several ways to increase the probability of securing a future of good work that was responsive to time, space, impact, purpose, and subject. Notice the slight but important modifier to work. "Good" always preceded what a worker thought a job should be. The adjective aligned with the International Labour Organization's (ILO) adoption in 1999 of the term "decent work" to promote a human-centered approach to the social impacts of a working life.[35] A future of any work or bad and indecent work was no future to plan for. My student-inspired recommendations aren't novel or exhaustive. In addition to the ILO, a number of organizations have put forward extensive plans for retethering the link between work and human dignity.[36] Nor do my ideas amount to a rigid prescription. But each idea is grounded in the work experiences of my students and the five categorical ways that workers experienced work. It's also predicated on the belief that you can't over prescribe what would strengthen the value of work and the dignity of those who do it.

While the changes that my students embrace largely focus on improving the objective features of work and are strongly supported by advocates conducting research on labor and employment issues, worker narratives offer something more than structural workplace reforms. In what workers tell us about their experience of work and how they come to know and think of labor, they express a version of work as a virtue that we are asked to defend. It shouldn't strike anyone as odd to suggest that work is a virtue. If done under the right conditions, work has properties that contribute to personal growth, happiness, a life well lived, and social wellbeing. For any person labor should measure up to Marx's claim that it "enable him to enjoy his personality, realize his natural capacities and spiritual aims."[37] However, if labor is reduced to a mere instrument or factor of production, then work can stunt the development of our moral values, cognitive skills, and emotional intelligence.

These dichotomous conditions represent different conceptions of human activity held by the Greek philosopher Aristotle that can be applied to a future understanding of work. He identified one form of activity (e.g., labor) as being good for its own sake and having largely intrinsic value. He called this activity *praxis,* and it is done for itself and no other reason. The work "action" is its own ends. A second form of work, *poiesis,* referred to activities that are a means to an end. In this case, the labor is performed mostly to procure external goods.[38] Neither activity perfectly describes how my students experienced work, but the duality roughly reflects a virtue continuum for situating work in our lives. Upon reflection, I find redolent within the worker essays an outline of a moral economy of labor. To understand how the themes of time, space, impacts, purpose, and subject contribute to the nature of work, it is useful to apply Aristotle's virtue ethics as a conceptual framework for how to approach working.[39] His ideas of what constitutes the things we call "the good" (*agathos*) are remarkably aligned with my students' experiences and the themes in this book. Here is Aristotle's description of how the good is typically spoken of; "What *sort* of thing something is, spoken of as the virtues; *how much* something is, it is spoken of as the measured amount; its *relation* to something, as what is useful; as regards *time*, as the opportune moment, as regards *place*, as the right location."[40]

Aristotle claimed that virtues were the most important habits for people looking to achieve the good life. Being virtuous was not just knowing the right thing to do but also developing that knowledge through practical experience. He further noted that virtuous behavior, which brought about individual and social flourishing, was only possible in the "polis" (i.e., city-state or society). Being virtuous required not only knowing what to do (e.g., the job) but then acting well with others (e.g., relations of production). Therefore, virtuous acts ought to be done both on behalf of the individual acting and also in the best interest of others in society. One additional aspect of acting virtuously, according to Aristotle, is to find the "golden mean" between extreme alternatives. The mean is a reference point between two bad quantities of something; one is a severe deficiency and the other an obsessive excess. While the mean does not necessarily lie equal distances from the ends, either extreme is a vice. Virtue is found in finding the sweet spot; neither too little nor too much. In their essays workers have revealed that their work profoundly influences their personal and social well-being. Here is where my student essays hew remarkably close to the idea of how work should be situated in society, both in the present and in the future.

Space and Time

Work is killing folks. Slowly and then all at once. Therefore, the *space* we occupy at work and the *time* we spend on the job must address the value of human life. A forty-hour workweek is an anachronistic artifact in the contemporary period of advanced technological efficiency and productivity. Capital has developed to the extent that workers needn't labor their life away. The concept of a "work-life balance" is too often little more than a disingenuous discourse perpetuated by employers, opportunistic politicians, and media sources. As workers repeatedly expressed, they needed an opportunity to work. But how much *time* is desired or healthy? What amount of time was consistent with subjective happiness and objective well-being?

If a person without the material means to avoid working has no employment time, life would likely be brutal. Exchanging their time for an income is the way that workers secure enough of the property they need to survive and perhaps to prosper. On the other hand, if you were constantly working, life would be oppressive, and you would forfeit all your time to the boss. Work is typically measured by labor time, but let's not forget that every minute you labor uses up an amount of human energy. More energy and time for production subtracts energy and time from other pursuits. Fishing, reading, watching horror movies, or taking walks with someone you love. The fact that work and life are juxtaposed as separate alien entities whose boundaries must be naturally negotiated, instead of understood as unified human activity, reflects the way that commercial ends have come to lord over workers. In September of 2022 railroad freight companies nearly subjected the country to a national strike because they refused to allow their employees to take an unpaid—let me write that again—*unpaid* day off to see a doctor.[41] These employers were so emboldened by their ability to control how workers experienced time that they recreated working conditions from the late nineteenth century. Somehow what we do for a living has come to be in opposition to the lives we seek to create. To have more of one is to have less of the other. Work is the negation of life. Life is the negation of work. Therefore, to give back to workers some control over their lives requires, at a minimum, placing limits on the time they spend as waged workers. As Marx said, "The shortening of the working-day is its basic prerequisite."[42] Certainly, time off without fear of job loss should be a basic human right. We need to also revisit the thirty-hour and four-day work week. Cambridge University Professor Brendan Burchell sees nothing inevitable or foreordained about the time we must work. "People often talk about the five-day week [as] if it's something that was in the book of Genesis. That's very far from the truth."[43]

Additionally, too many workers are clocking ridiculously long days and weeks and not earning overtime pay. They are often misclassified as exempt employees subsequently, don't qualify for overtime pay. The designation is yet another way that capital squeezes surplus labor value from workers. Employees should be properly classified under the law and receive the employment benefits they are entitled to under the law. If it was, workers would live longer. My students were resigned to working for practically forever. Their work had a temporal dimension with a distant horizon. But how long should be enough? If average life expectancy is shrinking, a fruitful retirement before sixty-five should be possible for people who have been employed since their teens. Thus, to allow for a virtuous job and post-employment life, we must create policies to balance work time with other life activities. We should put human life before profit, even under capitalism.

Workers would also live longer and be healthier if they were protected to the greatest degree possible from unhealthy work environments. Capital "is reckless of the health or length of life of the worker, unless under compulsion from society."[44] Employers should know that there is a reasonable probability that their workplaces will be inspected for health and safety violations. Increased unionization would both reduce structural dangers and increase oversight. A *workspace* that is underinvested in and too spartan would leave a worker without the capacity to learn the trade. Job sites, for example, that provided the requisite tools, equipment, lighting, and room to operate would be conducive to doing a good job. Spaces that lack supplies, good ventilation, portable toilets, and ergonomically sound design may save the employer money but will likely degrade the work.

Where the workplace is matters also. If work is done fully remotely, it can suppress the development of social relationships and hinder bonds of solidarity, but it may provide a welcome degree of scheduling flexibility for some workers. However, if the jobsite is massive (think a warehouse) work can be mind-numbingly routine or populated by more robots than people. The workplace can become joyless and uninspiring. Most concerning for finding the virtuous balance, the space could be too dangerous for human beings. Work sites are always contested spaces due to health concerns. Enough protections and they could be safe spaces; not enough and they were transmittal points for death and illness. Additionally, if a person is expected to work at and away from the jobsite (think K-12 teachers), the workspace effectively encroaches upon the sanctity of a personal domain. The practical effect is that a worker never truly leaves the job site. A workplace that demands unreasonable levels of effort is abusive on the body, mind, and emotions. Prohibiting forms of employment characterized by "physical and mental degradation ... premature death, [and] the torture of over-work" ought to be a high priority of the state.[45] Virtuous work requires a good workplace.

One of my students, Tom Walton, worked for the postal service in a small Illinois town and all his life was known as the "mail carrier's son." After about thirty years working as a postal clerk, he had a metaphysical sense of where work happened that echoed Aristotle's perspective on where virtue was found. "Work is somewhere between heaven and hell." What's needed is the right amount of well-organized, resourced, and safe workplaces. Government regulation should ensure that where we work brings out the best in human creativity and not be predicated on maximizing the crazed pursuit of profit.

Impacts

Work is far too important, too life forming, too critical to our humanity to leave to employers. The *impacts* are far too severe. It no doubt would surprise the majority of people, but except in limited ways for workers employed in the public sector, Americans lack constitutional rights on the job. Political philosopher Elizabeth Anderson equates the near-unfettered power employers have over workers to a "private government." What kind of government would that be? Consider that without a union a person is an "at will" employee—a judge-made designation—vulnerable to termination without "just cause." What this means is that as long as employers do not overtly fire a person on the grounds of some legally protective status (e.g., race, gender, age or disability), they have near carte blanche to discharge employees for any stated or unstated reason.

The ubiquitous nature of the boss's oversight has inspired technologies to rationalize the process of observing, evaluating, ranking, and disciplining workers. A front-page *New York Times* story under the banner headline "On the Clock and Tracked to the Minute," noted that eight of the ten largest private US employers "track the productivity metrics of individual workers, many in real time." Few if any state laws limit "how to implement these technologies to surveil workers."[46] The result of the employer using these technologies is to subject the worker to what the French philosopher Michel Foucault calls "disciplinary power."[47] Capital's insecurity about the edifice built on waged labor has generated an extensive intellectual school of human resource management. The field has morphed multiple times into a cacophony of management theories and business buzzwords.[48] From Foucault's perspective the point of all managerial tools broadly defined is not to enable the individual to expand their own potential but to normalize worker behavior to meet the employers' needs. "The code they [the worker] come to define is not that of law but that of normalization."[49]

The impact of this all-consuming employer control are workplaces filled with dissatisfied workers. Employee unhappiness with work is typically accompanied by a claustrophobic workplace climate and culture that almost ensures that people won't perform at their best. Instead, they will act defensively and not creatively. They will be extremely risk adverse and default to doing the familiar, safe thing that is dissatisfying but keeps them employed. They will get the job done, but many will experience burnout and the attendant physical and mental symptoms, like anxiety, lack of sleep, headaches, and muscle pain. It is the disquiet felt by millions of workers who are captured by the material need to sell their labor and can't find an escape from the realization that work truly is "taking over."

Further, the impact of utilizing the exploited labor of dissatisfied workers leaves individuals and society impoverished. It contributes to obscene inequality between capital and worker shares of wealth. Aristotle appreciated the value of possessing enough wealth and private property that "suffices for a good life" but no more than was consistently put to virtuous use. "The moneymaking life is characterized by a certain constraint, and it is clear that wealth is not the good being sought."[50] In defending the ownership of personal property, John Locke put forth the principal of "productive use" that placed some parameters around the acquisition of wealth.[51] You could own a lot as long as it was being used for constructive ends. However, the acquisition of extravagant wealth was not a virtue. A society with America's degree of economic disparity—especially as it correlates to race, gender, and class—is not virtuous or just. My students don't appear to want—at one end of the spectrum—to own the means of production, as much as they value doing challenging, well-compensated, and fulfilling work. And they want to avoid—at the other end of the line—laboring for minimum wage. Beyond pay, worker essays revealed that they also seek satisfying work environments. "Work is supposed to be fulfilling." Workers and managers should be able to construct employment opportunities that include a balance of sufficient material and psychological rewards. As researchers in psychology, economics, and organizational behavior have discovered, people who are challenged by their work and have some control over it feel good about how they earn a living.

One of the acts most threatening to a worker's livelihood is expressing support for a labor union. Avoiding and discouraging workers from joining unions is built into the DNA of American employers. Their success at thwarting worker organizing is the most damaging impact of the gross imbalance of power between labor and capital. Wearing a prounion button or even talking at work about better wages can be reason enough for an employer to push someone onto the unemployment line.[52] Union density in 2020 was 10.8 percent, roughly half of what it was in 1983, the first year for which comparable union data was available.[53] The steep drop led to media cover stories with apocalyptic titles, like the one in *Harper's Magazine*: "Labor's Last Stand: Is This The End of American Unions?"[54] The question has been asked before and the answer has always come back no. However, existing is one thing, effective existence is another.

Since most of my students were born, the country has steadily become less unionized. A higher proportion of workers today than when my dad retired in 1987 are treated as "at will" employees with little collective voice at work. But when, in 2018, the Supreme Court ruled in *Janus v AFSCME Illinois* that public-sector unions could not even collect fees—different from union dues—from workers benefiting from union representation, thereby imposing by legal fiat a national right-to-work regime on government employment, the threat of dissolution became more potent.[55] Timothy Noah, labor policy editor at *Politico*, said what seemed obvious, "The prognosis of the US labor movement is dismal—that's the reality."

Despite the paltry and decreasing numbers, over 70 percent of Americans approve of labor unions and most workers want a union in their workplace.[56] However, worker desires have been "effectively cancelled out by a combination of legal and illegal employer intimidation tactics."[57] Employers collectively spend $430 million per year on "union avoidance" consultants who teach them how to exploit weakness in federal labor law to effectively scare workers out of exercising their legal right to collective bargaining. Professor John Logan has noted that "aggressive employer opposition" facilitated by weak legal protection for labor rights is the single major cause of the "slow strangulation of private-sector unionism."[58] Anderson adds up this far-reaching authority wielded by the boss and concludes, "Most workers are governed by communist dictatorships in their work lives."[59] The result is that workers don't collectively resist the working conditions they dislike. Instead, they mostly tolerate bad jobs or a bad boss, or they push back individually. Some withhold productivity, come late, leave early, or just quit in record numbers. Professor of law and philosophy Scott Hershovitz recognizes a severe contradiction in our civic standing and economic reality: "Americans talk a good game about freedom. We love our constitutional rights. But if you care about freedom, the American workplace should seriously disturb you."[60]

However, even the best employers are still primarily interested in the cheapest, most controllable labor possible. It isn't personal; it's business. Importantly, the wages and working conditions that characterize employment are not the simple products of supply and demand; bargaining asymmetries are key. Recognizing the character of class relations, my colleague Professor Steven Ashby asserts that "labor unions are the most important vehicle to defend workers' rights in the world. The world would be a far better place if every worker who wanted could, without fear, join a labor union."[61] Therefore, work's physical, mental, and emotional impact, along with its necessity means that workers must have very strong labor unions representing them. Not weak ones. Not ones that look good on paper. These unions had to be willing to resist capital through strikes and nonviolent militant strategies. A strike, in principle, is an "expression of labor withdrawing cooperation from the unequal power relations at work." Political science professor Andrew Kolin points out that strikes symbolize that "workers do have interests that differentiate them from employers."[62]

My students were unequivocal that there was a critical need to grow the labor movement if work's purpose was to be realized. The social relations at work should be democratized so that workers are less yoked to their bosses and have a voice in how their employers operate. Labor unions don't have to disappear to fully subject workers to capital exploitation; they need only be reduced to irrelevancy. To be a countervailing power to capital and elevate the positive effects of work, unions had to organize new workers, have political influence, and negotiate strong contracts. Importantly, they also needed to be democratic and elect visionary leadership.

Work is responsible for all wealth; therefore compensation must properly reflect labor's contribution. Labor power would still be sold—the proletarian revolution might come someday, but not anytime soon—and it couldn't be offered cheaply. Capital will keep realizing financial returns beyond what it pays the workers. The only uncertainty is the size of the gap. Its grown substantially since I began to teach, and there is no empirical absolute end point. A US Treasury Department report investigating corporate power to set wages concluded that worker earnings were on average roughly 20 percent lower than they would be if employers were fully compensating their employees for the value they generate.[63] The *Harvard Business Review* recognized the problem: "The majority of Americans share in economic growth through the wages they receive for their labor, rather than through investment income. Unfortunately, many of these workers have fared poorly in recent decades. Since the early 1970s, the hourly inflation-adjusted wages received by the typical worker have barely risen, growing only 0.2% per year. In other words, though the economy has been growing, the primary way most people benefit from that growth has almost completely stalled."[64] Put simply, work just about no longer pays.

Purpose

Work without *purpose* is unthinkable and punitive. Human beings construct their world and develop their essence in part through their labor. They seek satisfying work and intellectual discretion over how to perform their tasks. Workers valued the development and exercise of more complex skills that allowed them to utilize all their faculties. "Work is a way to express individual talents." Self-realization was a good reason to work. However, jobs that sever any connection between conception and execution are far more likely to be monotonous and "stifle the human capacity for thought, imagination, and skill."[65] We should be able to find the appropriate degree of worker autonomy that exists in every job. Furthermore, no workers in my classes did worthless labor or toiled on a job for merely selfish reasons. I agree with Dr. Martin Luther King who said that "whenever you are engaged in work that serves humanity and is for the building of humanity, it has dignity, and it has worth."[66] Working to care and provide for family and community nestled comfortably within a web of social relationships enriches life. Nurses ministering to patients are helping to heal others. Yet with very rare exception, hospitals in this country do not enforce patient-nurse staffing ratios. Acting virtuously— for nurses and patients—would require establishing a reasonable workload. Teachers helping kids learn to read are helping generations. Universal Pre-K and full-day kindergarten, along with smaller classroom sizes, more social workers, and intervention specialist, are a few of the effective measures to educate our children. But despite knowing what's best for learning, classroom teacher-student ratios are too high, social workers bare a ridiculously large case load, and early learning educators earn shamefully low salaries.

We should invest in the infrastructure that supports a healthy and rational participation in work. Work's purpose extends to empowering individual workers, raising healthy families, and creating prosperous communities. Let's begin with providing paid leave to our labor force. Columnist Roxane Gay points out the disingenuous "elected leaders, many of whom extol the virtues of family," but "can't even agree on making parental leave a law."[67] The United States is one of only six nations recognized by the U.N. without a parental leave law. Establishing "fair workweek" rules that allow workers to have some voice and confidence in their weekly work schedules would also be beneficial. And if the pandemic taught capital and elected leaders anything, it was the essential need for childcare to keep the working class on the job. Why shouldn't employers who depend on workers to generate their profits fund childcare services for their employees? So few firms provide services that its clear employers have relied on individual families (whose wages were stagnant for four decades prior to fall 2021) and schools to perform the reproductive labor necessary to turn the economic wheel. Employers have gone as far as to actively circumvent federal legislation that was specifically designed to encourage them to build childcare centers in the United States.[68] Instead of expanding the availability of childcare, companies have utilized tax policy to subsidize citizens' use of inadequate and poorly paid market services rather than developing and providing public services. We should abide by Adam Smith's belief that legislation in favor of the worker is "always just and equitable."[69]

Student essays repeatedly linked work's objectives to building a healthy society. However, it would be nearly impossible to use work to develop and preserve the community if antiworker politicians continued to get elected. Work can only be a ladder into prosperity if corporate power is restrained. Since the 1970s class relations and neoliberal economics have degraded work and increased the precariousness of employment conditions in the United States. One large study revealed the "number of workers in high quality, full-time employment, with adequate wages and benefits, has decreased over the last 40 years, while the number with low-quality, precarious employment (PE) has increased."[70] The deterioration of working conditions causes cascading harm within the families and communities that harbored employers. For instance, insufficient income compromises a person's access to necessities that contribute to wellbeing, like nutritious foods, safe neighborhoods, public parks, dependable mass transportation, well-funded schools, suitable housing, clean air, and water, and good medical care. Poor quality jobs are also associated with greater exposure to adverse physical outcomes and psychosocial stress. The employer's rule we ascent to not only leads to worker abuse; it poisons our communities.

Adam Smith and Karl Marx pointed out that the social relations of work are artificially determined through state intervention. Employers have the means to manipulate legislatures to pass laws in their favor. The result was a concentration of wealth that Smith considered an "economic pathology."[71] Any policy recommendation from capital "ought to be listened to with great precaution." Smith warned that "It comes from an order of men whose interest is never exactly the same with the general public, who have generally an interest to deceive and even oppress the public, and accordingly have, upon many occasions, both deceived and oppressed it."[72] Work writ large is a social convention dependent on public policy. Who counts as an employee, what is the employment standard, how do we understand employment obligations, how are the outcomes distributed, and what participatory mechanisms do workers have to influence their employment destinies? These are just a few of the matters that policy determines—for good or for bad.[73]

Work is "a basic mode of being in the world," that also humanizes the world, but in William Morris's words, "Nothing should be made by man's labour which is not worth doing; or which must be made by labour degrading to the makers."[74] In other words, work cannot fulfill its function to raise the community's wellbeing if it deforms the worker. It follows then that a workplace where workers had the means to do well, required supporting a proworker political agenda. Ruth Yeoman has an idea for framing that agenda. She argues that "work is a mode of being in the world which transcends the employment relation to include all the activities which contribute to producing and reproducing a complex system of social cooperation." Thus, for work to avoid visiting "harms upon people, then the widespread institution of meaningful work is a proper moral and political project."[75]

Between treating work as just the "dull compulsion of economic relations" or as a calling, there is a medium that is respectful of the worker.[76] Work cannot fulfill, nor should it be expected to fulfill, every personal intrinsic drive. Work can and should, however, contribute mightily to our happiness. It may be more virtue signaling then virtue commitment, but the REI consumer cooperative declares on their website that the company believes in "putting purpose before profit."[77] Perhaps it's just a neat slogan because they also don't believe that "placing a union between the co-op and its employees is needed or beneficial."[78] Turns out their workers at a Manhattan store thought differently and voted to join a union.[79] Nonetheless, focusing on a noncommercial purpose should create the opportunity to identify a consensus reason for going to work. Finding out what people want from work is only possible if we listen to workers and then organize our employment relations to maximize virtue.

Subject

Worker essays demonstrated that the *subject* of their work included themselves but also workmates, family, consumers, taxpayers, and the larger community. People work for people they love and folks they don't even know. In truth, workers are a means for customers, taxpayers, children, the public, and other workers. Workers satisfy needs and wants, from a cup of coffee to heart surgery to clean streets. But if workers are treated only as a cost of production and there is no recognition that they and others are the subject of their own labor, then employment relations cannot be just. Workers are not merely a means. As human beings they are also a dignified ends and should be treated as such. There has been too much weight placed on the socially necessary labor-time side of the work-life equation and not enough on how work contributes to a virtuous lived experience. To achieve the Aristotelian mean there would need to be a better focus on work's contribution to the interdependent social nature of people living, playing, praying, and working together.

Work can't be done for one another if workers are not for one another. Labor's subject should include anyone who works for a living. My students agreed that divisions within the labor force over race, gender, language, nationality, and citizenship status were destructive. The labor movement took a giant step toward class solidarity in 2001 when the AFL-CIO shook off the shackles of its ugly past anti-immigrant stance. Affiliated unions attending the labor body's annual convention in Chicago, adopted Resolution 5. Its preamble left no doubt where organized labor stood on America's immigration policy: "Standing Up for Immigrant Workers—A Call to Action. Strengthening a Special Bond: Unions and Immigrants Building Community Coalitions and Civic Participation. Implementation of Immigration Law." Union leaders asked themselves a "question that every generation of trade unionists has asked: 'Which side are you on?'"[80] It was a long overdue rectification. From my vantage point the least welcomed point of education among union leaders, members, and nonunion workers was a focus on bias and the differential benefits of work based on race, gender, and language. Occupations vary in their demographic mix, but in many industries, like construction and high-tech, too few African Americans, Hispanics, and women are employed in unionized occupations.

Another area that workers found important to their subjectivity is the commercial media. Popular portrayals of the working class and specifically labor unions is a source of deep antipathy among workers. My students struggled to find honest, positive, or informative news about the working class. Workers are too often presented as one-dimensional and derivative subjects. There used to be dedicated and well-informed labor-beat reporters at all major metropolitan newspapers. I had the pleasure of being interviewed by several of them, including the *Chicago Tribune's* Steven Franklin, the *New York Time's* Steven Greenhouse, and Phil Dine at the *St. Louis Post-Dispatch*. Few of these positions exist any longer. Noam Schieber at the *New York Times* is a prominent exception. Major metropolitan newspapers have largely abandoned a "labor beat" focused on labor relations. In its place a new "beat" survived and told other stories.[81] Representation of labor on television and in movies is worse. Only occasionally do they portray a well-rounded, authentic worker or working-class life. One of the most popular and entertaining courses that I have taught is on the popular representations of labor in television and cinema. Students watched clips of shows and movies and then deconstructed the images and message. It was rare to find a representation that they judged as realistic or fair, particularly if the story was about collective worker action or unions. Far more common was the characterization embedded in the following lines spoken by television's most enduring working-class figure, Homer Simpson: "If you don't like your job you don't strike. You just go in every day and do it really half-assed. That's the American way."[82]

A big strike got attention in the mass media, at least for a while. In October and November of 2021, there was an upsurge in strikes. Press coverage was extensive, and the industry dubbed the frequency of job actions "Striketo-ber."[83] Additional stories pointed out how the pandemic had given workers increased leverage to improve the quality of their jobs. One headline went as far as to refer to a "Workers Economy," although the story quoted an expert who said, "We absolutely know the employers hold the cards."[84] Strike stories are appealing because they represent conflict, but no matter how they are covered, the focus on workers' concerns fades along with the picket lines. They inevitably give way to profiles of business executives, daily updates on the stock market returns, corporate decision-making and earnings, and industrial-sector reports on, of course, the section of the paper dedicated to capital—the business page. Television stays focused—no matter the socio-economic reality of modern capitalism—on its primary mission which is bringing consumers to advertisers or subscribers to investors. Happy friends, often guys in a beer commercial, are preferred. No ad revenue or subscribers, no favorite program to watch. Stories of everyday worker struggles don't fit the celebratory framework necessary to bring people with money to advertisers.

My students had no problem complaining about how toxic and delusional Washington politicians and ginned-up accounts of nonstories meant to feed outrage dominated the mainstream media's account of America. A more difficult task was identifying stories about what it meant to work in a class-based society growing rapidly more unequal. Cable and network news outlets and national print and virtual newspapers were still covering employment and economic conditions, but labor unions as a prime subject of interest to the nation's welfare had been marginalized. In truth, most previous writing had relied on strikes and scandals. But as one student in my class noted, "The problem isn't the bad stuff they publish, it's that they simply ignore us." Yes, as a general news story—except for Labor Day—labor unions have become invisible. Or at least they were until a postpandemic labor shortage and a significant rise in worker organizing in 2022 thrust unions into public consciousness. Nonetheless, except in the pages of a few alternative progressive journalistic sources, which relatively few workers read, did the workers regularly see themselves and the work they do reflected in an authentic way.[85] What was needed was a media by and for the working class.

Knowing and valuing the subject of work is further attenuated because society has ignored the role of work as a subject of study in educating people. The curricular absence of work is surprising but likely not unintentional. The business community has historically insisted that education serve their interest. Doing that meant treating students as objects to be prepared, shaped, and indoctrinated to become wage workers. In 1913 John D. Rockefeller sponsored the General Education Board, which funded public schools to the tune of millions of dollars. What they were buying, however, wasn't people who could think critically about a life of labor. "We shall not try to make these people or any of their children into philosophers or men of learning, or science. We are not to raise up from among them authors, orators, poets, or men of letters. We shall not search for embryo great artists, painters, musicians. Nor will we cherish even the humbler ambition to raise up from among them lawyers, doctors, preachers, politicians, statesmen, of whom we now have ample supply."[86] The elite and capitalists were aplenty; no more please. But there was an avaricious need for wage labor. It never satiated. In the mid-1980s the Committee for Education Development proclaimed that "Employers in both large and small businesses decry the lack of preparation for work among the nation's high school graduates."[87]

A decade later employers were even blunter about what they wanted from schools: "The primary purpose of education is to prepare students to work successfully in the global economy."[88] The objective is clear and myopic. Schools are not pre-employment training programs. Education is not resume planning. Work is an activity that allows a person to live a prosperous human life, and education should inspire human development. Education should enable the student to become the active subject of their own destiny. Teenagers overwhelmingly understand the relationship between work and well-being. More than nine in ten boys and girls say that "having a job or career they enjoy would be extremely or very important to them as an adult."[89] Educational theorist John Dewey believed that to "find out what one is fitted to do, and to secure an opportunity to do it, is the key to happiness." Accordingly, the "dominant vocation of all human beings at all times is living—intellectual and moral growth."[90] In 1957 the Association for Supervision and Curricular Development Committee offered the following counter perspective to the business chieftains: "The main purpose of the American school is to provide for the fullest possible development of each learner for living morally, creatively, and productively in a democratic society."[91] The organization further stressed that "The one continuing purpose of education, since ancient times, has been to bring people to as full a realization as possible of what it is to be a human being." Narrow special business interests like reproducing wage employees "imply a distorted human existence."[92]

Aside from the gross inaccuracy and self-serving quality of the employers' education claims, even if you accepted them at face value, the absence of curricula about work or working is conspicuous. Our nation's K-12 curriculum barely mentions workers or unions, and there are only a handful of higher-education programs like the Labor Education Program that I direct. As a result, worker rights literacy is woefully lacking in the United States. Educators at the turn of the twentieth century recognized the danger of converting schools into worker labs. Margaret Haley, President of the National Federation of Teachers, rang the warning bell.

> Two ideals are struggling for supremacy in American life today: one the industrial ideal, dominating thru the supremacy of commercialism, which subordinates the worker to the product and the machine; the other, the ideal of democracy, the ideal of the educators, which places humanity above all machines, and demands that all activity shall be the expression of life.[93]

Students should be taught about what work is, poetry and all, before they become the object of prose and study.

Finding work's virtuous mean is feasible, but it will not be uncontested. Abiding by it will be even more arduous. Employers, even the most self-proclaimed socially responsible ones, are driven principally to be profitable. In his annual letter to CEOs, titled "The Power of Capitalism," Blackrock Capital head Larry Fink made clear what my students never doubted: "Make no mistake, the fair pursuit of profit is still what animates markets; and long-term profitability is the measure by which markets will ultimately determine your company's success."[94] Aristotle would have granted that commercial striving for wealth is beneficial to well-being. But only as a device to constructing the good life for society. The so called "fair pursuit of profit" or what Aristotle called the "art of acquisition," is both the "necessary foundation of true human flourishing and the greatest danger to it."[95] Therefore, according to worker essays, the subject of our political economy should be the betterment and happiness of people brought about through virtuous productive activities. Instead of the profit motive driving production, the ends of our virtuous society should be the development of high-quality jobs and meaningful work. Ensuring that work is done for the common good requires, at minimum, strong independent labor unions, some democratic control over the nation's organizational assets, and effective corporate regulation. On this dimension, I'm confident that if given the opportunity workers would be most skillful in finding the Aristotelian mean, which would facilitate human flourishing. Therefore, educational, mass-media, cultural, legal, and legislative institutions should prioritize work's ability to help raise virtuous individuals and communities.

A Worker-Centered Future of Work Is Possible

My student-inspired recommendations are not unrealistic or implausible. The point of knowing what workers think "work is," is not simply to develop an explanatory body of knowledge. It's also to offer a critique of work and where needed, to propose changes. What my students' physical, cognitive, and emotional knowing have taught me is that social action is required to ensure that work in the future is less an Old Testament form of punishment and more a necessary way to realize our highest human potential. To paraphrase Marx, the point of what workers teach us is not to "interpret the world of work, in various ways . . . but to change it."[96] Once we have witnessed the substance and significance of our essential human activity, there's no going back to ignorance.

Work has a future. At some point in every class, I say "Someone is digging and getting in the hole." It's a shorthand way to point out that society will continue to require that a large class of people do the hard, dirty, dangerous, creative, and productive work essential to human community. The question is under what conditions, for what purpose, and to what ends will the digging occur. How much surplus value will be generated? What share of the wealth will be returned to the workers? Adam Smith had an answer. Keep wages high and profits low. The rate of profit, he warned, was "always highest in the countries which are going fastest to ruin."[97] In *An Inquiry Into the Wealth of Nations*, he wrote "The property which every man has in his own labour, as it is the original foundation of all other property, so it is the most sacred and inviolable."[98] Smith prioritized labor over capital because, unlike those who "live by profit" who do not have "the same connection with the general interest of society," those "who live by wages" are "strictly connected with the interest of the society."[99] And what if we honored workers and the fruits of their labor? "In that case," Marx concludes, "our products would be like so many mirrors, out of which our essence shone."[100]

The enormous dislocations caused by the pandemic and continuous technological interventions will relocate work and alter how it is done. But where and how won't change the fundamental need for productive labor to dig, lift, push, carry, drive, and make the ground ready literally and metaphorically. My students are resolute that "work is in the hands of the people." It is precariously held from one generation to the next by folks who don't own the country's capital and must live off their productive labor. If, as Philip Levine's ode to the working class defiantly declares, "you don't know what work is, then forget you." All of us who benefit from the labor of others—and that's all of us—are responsible for protecting the many hands, minds, and hearts who give birth to each day. We can't be indifferent to the barista, the delivery driver, the landscaper, the agricultural worker, the nurse, the warehouse packer, the teacher, the operating engineer, the janitor, the bus driver, the room attendant, or millwright. We owe our existence to the productive people who labor long hours over a lifetime. To put a sharper edge on the point, those of us who work at something other than an hourly wage or modest salary job are dependent on the working class for our opportunities to live a decent life. If every teacher, firefighter, electrician, bus driver, nurse, clerk, restaurant server, meatpacker, administrative aide, and mechanic simultaneously put down their tools, the world would stand still. Indeed, "work is what keeps the world working."

As interdependent and impermanent members of a society, we shouldn't be indifferent to how the world is being made and remade. The overwhelming majority of adults who have or will raise children will insert their kids into a social structure that principally values their future labor. They will be prepared to be productive workers, either as employees or perhaps independent contractors. A small percent will assume ownership status or work in professions that sell, manage, or legally protect the productive labor of millions. Michael Zwieg estimated in *Working Class Majority* that the American capitalist class makes up no more than 2 percent of the labor force.[101] The odds that future workers will become part of the wealthy fraction is just as small. In 2018 less than one in five people lived in "upper class" households.[102]

Truth is, folks are going to keep doing hard, not-always-enjoyable work. But that work doesn't have to be soul crushing. It can fill bellies and pantries and spirits and minds. It can be in exchange for money and be purposeful. It will use up and produce life. In the meantime, I'll keep asking students to write six-word essays. Their replies may change. We'll see. Whatever they write will be related to the structural and empirical conditions that they find at and through work.

After reading and reflecting on years of worker essays, I asked my father for his response. He didn't disappoint. According to my dad, retired union steelworker Robert Gabriel Bruno, "Work is doing what I had to do." Dad never did speak with a creative flourish. And yet my students and his son understood every word.

Notes

Introduction

1. Karl Marx quoted from *Capital, Volume 1* in David Harvey's *A Companion to Marx's Capital: The Complete Edition* (London: Verso Press, 2018), 372.

2. Herbert Applebaum, *The Concept of Work: Ancient, Medieval, Modern* (Albany: State University of New York Press, 1992), ix.

3. Bertrand Russell, "In Praise of Idleness," *Harper's Magazine*, October 1932 at https://harpers.org/archive/1932/10/in-praise-of-idleness/, accessed 4/2/2023.

4. The philosopher Maurice Merleau-Ponty was an important thinker within the phenomenological tradition. The text's sentence construction is borrowed and adapted from the following excerpt from Merleau-Ponty's *Phenomenology of Perception*: "The world is not what I think, but what I live through, I am open to the world" (London: Routledge, Kegan and Paul 1945/1962), 17.

5. Russell said that "Work is of two kinds: first, altering the position of matter at or near the earth's surface relatively to other such matter; second, telling other people to do so." The work I'm examining fits broadly within the first kind. Bertrand Russell, "In Praise of Idleness," *Harper's Magazine*, October 1932 at https://harpers.org/archive/1932/10/in-praise-of-idleness/, accessed 4/2/2023.

6. On the other hand, it is considered work because it often involves some combination of routine household tasks, household management, and emotional labor. Helen J. Mederer, "Division of Labor in Two-Earner Homes: Task Accomplishment versus Household Management as Critical Variables in Perceptions about Family," *Work Journal of Marriage and Family*, 55, no. 1 (February 1993): 133–45. Some analysts actually have considered household labor time in total work hours (e.g., Laura Leete and Juliet B. Schor, "Assessing the Time-Squeeze Hypothesis: Hours Worked in the United States, 1969–89," *Industrial Relations A Journal of Economy and Society*, 33, no. 1 (May 2008): 25–43.

7. Nationwide, for example, women are 3.8 percent of construction industry laborers, 4 percent of firefighters, 5.8 percent of machinists, and 32.7 percent of nonsupervisory assemblers and fabricators, but 94.8 percent of childcare providers, 87.4 percent of registered nurses, 79.6 percent of elementary and middle school teachers, 90 percent of health aides, 58.1 percent of food preparation employees, 71.5 percent of laundry and dry-cleaning workers, 88.3 percent of maids and housekeeping cleaners, 79.7 percent of flight attendants and 64 percent of bakers. Black workers, for instance make up 37.1 percent of postal service sorters; 37 percent of transit bus drivers; 24.6 percent of baggage porters, bellhops, and concierges; and 21.9 percent of hotel, motel, and resort desk clerks; but 6.9 percent of plumbers, pipefitters, and steamfitters; 10 percent of police officers; and 7 percent of special education teachers. By comparison, Hispanic workers make 36 percent of cooks, 37.6 percent of dishwashers, 44.5 percent of landscaping and groundskeeping workers, 46 percent of construction laborers, 51.2 percent of painters, 22.4 percent of telecommunications line installers and repairers, and 40 percent of meat-processing workers. For a complete list of occupations and workforce demographics, see "Labor Force Statistics from the Current Population Survey," *U.S. Bureau of Labor Statistics, Department of Labor*, https://www.bls.gov/cps/cpsaat11.htm.

8. "The Race Card-Six Word Essay," *National Public Radio*, accessed January 8, 2021, https://theracecardproject.com.

9. Just one contemporary book example is John Budd's *The Thought of Work* (Ithaca, NY: ILR Press, 2011).

10. In *The Rule of St. Benedict*, written by Saint Benedict of Nursia, Italy, founder of the Benedictine Order, prayer is referred to as "the work of God." Prayer is work and work is prayer in the economy of monastic life. See, Chris Sullivan, "Work and Prayer in the Style of St. Benedict," https://www.loyolapress.com/catholic-resources/prayer/personal-prayer-life/different-ways-to-pray/work-and-prayer-in-the-style-of-st-benedict/.

11. Charles McGrath, "Voice of the Workingman to Be Poet Laureate," *New York Times*, August 9, 2011, https://www.nytimes.com/2011/08/10/books/philip-levine-is-to-be-us-poet-laureate.html?_r=1&hp, Retrieved January 8, 2021.

12. McGrath, "Voice of the Workingman."

13. "The Poet of the Assembly Line," *The Attic*, https://www.theattic.space/home-page-blogs/2018/9/20/the-poet-of-the-assembly-line, Retrieved January 8, 2021.

14. Philip Levine, "What Work Is," in *What Work Is* (New York: Alfred A. Knopf, 1992), 77. Copyright © 1992 by Philip Levine. Used by permission of Alfred A. Knopf, a division of Random House, Inc.

15. Here's one: "Work is what my wife makes me do." The best example, was "work is a word."

16. Karl Marx quote from Marx's *Capital Volume I*, in David Harvey's *A Companion to Marx's Capital*, 293.

17. Bureau of Labor Statistics Report, February 2021, https://www.bls.gov/opub/reports/minimum-wage/2020/home.htm.

18. David Graeber, *Bullshit Jobs: A Theory* (New York: Simon and Schuster, 2018).

19. Sean Illing, "Bullshit Jobs: Why They Exist and Why You Might Have One," *VOX*, November 9, 2019, https://www.vox.com/2018/5/8/17308744/bullshit-jobs-book-david-graeber-occupy-wall-street-karl-marx.

20. Kathi Weeks, *The Problem with Work: Feminism, Marxism, Antiwork Politics, and Postwork Imaginaries* (Chapel Hill, NC: Duke University Press, 2011), 6.

21. The first published quote of this joke was by Don Marquis and appeared in the Weather Vane Column section of the *Buffalo Evening News*, February 15, 1921. A history of the quote can be seen at "When Croesus Tells You He Got Rich Through Hard Work, Ask Him 'Whose?,'" Quote Investigator, accessed March 19, 2023, https://quoteinvestigator.com/2020/01/01/hard-work/.

22. Kate Gibson, "DoorDash to Pay $2.5 Million for Allegedly Misusing Worker Tips," *CBS News*, November 24, 2020, https://www.cbsnews.com/news/doordash-worker-tips-2-5-million-settlement/.

23. Andy Newman, "My Frantic Life as a Cab-Dodging, Tip-Chasing Food App Deliveryman," *New York Times*, July 21, 2019, https://www.nytimes.com/2019/07/21/nyregion/doordash-ubereats-food-app-delivery-bike.html.

24. Stan Choe, "CEO Pay Rose 17% in 2021 as Profits Soared; Workers Trailed," *Associated Press*, May 27, 2022, https://apnews.com/article/2021-median-ceo-pay-df8a253483aebd48be99f50826ef2b49.

25. Peter Eavis, "Meager Rewards for Workers, Exceptionally Rich Pay for C.E.O.s," *New York Times*, June 11, 2021, https://www.nytimes.com/2021/06/11/business/ceo-pay-compensation-stock.html.

26. Folks like Elon Musk, Jeffrey Bezos, Alexander Karp, Steven Schwarman Brian Chesky.

27. From a poem by Tom Wayman, "Paper, Scissors, Stone," in *For a Living: The Poetry of Work*, edited by Nicholas Coles and Peter Oresick (Champaign: University of Illinois Press, 1995), 362.

28. Just one example of exploitation is Amazon. First, note that Bezos has a $170 billion stake in the firm. Now consider that during the pandemic, Amazon's profits leaped 84 percent. The median employee however earned just $29,007. The 2020 pay was merely $159 above the 2019 pay. Eavis, "Meager Rewards for Workers, Exceptionally Rich Pay for C.E.O.s."

29. From Lincoln's First Annual Message to Congress, December 3, 1861, https://rogerjnorton.com/Lincoln97.html.

30. David Von Drehle, *Triangle: The Fire That Changed America* (Grove Press, 2004).

31. "The National Labor Relations Act, 1935," *The National Labor Relations*

Board, https://www.nlrb.gov/guidance/key-reference-materials/national-labor
-relations-act.

32. Jonathan Levy, *Ages of American Capitalism: A History of the United States* (New York: Random House, 2022), 266.

33. Michael Sandel, *Democracy's Discontent: America in Search of a Public Philosophy* (Cambridge, MA: Belknap Press, 1996), 181–84 and "Wage Slavery or Social Slavery?" *New York Times*, September 25, 1915, https://www.nytimes.com/1919/09/25/archives/wage-slavery-or-social-slavery.html.

34. Lawrence B. Glickman, *A Living Wage: American Workers and the Making of Consumer Society* (Ithaca, NY: Cornell University Press, 2019), 19.

35. Francis Patrick Walsh and Basil M. Manly, *Final Report of the Commission on Industrial Relations*, and United States Commission on Industrial Relations, Washington, D.C., 1915, 2 and 8, https://go-gale-com.proxy2.library.illinois.edu/ps/i.do?p=MOML&u=uiuc_uc&id=GALE%7CF0151918949&v=2.1&it=r.

36. Graham L. Staines and Robert P. Quinn, "American Workers Evaluate the Quality of Their Jobs," *Monthly Labor Review* 102, no. 1 (January 1979): 3–12, https://www.jstor.org/stable/41840853.

37. "Worker Alienation, 1972" in *Hearings Before The Subcommittee On Employment, Manpower, And Poverty Of The Committee On Labor And Public Welfare United States Senate Ninety-Second Congress*, United States. Congress. Senate. Committee on Labor and Public Welfare. Subcommittee on Employment, Manpower, and Poverty, US Government Printing Office, 8, https://babel.hathitrust.org/cgi/pt?id=ucl.a0000415182&view=page&seq=3.

38. James O'Toole et al., *Work in America*, 1972, report of the Special Task Force to the Secretary of Health, Education, and Welfare, Washington, DC, Special Task Force on Work in America, Abstract at https://files.eric.ed.gov/fulltext/ED070738.pdf.

39. O'Toole, *Work in America*, table of contents.

40. John Schmitt, "Did Job Quality Deteriorate in the 1980s and 1990s?" in *Sourcebook of Labor Markets: Evolving Structures and Processes*, ed. Ivar Berg and Arne L. Kalleberg (New York: Kluwer Academic/Plenum Publishers, 2001), 387–405.

41. Quote appeared in Jonathan Levy's *Ages of American Capitalism: A History of the United States* (New York: Random House, 2022), 650.

42. David R Howell and Arne L. Kalleberg, "Declining Job Quality in the United States: Explanations and Evidence," *RSF: The Russell Sage Foundation Journal of the Social Sciences* 5, no. 4 (2019): 1–53, DOI: 10.7758/RSF.2019.5.4.01.

43. The Department of Labor's Good Jobs Initiative can be found at https://www.dol.gov/general/good-jobs.

44. See, the Good Jobs Summit agenda at https://www.dol.gov/sites/dolgov/files/goodjobs/Good-Jobs-Summit-Agenda.pdf. I was an invited academic.

45. Matt Davis, "Maslow's Forgotten Pinnacle: Self-Transcendence," *Big Think*, August 9, 2019, https://bigthink.com/neuropsych/maslow-self-transcendence;

and Richard Kraut, "Aristotle's Ethics," *Stanford Encyclopedia of Philosophy* (Summer 2022), edited by Edward N. Zalta, https://plato.stanford.edu/entries/aristotle-ethics/#HumaGoodFuncArgu.

46. Barry Schwartz, *Why We Work* (TED Books) (New York: Simon and Schuster, 2015).

47. Barry Schwartz, "'Wealth of Nations' Stole Happiness from Workers—Here's How We Steal It Back," *Quartz*, February 18, 2016, https://qz.com/531996/wealth-of-nations-stole-happiness-from-workers-heres-how-we-steal-it-back/.

48. David Harvey, "Universal Alienation," *Journal for Cultural Research* 22, no. 2 (2018): 137—50, https://doi.org/10.1080/14797585.2018.1461350.

49. See, Google Books Ngram Viewer, https://books.google.com/ngrams/graph?content=wage+slavery&year_start=1800&year_end=2019&corpus=26&smoothing=3&direct_url=t1%3B%2Cwage%20slavery%3B%2Cc0#t1%3B%2Cwage%20slavery%3B%2Cc0/.

50. Ruth Yeoman, "Conceptualising Meaningful Work as a Fundamental Human Need," *Journal of Business Ethics* 125 (October 2014): 235–51, DOI 10.1007/s10551-013-1894-9.

51. The actual statement is "Philosophers have only interpreted the world in various ways; the point, however, is to change it." In "Theses on Feuerbach," in *The Marx-Engels Reader*, ed. Robert C. Tucker (New York: W.W. Norton, 1978), 145.

Chapter 1. The Time of Work

1. US Bureau of Labor Statistics, *American Time Use Survey News Release*, June 23, 2022, https://www.bls.gov/news.release/atus.htm.

2. Lonnie Golden and Morris Altman, "Why Do People Overwork? Over-Supply of Hours of Labor, Labor Market Forces and Adaptive Preferences," in *The Long Work Hours Culture: Causes, Consequences and Choices*, ed. Ronald Burke and Cary Cooper (Bingley, UK: Emerald Group Publishing, 2008), 61–83.

3. The hospital chain's referenced "dedication" was likely to the billions in profits it made after slashing staffing cost by $500 million. See Rebecca Robbins, Katie Thomas, and James Silver-Greenberg, "Big Hospital Chain's Cuts Ignited Its Staffing Crisis," *New York Times*, December 16, 2022, https://www.nytimes.com/2022/12/15/business/hospital-staffing-ascension.html.

4. Lonnie Golden and Alison Dickson, *Precarious Times at Work: Detrimental Hours and Scheduling in Illinois and How Fair Workweek Policies Will Improve Workers' Well-Being*, December 9, 2020, http://publish.illinois.edu/projectfor middleclassrenewal/files/2020/12/PMCR-PRECARIOUS-TIMES-AT-WORK_FINAL_pages-FINAL.pdf.

5. Tom W. Smith, Michael Davern, Jeremy Freese, and Stephen Morgan, *General Social Surveys*, 1972–2018, sponsored by National Science Foundation.—NORC ed.—Chicago: NORC, 2018: NORC at the University of Chicago

[producer and distributor]. Data accessed from the GSS Data Explorer website at gssdataexplorer.norc.org.

6. A couple of examples among many studies that show how the association between level of job satisfaction influences health and happiness are F. Olcer and M. Florescu, "Mediating Effect of Job Satisfaction in the Relationship Between Psychological Empowerment and Job Performance," *Business Excellence and Management* 5, no. 1 (2015): 5–32; G. Ozbag and G. Ceyhun, "The Impact of Job Characteristics on Burnout; The Mediating Role of Work Family Conflict and the Moderating Role of Job Satisfaction," *International Journal of Academic Research in Management* 3 no. 3 (2014): 291–309; J. Greenhaus, K. Collins, and J. Shaw, "The Relation Between Work-life Balance and Quality of Life," *Journal of Vocational Behavior* 63, no. 3 (2002): 510–31; F. F. Reichheld *The Loyalty Effect: The Hidden Force Behind Growth, Profits, and Lasting Value* (Boston: Harvard Business School Press, 1996).

7. Juliet B. Schor, *The Overworked American: The Unexpected Decline of Leisure* (New York: Basic Books, 1993).

8. Adam Smith, *An Inquiry into the Nature and Causes of the Wealth of Nations*, edited by S. M. Soares, MetaLibri Digital Library, 2007, book 1, chapter 8.

9. From a poem by Trinidad Sanchez, Jr., "Work, Work, Work," in *Working Words: Punching the Clock and Kicking Out the Jams*, ed. M. L. Liebler (Minneapolis, MN: Coffee House Press, 2020), 190.

10. Peter Goodman, "Risk of Rail Strike Looms Over Sick Pay," *New York Times*, October 29, 2022.

11. Claire Cain Miller, "The World 'Has Found a Way to Do This': The U.S. Lags on Paid Leave," *New York Times*, October 25, 2021, https://www.nytimes.com/2021/10/25/upshot/paid-leave-democrats.html.

12. Gretchen Livingston and Deja Thomas, "Among 41 Countries, Only U.S. Lacks Paid Parental Leave," *Pew Research Center*, December 16, 2019, https://www.pewresearch.org/fact-tank/2019/12/16/u-s-lacks-mandated-paid-parental-leave/.

13. Kathi Weeks, *The Problem with Work: Feminism, Marxism, Antiwork Politics, and Postwork Imaginaries* (Durham, NC: Duke University Press, 2011), 1.

14. John Stuart Mill, "Essay IV. On Profits and Interest," *in Essays on Some Unsettled Questions of Political Economy*, Create Space Independent Publishing Platform, 2016.

15. Adam Smith, *Wealth of Nations*, book 3, 383.

16. David McLellan, "Wage-Labour and Capital," in *Karl Marx Selected Writings*, 2nd ed. (Oxford: Oxford University Press, 2000), 276.

17. However, out of the three shifts (7:00 a.m.–3:00 p.m., 3:00 p.m.–11:00 p.m., and 11:00 p.m.–7:00 a.m.) my dad preferred the morning one because it meant he would be able to attend family and social functions more easily on the days he was working.

18. Friedrich Engels, *The Part Played by Labour in the Transition from Ape to Man* (Peking, China: Foreign Languages Press, 1975).

19. James O'Toole, *Work in America: Report of a Special task Force to the Secretary of Health, Education, and Welfare*, Department of Health, Education, and Welfare, Washington, DC (Cambridge, MA: MIT Press, 1973), 8.

20. Samuel A. Butler, "Postlapsarian Meditations: Labor and Political Participation in Socrates and Aristotle, with a Kantian Footnote," *Constellations* 22, no. 1 (2015): 126.

21. Karl Marx, *Grundrisse: Foundations of the Critique of Political Economy*, trans. Martin Nicolaus, sect. 1 (New York: Penguin Books, 1973). Available online at Marxists Internet Archive, https://www.marxists.org/archive/marx/works/1857/grundrisse/index.htm, 8.

22. Karl Marx, *Wage Labour and Capital*, original 1891 pamphlet available online at Marxists Internet Archive, https://www.marxists.org/archive/marx/works/download/pdf/wage-labour-capital.pdf, 9.

23. Karl Marx, "The Rate of Surplus-Value," in *Capital*, vol. 1, trans. Samuel Moore and Edward Aveling, Moscow: Progress Publishers, 1867. Available online at Marxists Internet Archive, https://www.marxists.org/archive/marx/works/download/pdf/Capital-Volume-I.pdf, 152.

24. Gerry. A. Cohen, *Karl Marx's Theory of History: A Defense* (Princeton, NJ: Princeton University Press, 1978), 189.

25. The International Union of Operating Engineers, Local 150, https://local150.org.

26. Adrian Bardon, *A Brief History of the Philosophy of Time* (Oxford: Oxford University Press, 2013).

27. Naomi Replansky, "Factory Poem," in *The Dangerous World: New and Selected Poems, 1934–1994* (Chicago: Another Chicago Press, 1994), 62.

28. The original rallying cry, "Eight hours labour, eight hours recreation, eight hours rest" came from British socialist and utopian Robert Owen in 1811.

29. A good history of labor organizing and militancy around the issue of work time is Philip S. R. Foner and David R. Roediger, *Our Own Time: A History of American Labor and the Working Day* (London: Verso Press, 1989).

30. Samuel Gompers, *What Does Labor Want?*, Paper Read Before the International Labor Congress, Chicago, Illinois, September 1893 (New York, n.d.).

31. Benjamin Kline Hunnicutt, *Work Without End: Abandoning Shorter Hours for the Right to Work* (Philadelphia, PA: Temple University Press, 1988).

32. Benjamin Hunnicutt, *Free Time: The Forgotten American Dream* (Philadelphia, PA: Temple University Press, 2013).

33. Derek Thompson, "Workism Is Making Americans Miserable," *The Atlantic*, February 24, 2019, https://www.theatlantic.com/ideas/archive/2019/02/religion-workism-making-americans-miserable/583441/.

34. John de Gaaf, "When Americans Came This Close to Establishing a 30-Hour Workweek," *Alter Net*, April 2, 2013, https://www.alternet.org/2013/04/when-america-came-close-establishing-30-hour-workweek/.

35. Jerry Jacobs and Kathleen Gerson, "Who Are the Overworked Ameri-

cans?" in *Working Time: International Trends, Theory, and Policy Perspectives*, ed. L. Golden and D. Figart (New York: Routledge, 2001), 89–105. P. Kuhn and F. Lozano, "The Expanding Workweek? Understanding Trends in Long Work Hours Among U.S. Men, 1979–2004," *Journal of Labor Economics*, vol. 26, 2, April 2008, 311–43; and "Work and Workplace," *GALLUP*, https://news.gallup .com/poll/1720/work-work-place.aspx.

36. Since beginning at the University of Illinois I have taught in union summer schools with the United Steelworkers Union (USW). My conversation about working overtime occurred with USW members from an Arconic plant in Indiana.

37. Hannah Sampson, "What Does America Have Against Vacation?" *Washington Post*, August 28, 2019, https://www.washingtonpost.com/travel/2019/08/28/ what-does-america-have-against-vacation/; Adewale Maye, "No Vacation Nation, Revised," Center for Economic and Policy Research, 2019, https://cepr.net/ documents/publications/nvn-summary.pdf.

38. Tom Wayman, "Factory Time," in *Working Classics: Poems on Industrial Life*, ed. Peter Oresick and Nichols Coles (Urbana: University of Illinois Press, 1990), 228–30.

39. Robert Bruno, Steven Ashby, and Frank Manzo IV, *Beyond the Classroom: An Analysis of a Chicago Public School Teacher's Actual Workday*, Project for Middle Class Renewal, School of Labor and Employment Relations, University of Illinois, April 9, 2012, https://lep.illinois.edu/research-and-publications/policy -reports/.

40. YoungAh Park, Robert Bruno, and Lucille Headrick, *Elementary Teachers' Work-Related Stressors and Strain*, Project for Middle Class Renewal, School of Labor and Employment Relations, University of Illinois, October 14, 2017, https://lep .illinois.edu/research-and-publications/policy-reports/.

41. In *Metaphysics*, Aristotle lays out the following four forms of causes: the material, formal, efficient, and final. See, Boris Henning, "The Four Causes," *Journal of Philosophy*, 106 (2009): 137–60.

42. Six Flags Great America is an amusement park with a location in Gurnee, Illinois.

43. Theresa Andrasfay and Noreen Goldman, "Reductions in 2020 US Life Expectancy Due to COVID-19 and the Disproportionate Impact on the Black and Latino Populations," *Proceedings of the National Academy of Sciences of the United States of America*, February 2, 2021, 118, no. 5, https://doi.org/10.1073/ pnas.2014746118.

44. Steven Johnson, *Extra Life: A Short History of Living Longer* (New York: Riverhead Press, 2021).

45. Mitra Toossi and Elka Torpey, "Older Workers: Labor Force Trends and Career Options, US Bureau of Labor Statistics, May 2017, https://www.bls.gov/ careeroutlook/2017/article/older-workers.htm; Teresa Ghilarducci, "Older Workers' Bureau Gains Momentum in Congress," *Forbes*, December 12, 2022, https://

www.forbes.com/sites/teresaghilarducci/2022/12/12/older-workers-bureau-gains-momentum-in-congress/?sh=2ec0533753a8.

46. *Joint Economic Committee Democrats,* "The Number of Older Workers Is Growing Quickly as They Continue to Face Economic Challenges," December 21,2022 at https://www.jec.senate.gov/public/_cache/files/54390cda-da1f-4e9c-aea1-d236a7cba214/older-workers-report-final.pdf.

47. Adrianna Kezar, Tom DePaola, and Daniel T. Scott, *The Gig Academy: Mapping Labor in the Neoliberal University (Reforming Higher Education: Innovation and the Public Good),* Johns Hopkins University Press, 2019; For an understanding on the precariousness of employment as a teacher in higher education see also, *An Army of Temps: AFT Adjunct Faculty Quality of Work/Life Report,* American Federation of Teachers at https://www.aft.org/sites/default/files/media/2022/qualitylifereport_feb2022.pdf.

48. PEW Research Center, "How American View Their Jobs," October 6, 2016, https://www.pewresearch.org/social-trends/2016/10/06/3-how-americans-view-their-jobs/.

49. U.S. Bureau of Labor Statistics, "Number of Jobs, Labor Market Experience, and Earnings Growth: Results from a National Longitudinal Survey," August 29, 2020, https://www.bls.gov/news.release/pdf/nlsoy.pdf.

50. U.S. Bureau of Labor Statistics, "Employee Tenure In 2020," September 22, 2020, https://www.bls.gov/news.release/tenure.nr0.htm.

51. U.S. Bureau of Labor Statistics, "Average Weekly Hours and Overtime of All Employees on Private Nonfarm Payrolls by Industry Sector, Seasonally Adjusted," January 8, 2021, https://www.bls.gov/news.release/empsit.t18.htm.

52. Carol Greenwald and Dorie Krauss, dir., *Shout Youngstown* (New York: Cinema Guild, 1984), 45 minutes, http://store.cinemaguild.com/nontheatrical/product/1537.html. Also available on YouTube at https://www.youtube.com/watch?v=6jk4ARquynE.

53. PEW Research Center, "The State of American Jobs," October 6, 2016, https://www.pewsocialtrends.org/2016/10/06/3-how-americans-view-their-jobs/.

Chapter 2. Work and Space

1. "The Way We Worked," Museum on Main Street (website), Smithsonian Institution, https://museumonmainstreet.org/content/way-we-worked.

2. "The Way We Worked Exhibition Outline" Museum on Main Street (website), Smithsonian Institution, https://museumonmainstreet.org/sites/default/files/twww_exhibition_outline.pdf.

3. Kathi Weeks, *The Problem with Work: Feminism, Marxism, Antiwork Politics, and Postwork Imaginaries* (Durham, NC: Duke University Press, 2011), 2.

4. Karl Marx, "The Labour-Process and the Process of Producing Surplus-Value," in *Capital: A Critique of Political Economy,* vol. 1, trans. Ben Fowkes (New York: Vintage, 1977), 283–306.

5. Karl Marx, *Economic and Philosophic Manuscripts of 1844*, trans. Martin Milligan (Moscow: Progress Publishers, 1959), https://www.marxists.org/archive/marx/works/download/pdf/Economic-Philosophic-Manuscripts-1844.pdf, 30.

6. Marx, *Economic and Philosophic Manuscripts*, 30.

7. Marx, *Economic and Philosophic Manuscripts*, 51

8. "24 Percent of Employed People Did Some or All of Their Work at Home in 2015," US Bureau of Labor Statistics, July 8, 2016, https://www.bls.gov/opub/ted/2016/24-percent-of-employed-people-did-some-or-all-of-their-work-at-home-in-2015.htm.

9. Matthew Day, Harley Frazis, Mark Lowenstein, and Hugette Sun, "Ability to Work from Home: Evidence from Two Surveys and Implications for the Labor Market in the COVID-19 Pandemic," *Monthly Labor Review*, US Bureau of Labor Statistics, June 2020, accessed February 23, 2023, https://www.bls.gov/opub/mlr/2020/article/pdf/ability-to-work-from-home.pdf.

10. Excerpt from a letter from an employee at Kinder Morgan titled "Emergency Access Credentials COVID-19," March 20, 2020.

11. Arthur L. Stinchcombe, "Work Institutions and the Sociology of Everyday Life," in *The Nature of Work: Sociological Perspectives*, ed. Kai Erikson and Steven Peter (New Haven, CT: Yale University Press, 1990), 100.

12. "Chicago Bean History: The Inside Story behind Cloud Gate," The Clare (website), accessed March 19, 2023, https://theclare.com/chicago-bean-history-inside-story-behind-cloud-gate/.

13. Karl Marx, *The Marx-Engels Reader*, 2nd ed., *Economic and Philosophic Manuscripts*, edited Robert C. Tucker (New York: W.W. Norton, 1978), 71.

14. Kevin Bernard Moultrie Daye, "The Missing Bodies in Architecture's Talk of Embodied Energy," Failed Architecture (website), accessed March 11, 2023 https://failedarchitecture.com/the-missing-bodies-in-architectures-talk-of-embodied-energy/.

15. Mike Rose, *The Mind at Work: Valuing the Intelligence of the American Worker* (New York: Penguin Books, 2005).

16. Erving Goffman, *The Presentation of Self in Everyday Life* (New York: Anchor Books, 1959), 124.

17. Goffman, *The Presentation of Self*, 124.

18. Rose, introduction to *The Mind at Work*, xv.

19. Antonio Gramsci, *Selections from the Prison Notebooks*, ed. and trans. Quintin Hoare and Geoffrey Nowell Smith (London: Lawrence and Wishart, 1971).

20. Robert M. Pirsig, *Zen and the Art of Motorcycle Maintenance: An Inquiry into Values* (New York: William Morrow Paperbacks, 2006), 99.

21. Matthew Crawford, *Shop Class as Soulcraft: An Inquiry into the Value of Work* (New York: Penguin Press HC, 2009).

22. Many jobs formally require a college degree to apply, but in practice it isn't necessary to do the work. For instance, according to Byron Auguste, president and cofounder at Opportunity@Work, two-thirds of administrative assistants

don't have bachelor's degrees, but "three-quarters of the new job postings for administrative assistants say you have to have a bachelor's degree to be considered for that job. So, two-thirds of the people who currently do that job can't apply for three-quarters of the new jobs in the field." See "Jobs Requiring College Degrees Disqualify Most U.S. Workers—Especially Workers Of Color," *PBS News Hour*, October 26, 2021, ahttps://www.pbs.org/newshour/show/jobs-requiring-college-degrees-disqualify-most-u-s-workers-especially-workers-of-color).

23. Chris Warhurst, Chris Tilly, and Mary Gatta, "A New Social Construction of Skill," in *The Oxford Handbook of Skills and Training*, ed. John Buchanan, David Finegold, Ken Mayhew, and Chris Warhurst (Oxford: Oxford University Press, 2022); Ronnie J. Steinberg, "Social Construction of Skill," *Work and Occupations* 17, no. 4 (November 1990): 449–82.

24. Natasha Iskander, *Does Skill Make Us Human?: Migrant Workers in 21st-Century Qatar and Beyond* (Princeton, NJ: Princeton University Press, 2021).

25. Tom W. Smith, Michael Davern, Jeremy Freese, and Stephen Morgan, General Social Surveys, 1972–2018 Sponsored by National Science Foundation, National Opinion Research Center (NORC) at the University of Chicago. (Chicago: NORC, 2018). NORC at the University of Chicago [producer and distributor]. Data accessed from the GSS Data Explorer which houses the General Social Survey website on the NORC website at ssdataexplorer.norc.org.

26. Historians suspect that Schmidt was a fabrication of Taylor's to bolster his claims for the "efficiency" of scientific management. See James Hoopes, *False Prophets: The Gurus Who Created Modern Management and Why Their Ideas Are Bad for Business Today* (New York: Basic Books, 2003).

27. Taylor is quoted in Rose, *The Mind At Work*, 144.

28. Cesar Chavez, "What the Future Holds," Big Think (website), October 31, 2014, https://bigthink.com/words-of-wisdom/cesar-chavez-farm-workers-are-not-beasts-of-burden-to-be-used-and-discarded/.

29. Tim Worstall, "The Story of Henry Ford's $5 a Day Wages: It's Not What You Think," *Forbes*, May 4, 2012, https://www.forbes.com/sites/timworstall/2012/03/04/the-story-of-henry-fords-5-a-day-wages-its-not-what-you-think/?sh=4bd7b208766d.

30. Samuel Gompers, "What Does Labor Want?" 1893, The Samuel Gompers Papers, http://www.gompers.umd.edu/More.htm.

31. Daniel Rodgers, *The Work Ethic in Industrial America, 1850–1920* (Chicago: University of Chicago Press, 1978), 14.

32. Rose's, *The Mind at Work*, 145.

33. Herbert Applebaum, *Royal Blue: The Culture of Construction Workers* (New York: Holt, Rinehart and Winston, 1991), 23.

34. William Morris, "Useful Work Versus Useless Toil," in *William Morris on Art and Socialism*, ed. Norman Kelvin (New York: Dover Press, 1999), 128–43.

35. Arlie Hochschild, *The Time Bind: When Work Becomes Home and Home Becomes Work* (New York: Metropolitan Books, 1997.)

36. *Transformers*, directed by Michael Bay (United States: DreamWorks SKG, Paramount Pictures International, Di Bonaventura Pictures, 2007), DVD.

37. Karl Marx quoted in John Bellamy Foster, "Marx as a Food Theorist" *Monthly Review*, December 1, 2016, https://monthlyreview.org/2016/12/01/marx -as-a-food-theorist/#fn6.

38. Karl Marx and Frederick Engels, *The German Ideology* (New York: International Publishers, 1970).

39. David Hume, *Treatise of Human Nature*, book 1 (Oxford: Oxford Press, 1689), 35. Available online at the Online Library of Liberty a digital library of scholarly works at http://files.libertyfund.org/files/342/0213_Bk.pdf.

40. US Bureau of Labor Statistics, *Employer-Reported Workplace Injury and Illnesses, 2019*, Economic News Release, November 4, 2020, https://www.bls.gov/ news.release/osh.nr0.htm.

41. US Bureau of Labor Statistics, *Census of Fatal Occupational Injuries Summary, 2019*, Economic News Release, December 16, 2020, https://www.bls.gov/ news.release/cfoi.nr0.htm.

42. Jane Spencer and Christina Jewett, "12 Months of Trauma: More Than 3,600 US Health Workers Died in Covid's First Year," *The Guardian*, April 8, 2021, https://khn.org/news/article/us-health-workers-deaths-covid-lost-on-the -frontline/.

43. Charles A. Taylor, Christopher Boulos, and Douglas Almond, "Livestock Plants and COVID-19 Transmission," *Proceedings of the National Academy of Sciences of the United States of America*, December 15, 2020, https://www.pnas .org/content/117/50/31706.

44. Quote is from Jim Zarroli, "'Deaths of Despair' Examines the Steady Erosion of U.S. Working-Class Life," NPR, March 18, 2020, https://www.npr.org/ 2020/03/18/817687042/deaths-of-despair-examines-the-steady-erosion-of-u-s -working-class-life.

45. OSHA is the federal Occupational, Safety and Health Administration which is charged with setting and enforcing workplace safety standards.

46. Erving Goffman, *The Presentation of Self in Everyday Life* (New York: Anchor Books, 1959), 27.

47. Sylvia Allegretto, "The Teacher Pay Penalty Has Hit a New High: Trends in Teacher Wages and Compensation Through 2021," Economic Policy Institute (website), August 16, 2022, https://files.epi.org/uploads/251657.pdf.

48. Marx, *Marx-Engels Reader*, 71.

49. Jim Daniels, "Still Lives in Detroit: #2, Parking Lot, Ford Sterling Plant," in *Working Classics: Poems on Industrial Life*, ed. Peter Oresick and Nicholas Coles (Urbana: University of Illinois Press, 1990), 54.

50. Marx quoted from "Economic and Philosophic Manuscripts of 1844" in *Alienation: Marx's Conception of Man in a Capitalist Society*, ed. Bertel Ollman, 2nd ed. (Cambridge: Cambridge University Press, 1977), 98.

51. Marx, "Economic and Philosophic Manuscripts," qtd. in *Alienation*, 141.

Chapter 3. Work's Impact

1. Bob Black, *The Abolition of Work* (self-published), 1996, 18.

2. *2019 Employer Health Benefits Survey*, Kaiser Family Foundation, 2019, February 12, 2023, https://www.kff.org/report-section/ehbs-2019-summary-of-findings/.

3. Karl Marx, *Economic and Philosophic Manuscripts of 1844*, trans. by Martin Milligan (Moscow: Progress Publishers 1959), 29. Available online at the Marxists Internet Archive, https://www.marxists.org/archive/marx/works/download/pdf/Economic-Philosophic-Manuscripts-1844.pdf.

4. Karl Marx, "The Buying and Selling of Labour-Power," in *Capital*, vol. 1, book 1, trans. Samuel Moore and Edward Aveling, ed. by Frederick Engels (Moscow: Progress Publishers, 1887), 118–24. Also available at the Marxists Internet Archive, https://www.marxists.org/archive/marx/works/download/pdf/Capital-Volume-I.pdf, 122.

5. Jan Beaty, "My Father Teaches Me to Dream," *Working Worlds: Punching the Clock and Kicking Out the Jams*, ed. M. L. Leibler (Coffee House Press: Minneapolis, 2010), 20.

6. Karl Marx, *Capital*, vol. 1.

7. J. M. Berg, J. E. Dutton, and A. Wrzesniewski, "Job Crafting and Meaningful Work," in *Purpose and Meaning in the Workplace,* ed. B. J. Dik, Z. S. Byrne, and M. F. Steger (Washington, DC: American Psychological Association, 2013), 81–104.

8. The phrase "bread and roses" preceded the strike, appearing in a poem by James Oppenheim published in *The American Magazine* in December 1911.

9. Judy Collins recorded a popular version of the song in in 1976 on an album, titled "Bread and Roses" that reached number 25 on the Billboard Pop Album charts (see "Bread and Roses," Wikimedia Foundation, last modified March 1, 2023, https://en.wikipedia.org/wiki/Bread_and_Roses_[album].)

10. Martin Heidegger, *Being and Time* (1927), revised by Dennis J. Schmidt (New York: SUNY Press, 2010).

11. Al Gini, *My Job, My Self: Work and the Creation of the Modern Individual* (New York: Routledge Press, 2001), 5.

12. Albert Camus, *The Myth of Sisyphus*, trans. Justin O'Brien (New York: Knopf Doubleday, 2018).

13. Charles Duhigg, "Wealthy, Successful and Miserable," *New York Times Magazine*, February 24, 2019, 26.

14. "How to Build a Better Job," episode 25 of *Hidden Brain Podcast*, March 29, 2016. Transcripts available at https://www.npr.org/transcripts/471859161.

15. "The Brotherhood of the Barrel," is synonymous with the Chicago Firefighters' Strike of 1980. According to the union, "the phrase stems from the men who were on strike from February 14 to March 7, 1980. To keep warm in frigid temperatures, the striking firefighters gathered around makeshift heaters which were

fifty-five-gallon drums set afire. Despite the cold, the picket lines were never abandoned for the full 23 days of the strike." See "Brotherhood of the Barrel," the Button Museum, Chicago, Illinois (website), accessed March 19, 2023, https://button museum.org/buttons/brotherhood-barrel.

16. Ernst Langthaler and Elke Schüßler, "Commodity Studies with Polanyi: Disembedding and Re-Embedding Labour and Land in Contemporary Capitalism," *Österreich Z Soziol* 44 (2019): 209–23, https://doi.org/10.1007/s11614-019-00339-2.

17. In 1946 Congress passed the Taft-Hartley Act, which included a provision allowing states to pass government regulations that prohibit unions and employers from voluntarily including union security clauses in negotiated contracts. This provision is colloquially called a "right-to-work" law. It permits and incentivizes workers who are represented by a union to receive all the services and benefits of collective bargaining (e.g., higher wages, better benefits, and legal representation) without paying anything for them. State right-to-work laws are associated with lower unionization rates and worse economic outcomes for workers. See Frank Manzo IV and Robert Bruno, *Promoting Good Jobs and a Stronger Economy: How Free Collective-Bargaining States Outperform "Right-to- Work" States,* February 9, 2021, at https://illinoisepi.files.wordpress.com/2020/05/ilepi-pmcr-promoting -good-jobs-and-a-stronger-economy-final.pdf, accessed May 22, 2023.

18. Jean Jacques Rousseau, *The Social Contract Or Principles Of Political Right* (1762), trans. G. D. H. Cole, public domain, International Relations and Security Network, ETH Zurich 39, https://discoversocialsciences.com/wp-content/ uploads/2018/07/Rousseau-Social-Contract.pdf.

19. *Downton Abbey* (2010–2015), season 4, episode 8. Full transcript at https://sub-slikescript.com/series/Downton_Abbey-1606375/season-4/episode-8-Episode _48.

20. YoungAh Park, Robert Bruno, and Lucille Headrick, *Elementary Teachers' Work-Related Stressors and Strain,* October 14, 2017, https://lep.illinois.edu/ wp-content/uploads/2021/08/Teacher-union-technical-report.pdf.

21. Home Health Care Data, "National Center for Health Statistics," *The Center for Disease Control and Prevention,* accessed February 12, 2023, https://www.cdc .gov/nchs/fastats/home-health-care.htm.

22. Liz Donovan and Muriel Alarcon, "In a Booming Industry, Workers Feel the Stress," *New Your Times,* September 26, 2021, Sunday Business.

23. Jodi Kantor, Karen Weise, and Grace Ashford, "The Amazon That Customers Don't See," *New York Times,* June 12, 2001.

24. Frederick W. Taylor, *The Principles of Scientific Management,* 1911.

25. The pay increase was not a raise per se; it was a profit-sharing plan. For example, if you made two dollars a day under the old pay schedule, you continued to earn that amount under the "Five-Dollar" plan. But if a worker met all the company's requirements, Ford gave you a bonus of three dollars. There were other rather invasive conditions. As stated on the Ford Archive website, "To qualify for the pay increase, workers had to abstain from alcohol, not physically

abuse their families, not take in boarders, keep their homes clean, and contribute regularly to a savings account. Ford Motor Company inspectors came to workers' homes, asked probing questions, and observed general living conditions. If 'violations' were discovered, the inspectors offered advice and pointed the families to resources offered through the company. Not until these problems were corrected did the employee receive his full bonus." See, "Ford's Five-Dollar Day," The Henry Ford Archive, January 3, 2014, https://www.thehenryford.org/explore/blog/fords-five-dollar-day/.

26. "The Middle Class Took Off 100 Years Ago. Thanks to Henry Ford," NPR, *All Things Considered*, January 27, 2014, https://www.npr.org/2014/01/27/267145552/the-middle-class-took-off-100-years-ago-thanks-to-henry-ford.

27. Despite enormously long odds, workers at the largest Amazon facility in Staten Island did the unthinkable and voted to unionize. (Andrea Shu, "In a stunning victory, Amazon workers on Staten Island vote for a union," NPR, April 1, 2021, https://www.npr.org/2022/04/01/1089318684/amazon-labor-union-staten-island-election-bessemer-alabama-warehouse-workers). However, just a week after ballots were tallied the company filed a raft of objections to the election. (Shu, "Amazon seeks to overturn historic Staten Island union victory at labor hearing," NPR, June 13, 2022, https://www.npr.org/2022/06/13/1104549165/amazon-labor-union-election-hearing-staten-island-objection-nlrb-warehouse). Among its complaints was a very unusual and desperate one. Amazon charged that union organizers handed out marijuana to workers in return for their support. Union leaders had spoken openly about providing workers with marijuana, not as an inducement to vote yes but to ease the physical pain of working in a warehouse. The federal agency responsible for enforcing the nation's labor law governing labor-management relations, the National Labor Relations Board, rejected the firm's complaints, finding that Amazon had not established that the agency, the union, or any other parties "engaged in objectionable conduct affecting the results of the election." (Annie Palmer, "Amazon Loses Effort to Overturn Historic Union Election at Staten Island Warehouse," CNBC, September 1, 2022, https://www.cnbc.com/2022/09/01/amazon-loses-effort-to-overturn-union-win-at-staten-island-facility.html).

28. Mary Tyler March, "Construction Workers Among Most Susceptible to Opioid Abuse," *Construction Drive*, October 31, 2017, https://www.construction dive.com/news/construction-workers-among-most-susceptible-to-opioid-abuse/508546/; "Construction Workers and Addiction: Statistics, Recovery and Treatment," https://americanaddictioncenters.org/rehab-guide/workforce/blue-collar-workers/construction-workers; Donna M. Bush and Rachel N. Lipari, "Substance Use and Substance Use Disorder By Industry," 2015, https://www.Samhsa.Gov/Data/Sites/Default/Files/Report_1959/Shortreport-1959.html; and Danielle C. Ompad, Robyn R. Gershon, Simon Sandh, Patricia Acosta, and Joseph J. Palamar, "Construction Trade and Extraction Workers: A Population at High Risk for Drug Use in the United States," 2005–2014, National Institute

of Health Library of Medicine, Department of Health and Human Services, Washington, DC, accessed March 19, 2023, https://www.ncbi.nlm.nih.gov/pmc/articles/PMC6910220/.

29. Harduar Morano L, Steege AL, Luckhaupt SE. Occupational Patterns in Unintentional and Undetermined Drug-Involved and Opioid-Involved Overdose Deaths- United States, 2007–2012. MMWR Morb Mortal Wkly Rep 2018; 67: 925–30. DOI: http://dx.doi.org/10.15585/mmwr.mm6733a3external icon.

30. See quote in G. A. Cohen's, *Karl Marx's Theory of Labor History: A Defense* (Princeton, NJ: Princeton University Press, 1978), 25.

31. Jody Heymann, Hye Jin Rho, John Schmitt, and Alison Earle, "Contagion Nation: A Comparison of Paid Sick Day Policies in 22 Countries," *Center for Economic and Policy Research*, Washington, DC, 2009, 1.

32. Heymann, Rho, Schmitt, and Earle, "Contagion Nation," 2.

33. The 1993 Family and Medical Leave Act requires a subset of employers (those with fifty or more employees) to provide a subset of employees (those who have worked for their employer for at least 1,250 hours in the twelve months prior to the leave) with unpaid leave to address a subset of circumstances, when a close family member (limited to a child, parent, or spouse) has a "serious health condition" (not a common illness). See "Family and Medical Leave Act," US Department of Labor, Wage and Hour Division, Washington, DC, accessed March 19, 2023, https://www.dol.gov/agencies/whd/fmla.

34. Scott Brown, Jane Herr, Radha Roy, and Jacob Alex Klerman, "Employee and Worksite Perspectives of the FMLA Who Is Eligible?" July 2020, https://www.dol.gov/sites/dolgov/files/OASP/evaluation/pdf/WHD_FMLA2018PB1 WhoIsEligible_StudyBrief_Aug2020.pdf

35. Jacob Alex Klerman, Kelly Daley, and Alyssa Pozniak, "Family and Medical Leave in 2012: Executive Summary," Abt Associates Inc., Prepared for the U.S. Department of Labor, 2013.

36. "Paid Family and Medical Leave: By the Numbers," The Center for American Progress, Women's Initiative, September 27, 2017, https://cdn.americanprogress.org/content/uploads/2017/09/26120405/PaidFamilyMedicalLeave-factSheet.pdf?_ga=2.58157290.1382222010.1623363619–439507432.1623363619.

37. Grace Dunn, Larissa Petrucci, Frank Manzo, and Robert Bruno, *Registered Nursing in Crisis National Survey Reveals Insufficient Staffing, Severe Moral Distress, and High Turnover*, Project for Middle Class Renewal, School of Labor and Employment Relations, University of Illinois, June 23, 2022, https://lep.illinois.edu/wp-content/uploads/2022/06/PMCR-ILEPI-Registered-Nurses-in-Crisis.pdf.

38. Elizabeth D. Steiner, Sy Doan, Ashley Woo, Allyson D. Gittens, Rebecca Ann Lawrence, Lisa Berdie, Rebecca L. Wolfe, Lucas Greer, and Heather L. Schwartz, *Restoring Teacher and Principal Well-Being Is an Essential Step for Rebuilding Schools Findings from the State of the American Teacher and State of the American Principal Surveys, 2022*, Rand Corporation, Santa Monica, California, https://www.rand.org/pubs/research_reports/RRA1108-4.html.

39. "Universal Paid Sick Leave is Essential for Combating the Pandemic and Protecting the Economy," Report from the *U.S. Congress Joint Economic Committee*, Congressman Don Byer, Vice Chair, accessed February 13, 2023, https://www.jec.senate.gov/public/_cache/files/013a1720-1cf4-4fcd-baf1-1874fad51dcf/paid-sick-leave-the-coronavirus-final.pdf.

40. Pedro Pierti, "Puerto Rican Obituary," in *The Young Lords: A Reader*, ed. Darrel Enck-Wanzer (New York: New York University Press, 2010), 71–80.

41. O*NET US Department of Labor at https://www.dol.gov/agencies/eta/onet.

42. "Hosts and Hostesses, Restaurant, Lounge, and Coffee Shop," O*NET, US Department of Labor, accessed March 19, 2023, https://www.onetonline.org/link/summary/35-9031.00.

43. O-NET OnLine, Summary Report for: 51-2041.00- Structural Metal Fabricators and Fittershttps://www.onetonline.org/link/summary/51-2041.00; O-NET OnLine, Summary Report for: 47-2011.00-Boilermakers at https://www.onetonline.org/link/summary/47-2011.00.

44. Emma García and Elaine Weiss, "U.S. Schools Struggle to Hire and Retain Teachers," *Economic Policy Institute*, April 16, 2019, https://files.epi.org/pdf/164773.pdf.

45. Daniel J. Madigan and Lisa E. Kim, "Does Teacher Burnout Affect Students? A Systematic Review of its Association with Academic Achievement and Student-Reported Outcomes," *International Journal of Educational Research* (November 2020), https://www.researchgate.net/profile/Daniel-Madigan/publication/345983498_Does_Teacher_Burnout_Affect_Students_A_Systematic_Review_of_its_Association_with_Academic_Achievement_and_Student-Reported_Outcomes/links/5fc4c663a6fdcc6cc6850b03/Does-Teacher-Burnout-Affect-Students-A-Systematic-Review-of-its-Association-with-Academic-Achievement-and-Student-Reported-Outcomes.pdf.

46. Arlie Russell Hochschild, *The Managed Heart Commercialization of Human Feeling* (Berkeley: California University Press, 2012).

47. Joana Lima, Barbara Rohregger, and Chris Brown, *Health, Decent Work, and the Economy*, World Health Organization, Policy Brief, accessed March 10, 2023, https://www.euro.who.int/data/assets/pdffile/0011/397793/SDG-8-policy-brief_4.pdf. 1–17.

48. AFL-CIO 2022, *Death on the Job: The Toll of Neglect a National and State-by-State Profile of Worker Safety and Health in the United States*, 30th ed., AFL-CIO Safety and Health Office, May 2021, Washington, DC, https://aflcio.org/reports/death-job-toll-neglect-2021.

49. "Worker Safety in Crisis: The Cost of a Weakened OSHA," *The National Employment Law Project*, April 2020, https://s27147.pcdn.co/wp-content/uploads/Worker-Safety-Crisis-Cost-Weakened-OSHA.pdf.

50. J. Paul Leigh, "Economic Burden of Occupational Injury and Illness in the United States," *Milbank Quarterly* 89, no. 4 (2011): 728–72.

51. Marx, "The Buying and Selling of Labour-Power," https://www.marxists .org/archive/marx/works/1867-c1/ch06.htm.

52. The industries with the highest fatality rates in 2019 were agriculture, forestry, and fishing and hunting; mining, quarrying, and oil and gas extraction; and transportation and warehousing (AFL-CIO 2022, *Death on the Job*).

53. Derek Thompson, "Workism Is Making Americans Miserable," *The Atlantic*, February 24, 2019, https://www.theatlantic.com/ideas/archive/2019/02/ religion-workism-making-americans-miserable/583441/.

54. Karl Marx's *Wage, Labour and Capital* was a pamphlet published in 1891. Available online at Marxists Internet Archive, https://www.marxists.org/archive/ marx/works/download/pdf/wage-labour-capital.pdf.

55. David B. Raymond, "The Philosophy of Work in Robert Frost's 'Two Tramps in Mud Time,'" *The Explicator*, 74, no. 2 (2016): 77–79, DOI: 10.1080/00144940 .2016.1169496 at https://doi.org/10.1080/00144940.2016.1169496.

56. "Reason to Believe" written by Bruce Springsteen, published by Sony/ ATV Music Publishing LLC, 1982, lyrics licensed and provided by LyricFind at Songfacts (website), accessed March 19, 2023, https://www.songfacts.com/lyrics/ bruce-springsteen/reason-to-believe/.

57. Pope John Paul II, *Laborem Exercens*, 1981, https://www.vatican.va/content /john-paul-ii/en/encyclicals/documents/hf_jp-ii_enc_14091981_laborem-exer cens.html.

58. Oren Cass, *The Once and Future Worker: A Vision for the Renewal of Work in America* (New York: Encounter Books, 2018).

59. In a thirty-country study, researchers Milena Nikolova and Femke Cnossen found much the same. They listed "competence," "autonomy," and "relatedness" as the top three needs. See, "What Makes Work Meaningful?" *IZA Institute for Labor Economics*, Discussion Paper Series, IZA DP No. 13112, Bonn, Germany, April 8, 2020, 1–32, http://ftp.iza.org/dp13112.pdf. See also E. Deci and R. Ryan, "Self-Determination Theory," in *Handbook of Theories of Social Psychology*, vol. 1, ed. P. A. Van Lange, E. Tory Higgins, and Arie W. Kruglanski 416–37 (London: SAGE, 2012); Marylène Gagné, "Self-Determination Theory in the Work Domain: This is Just the Beginning," in *The Oxford Handbook of Work Engagement, Motivation, and Self-Determination Theory* (New York: Oxford University Press, 2014), 414–32.

60. Karl Marx, *The German Ideology*, ed. C. J. Arthur (New York: International Publishers, 1985), 42.

61. Steven Peter Vallas, "Comments and Observations on the Nature of Work," *The Nature of Work: Sociological Perspectives*, ed. Steven Peter Vallas and Kai Erikson (New Haven, CT: Yale University Press, 1990), 345.

Chapter 4. The Purpose of Work

1. "The Jumpin Jive," *Salem Quaker*, 1940, http://history.salem.lib.oh.us/SalemHistory//Quakernewspapers/1939/Vol_20_No_3_Sep_1939_Part4.pdf.

2. Spivak appeared on the cover of *The Billboard: The World's Foremost Amusement Weekly*, August 23, 1941, and the story was on page 4. News of Spivak's being voted number two by "campus dancers" was reported in *Billboard's*, June 19, 1943, issue, which again featured him on the cover.

3. Lynn is also a veteran who served in the Military Police for five years. In speaking with her I realized she was one of our most distinguished students. She completed two University of Illinois Labor Education union women leadership programs—POLK Women's Leadership Conference and the advanced Women Empowerment Training—and a six-session certificate in labor studies. She has always dreamed about being a teacher. I'm confident she would make an inspiring instructor for a K-12 school district or for AFSCME. Interview on August 4, 2022.

4. Melody Wilding, "5 Signs You're About to Make a Bad Career Decision," *Forbes*, November 14, 2016, https://www.forbes.com/sites/melodywilding/2016/11/14/5-signs-youre-about-to-make-a-bad-career-decision/?sh=4e07bd71207c.

5. Josh Bivens, "Walton Family Net Worth is a Case Study Why Growing Wealth Concentration Isn't Just an Academic Worry," *Economic Policy Institute*, October 3, 2014, https://www.epi.org/blog/walton-family-net-worth-case-study-growing/.

6. The National Opinion Research Center at the University of Chicago has conducted the General Social Survey, a study that in part focuses on work issues.

7. "Take This Job and Shove It," written by David Allen Cole, lyrics © Warner Chappell Music, Inc. at Lyric Find.

8. Studs Terkel, *Working* (London: Wildwood House, 1975), 1.

9. Albert Camus, *The Myth of Sisyphus*, trans. Justin O'Brien (New York: Knopf Doubleday, 2018).

10. Burrow is the Ferris Family Associate Professor of Life Course Studies in the Department of Psychology at Cornell University. The quote was taken from Jackie Swift, "The Benefits of Having a Sense of Purpose," Blog Post, Cornell Research, December 7, 2020, https://medium.com/@CornellResearch/the-benefits-of-having-a-sense-of-purpose-ae05232cf5c8.

11. Jonathan Malesi, "Our Relationship to Work Is Broken," *New York Times*, September 26, 2021, Sunday Review, 4.

12. Many also used the word *support*.

13. Adam Smith, *The Theory of Moral Sentiments*, 6th ed. (1759; Project Gutenberg, 2018), chap. 2, https://www.econlib.org/library/Smith/smMS.html?chapter_num=8#book-reader.

14. Karl Marx, *German Ideology*, ed. C. J. Arthur (New York: International Publishers, 1985), 42.

15. Tom W. Smith, Michael Davern, Jeremy Freese, and Stephen Morgan, *General Social Surveys*, 1972–2018 [machine-readable data file] /Principal Investigator, Smith, Tom W.; Co-Principal Investigators, Michael Davern, Jeremy Freese, and Stephen Morgan; Sponsored by National Science Foundation.—NORC ed.—Chicago: NORC, 2018: NORC at the University of Chicago [producer and distributor]. Data accessed from the GSS Data Explorer website at gssdataexplorer.norc .org.

16. Tom W. Smith, Michael Davern, Jeremy Freese, and Stephen Morgan, *General Social Surveys*, 1972–2018 [machine-readable data file] /Principal Investigator, Smith, Tom W.; Co-Principal Investigators, Michael Davern, Jeremy Freese, and Stephen Morgan; Sponsored by National Science Foundation.—NORC ed.—Chicago: NORC, 2018: NORC at the University of Chicago [producer and distributor]. Data accessed from the GSS Data Explorer website at gssdataexplorer.norc.org.

17. Chris Higgins, "Labour, Work, and Action: Arendt's Phenomenology of Practical Life," *Journal of Philosophy of Education* 44, no. 2–3 (2010): 282.

18. Marx quoted in David Harvey, *A Companion to Marx's Capital, The Complete Edition* (London: Verso, 2018), 113.

19. Arendt distinguishes "work" from "labor." She considers laboring simply what we do to survive. It is, nonetheless, an essential part of the human condition because it is not only what humans need simply to live, but also to find happiness. Work, however, gives collective meaning to what we do. When workers produce something they both put a part of themselves into and leave something lasting in the world. My students' experiences nicely collapse Arendt's understanding and I use the terms labor and work synonymously. Hannah Arendt, *The Human Condition* (Chicago: University of Chicago Press, 1958), 94

20. Aristotle sketches two versions of "beauty" in the *Metaphysics* and *Poetics*. I find both versions can be a way to describe a job well done and the good it achieves.

21. Todd Jailer, "Bill Hastings," in *Working Classics: Poems On Industrial Life*, ed. Peter Oresick and Nicholas Coles (Urbana: University of Illinois Press, 1991), 14.

22. *Executive Paywatch*, AFL-CIO, accessed February 14, 2023, https://aflcio.org/ paywatch,

23. "Walmart Will Raise Pay For 565,000 Workers," *New York Times*, September 3, 2021, B2.

24. Alan Rapperport, "Deep Wounds Overshadow A Plan to Bolster the IRS," *New York Times*, July 24, 2021, B3.

25. Sydney Czyzon, "Iowa Meatpacking Plants Put Lives on the Line in COVID Pandemic," *Waterloo-Cedar Falls Courier*, March 15, 2021, https://www.thegazette .com/health-care-medicine/iowa-meatpacking-plants-put-lives-on-the-line-in -covid-pandemic/.

26. Clark Kauffman, "Lawsuit: Tyson Managers Bet Money on How Many Workers Would Contract COVID-19," *Iowa Capital Dispatch*, November 18,

2020, https://iowacapitaldispatch.com/2020/11/18/lawsuit-tyson-managers-bet -money-on-how-many-workers-would-contract-covid-19/.

27. "Lost on the Frontline," *The Guardian*, accessed February 14, 2023, https://www .theguardian.com/us-news/ng-interactive/2020/aug/11/lost-on-the-frontline -covid-19-coronavirus-us-healthcare-workers-deaths-database.

28. Hinda Mandall, "In Times of War (And Coronavirus) We've Always Relied on Women to Sew," *Commentary*, WBUR, April 6, 2020, https://www.wbur.org/ cognoscenti/2020/04/06/sewing-homemade-masks-hinda-mandell.

29. A good historical examination of these campaigns is Jack Schneider and Jennifere Berkshire, *A Wolf at the Schoolhouse Door: The Dismantling of Public Education and the Future of School* (New York: New Press, 2020).

30. The quote is from the late great Chicago teacher union president, Karen Lewis, and served as the title of the book I coauthored with Steven Ashby, *A Fight for the Soul of Public Education, the Chicago Teachers Strike* (Ithaca, NY: ILR Press, 2016).

31. "Educators We've Lost to the Coronavirus," *Education Week*, August 11, 2021, https://www.edweek.org/teaching-learning/educators-weve-lost-to-the-corona virus/2020/04.

32. Press Release, "Educators Say COVID-19 Has Greatly Exacerbated the Grief Support Crisis in Schools, According to New Survey, American Federation of Teachers and New York Life Foundation, October 21, 2020," https://www.aft .org/press-release/educators-say-covid-19-has-greatly-exacerbated-grief-support -crisis-schools.

33. Melissa Kay Diliberti and Heather L. Schwartz, "The K-12 Pandemic Budget and Staffing Crises Have Not Panned Out—Yet," Selected Findings from the Third American School District Panel Survey, *Rand Corporation*, 2021, https:// www.rand.org/pubs/research_reports/RRA956-3.html.

34. Denisa R. Superville, "Many Feared an Educator Exodus from the Pandemic. It Doesn't Seem to Have Happened. Yet." August 16, 2021, *Education Week*, https://www.edweek.org/leadership/many-feared-an-educator-exodus-from -the-pandemic-it-doesnt-seem-to-have-happened-yet/2021/08?utm_sourc e=nl&utm_medium=eml&utm_campaign=tu&M=62821346&U=2663666& UUID=537a13c2d974f51d353aefa2db21835e.

35. Sigmund Freud, *Civilization and Its Discontents*, trans. James Strachey (1930; Stephen Hicks, PhD [website]), https://www.stephenhicks.org/wp-content/ uploads/2015/10/FreudS-CIVILIZATION-AND-ITS-DISCONTENTS-text-final .pdf, 12.

36. Meister Eckhart quoted in Matthew Fox, *The Reinvention of Work* (San Francisco: Harper, 1994), 34.

37. Fox, *Reinvention of Work*, 244.

38. Baldwin quoted in Al Gini, *My Job, My Self: Work and the Creation of the Modern Individual* (New York: Routledge Press, 2009).

39. Organization for Economic Development, https://www.oecd.org/employ ment/job-quality.htm.

40. Daniel Alpert, Jeffrey Ferry, Robert C. Hockett, Amir Khaleghi, *The U.S. Private Sector Job Quality Index®*, Cornell Law School, November 2019, https:// d3n8a8pro7vhmx.cloudfront.net/prosperousamerica/pages/5467/attachments/ original/1573727821/U.S. Private_Sector_Job_Quailty_Index_White_Paper.pdf? 1573727821.

41. Rob Atkinson, "Potato Chips, Computer Chips: Yes, There Is a Difference," *The Commons*, December 23, 2020, https://americancompass.org/the-commons/ potato-chips-computer-chips-yes-there-is-a-difference/.

42. Steve Denning, "Understanding the U.S. Economy: Lots of Rotten Jobs," *Forbes*, December 5, 2019, https://www.forbes.com/sites/stevedenning/2019/12/05/ understanding-the-us-economy-lots-of-rotten-jobs/?sh=4aba3382d970.

43. David R. Howell and Arne L. Kalleberg, "Declining Job Quality in the United States: Explanations and Evidence," *Russell Sage Foundation Journal of the Social Sciences* 5, no. 4 (2019): 1–53, DOI: 10.7758/RSF.2019.5.4.01.

44. Jonathan Rothwell and Steve Crabtree, *How COVID-19 Affected the Quality of Work*, GALLUP, 2021, https://www.gallup.com/education/267590/great-jobs -report.aspx.

45. Steve Denning, "Understanding the U.S. Economy: Lots of Rotten Jobs," *Forbes*, December 5, 2019, https://www.forbes.com/sites/stevedenning/2019/12/05/ understanding-the-us-economy-lots-of-rotten-jobs/?sh=4aba3382d970.

46. An account of the auto industry bailout agreement can be found in fellow labor educator Tom Juravich's *At the Alter of the Bottom Line: The Degradation of Work in the 21st Century* (Amherst: University of Massachusetts Press, 2009), 188–92.

47. Catherine Ruckelshaus and Sarah Leberstein, "Manufacturing Low Pay: Declining Wages in the Jobs That Built America's Middle Class," National Em ployment Law Project, November 2014, https://s27147.pcdn.co/wp-content/ uploads/2015/03/Manufacturing-Low-Pay-Declining-Wages-Jobs-Built-Middle -Class.pdf.

48. *The State of American Jobs Report*, PEW Research, October 6, 2016, https:// www.pewresearch.org/social-trends/2016/10/06/3-how-americans-view-their -jobs/.

49. Quotes appear in Iring Fetscher, "Karl Marx on Human Nature," *Human Nature: A Reevaluation*, special edition, *Social Research* 40, no. 3 (Autumn 1973): 443–67, https://www.jstor.org/stable/40970148.

50. John Locke, *Two Treatise on Government* (Cambridge: Cambridge Uni versity Press, 1970), 187.

51. Jean-Jacques Rousseau, *Social Contract or Principles of Political Right*, trans. G. D. H. Cole (1762; Discover Social Sciences by Krzysztof Wasniewski [website]), book 2, ch. 11, https://discoversocialsciences.com/wp-content/uploads/2018/07/ Rousseau-Social-Contract.pdf.

52. Frank Manzo IV, Michael Jekot, and Robert Bruno, "The Impact of Unions on Construction Worksite Health and Safety Evidence from OSHA Inspections," *Illinois Economic Policy Institute* and *the Project for Middle Renewal*, School of Labor and Employment Relations, University of Illinois, September 13, 2021, https://lep.illinois.edu/research-and-publications/policy-reports/.

53. Adam Dean, Jamie McCallum, and Atheendar Venkataramani, "Unions in the United States Improve Worker Safety and Lower Health Inequality: The Latest Research On Unions Demonstrates that they Reduce the Spread of COVID-19 for Workers and the Broader Public," *Washington Center for Equitable Growth*, December 2022, https://equitablegrowth.org/research-paper/unions-in-the -united-states-improve-worker-safety-and-lower-health-inequality/?mkt_tok= MDE2LVpUSy0yMjYAAAGIq7WVShjY0G3fB7khpY2iN3PKidUCRPYCT6iBy 9z-hthmY2Czu9mbmELvl28kFlJ3Q4pHSGI0Fyqixq99VoE6JfI9O6uMdIINT NZ09XJx.

54. An example based on 2021 data is our report *The State of the Unions 2022, A Profile of Unionization in Chicago, in Illinois, and in the United States*, September 6, 2022, https://lep.illinois.edu/wp-content/uploads/2022/09/ILEPI -PMCR-State-of-the-Unions-Illinois-2022-FINAL.pdf.

55. Mike Konczal, *Freedom from the Market: America's Flight to Liberate Itself from the Grip of the Invisible Hand* (New York: New Press, 2022), 9.

56. Isiah Berlin, *Two Concepts of Liberty* (Oxford University Press, 1969; professional website of Professor Steven Levine, University of Massachusetts, Boston), http://faculty.www.umb.edu/steven.levine/Courses/Action/Berlin.pdf, 23.

57. Brent D. Rosso, Kathryn H. Dekas, Amy Wrzesniewski, "On the Meaning of Work: A Theoretical Integration and Review," *Research in Organizational Behavior* 30 (2010): 91–127.

58. Daniel Rodgers, *The Work Ethic in Industrial America, 1850–1920* (Chicago: University of Chicago Press, 1979, 14.

59. Brent Rosso, Kathryn H. Dekas, and Amy Wrzesniewski, "On the Meaning of Work," 99.

60. *Aristotle's Nicomachean Ethics*, trans. Robert C. Bartlett and Susan D. Collins, bk. 2, chap. 6, 1106a25, 33.

61. Pope John Paul II, *Laborem Exercens (On Human Work)*, Washington, DC: United States Catholic Conference, 1981), file:///Users/bobbruno/Desktop/ What%20Work%20Is/Laborem%20Exercens%20(14%20September%201981)%20 %7C%20John%20Paul%20II.webarchive.

62. Reverend Patrick Flanagan, "Sustaining the Import of Labor Unions: A Common Good Approach," *Journal of Catholic Legal Studies* 50, no. 1 (2011): 205–26, https://scholarship.law.stjohns.edu/cgi/viewcontent.cgi?article =1145&context=jcls.

63. Donna Summer and Omartian Michael, songwriters, "She Works Hard for the Money," 1983 lyrics © See This House Music, Sweet Summer Night Music, Mercury Records.

64. Pope Leo XIII, *Rerum Novarum Encyclical of Pope Leo XIII on Capital and Labor* (1891; The Holy See [website]), https://www.vatican.va/content/leo-xiii/en/encyclicals/documents/hf_l-xiii_enc_15051891_rerum-novarum.html.

65. Marx, *German Ideology.*

66. Amy Wrzesniewski, Justin M. Berg, and Jane E. Dutton, "Managing Yourself: Turn the Job You Have into the Job You Want," *Harvard Business Review*, June 2010, https://hbr.org/2010/06/managing-yourself-turn-the-job-you-have-into-the-job-you-want.

67. Wrzesniewski, Berg, and Dutton, "Managing Yourself."

68. Karl Marx, "Economic and Philosophic Manuscripts of 1844," in *The Marx-Engel Reader,* ed. Robert C. Tucker, 2nd ed. (New York: W.W. Norton, 1978), 74.

Chapter 5. The Subject of Work

1. See the Bracero Program, UCLA Labor Center, https://www.labor.ucla.edu/what-we-do/research-tools/the-bracero-program/; and the Bracero Program, 1942–1964, https://www.unco.edu/colorado-oral-history-migratory-labor-project/pdf/Bracero_Program_PowerPoint.pdf.

2. From Pauline R. Kibbe, *Latin Americans in Texas* (Albequerque: University of New Mexico Press, 1948).

3. Joanne B. Ciulla, *The Working Life: The Promise and Betrayal of Modern Work* (New York: Three Rivers Press, 2000), 3.

4. Ciulla, *Working Life,* 7.

5. Sigmund Freud, *Civilization and Its Discontents*, trans. James Strachey (1930; Stephen Hicks, PhD [website]), https://www.stephenhicks.org/wp-content/uploads/2015/10/FreudS-CIVILIZATION-AND-ITS-DISCONTENTS-text-final.pdf, 12.

6. "Raising Kids and Running a Household: How Working Parents Share the Load," *PEW Research*, November 4, 2015, https://www.pewresearch.org/social-trends/2015/11/04/raising-kids-and-running-a-household-how-working-parents-share-the-load/#who-does-more.

7. "Raising Kids and Running a Household," https://www.pewresearch.org/social-trends/2015/11/04/raising-kids-and-running-a-household-how-working-parents-share-the-load/#who-does-more.

8. "Inheritances by Age and Income Group," Penn Wharton, University of Pennsylvania, Budget Model, July 16, 2021, https://budgetmodel.wharton.upenn.edu/issues/2021/7/16/inheritances-by-age-and-income-group.

9. Victoria Osorio and Jon Huntley, "Inheritances by Age and Income Group," Penn Wharton, University of Pennsylvania Budget Model, July 16, 2021, https://budgetmodel.wharton.upenn.edu/issues/2021/7/16/inheritances-by-age-and-income-group.

10. Hayan Charara, "Cement," in *Working Words: Punching the Clock and*

Kicking Out the Jams, ed. M. L. Liebler (Minneapolis: Coffee House Press, 2010), 34–35.

11. Steve Rayshich, "The Gates," in *Overtime: Punchin Out With the Mill Hunk Herald: Worker Writer Anthology, 1979–1989* (Albequerque: West End Press; Pittsburgh: Piece of the Hunk), 92–93.

12. New King James Bible, Matthew 7:15–20, Bible Gateway, https://www.bible gateway.com/passage/?search=Matthew%207%3A15-20&version=NKJV.

13. Frederich Engels, "The Part Played by Labour in the Transition from Ape to Man," *Works of Frederich Engels, 1876*, appeared as the ninth chapter of the unfinished *Dialectics of Nature* written in 1883. It was however published by Progress Publishers in Moscow in 1934 and is available online at Marxists Internet Archive, https://www.marxists.org/archive/marx/works/1876/part-played-labour/index .htm.

14. Karl Marx, *The Eighteenth Brumaire of Louis Bonaparte*, in *The Marx-Engels Reader*, ed. Robert C. Tucker, 2nd ed., (New York: W. W. Norton, 1978), 595.

15. Karl Marx, *Capital*, trans. Ernest Unterm, vol. 3 (New York: International Publishers 1977), 820.

16. Fredrich Nietzsche, *Will to Power*, trans. Walter Kaufmann, (New York: Vintage Books, 1968).

17. Richard Sennet, *The Craftsman* (New Haven, CT: Yale University Press, 2008), 9.

18. Sennet, *The Craftsman*, 11.

19. David McLellan, "Economic and Philosophic Manuscripts," in Karl Marx, *Selected Writing*, 2nd ed. (Oxford: Oxford University Press, 2000), 91.

20. Theodore Roosevelt, *The New Nationalism*, 1910, Origins: Current Events in Historical Perspective, Department of History, Ohio State University https:// ehistory.osu.edu/exhibitions/1912/1912documents/thenewNationalism.

21. During a Yale Law School Speech, past AFL-CIO President Richard Trumka warned that America was at risk of becoming a "company nation" if anti-worker Supreme Court decisions continued. See, "Trumka Calls for New Supreme Court Direction at Yale Law School," September 7, 2018, at https:// aflcio.org/speeches/trumka-calls-new-supreme-court-direction-yale-law-school, accessed May 22, 2023.

22. John Logan, "The Union Avoidance Industry in the United States," *British Journal of Industrial Relations* 44 no. 4 (December 2006): 651–75.

23. Celine McNicholas, Margaret Poydock, Julia Wolfe, Ben Zipperer, Gordon Lafer, and Lola Loustaunau, "Unlawful U.S. Employers are Charged with Violating Federal Law in 41.5% of all Union Election Campaigns," *Economic Policy Institute Report*, December 11, 2019, https://www.epi.org/publication/unlawful -employer-opposition-to-union-election-campaigns/.

24. John J. Castellani, *Hearings Before the Committee on Banking, Housing, and Urban Affairs, United States Senate, One Hundred Eighth Congress, First Session,*

October 2, 2003, accessed February 15, 2023, https://www.govinfo.gov/content/pkg/CHRG-108shrg99603/html/CHRG-108shrg99603.htm.

25. Kathi Weeks, *The Problem with Work: Feminism, Marxism, Antiwork Politics, and Postwork Imaginaries* (Durham, NC: Duke University Press, 2001), 2.

26. *Collective Bargaining Agreement Between International Brotherhood of Electrical Workers (AFL-CIO) Local Union No. 9 and Middle States Electrical Contractors Association of the City of Chicago, May 30, 2021-May 31, 2025*, Article I, "Preamble and Declaration of Principles," p. 2, in author's possession.

27. Patrick Flavin and Gregory Shufeldt, "Labor Union Membership and Life Satisfaction in the United States," *Labor Studies Journal*, 41, 171–84.

28. Clarence Darrow, "Trade Unions in Conjunction with Closed Shop," in *The Bricklayer and the Mason, Official Journal of the Bricklayers and Masons International Union of America*, vol. 11, December 12, 1908, in *The Bricklayer and Mason*, vol. 10–11 Bricklayers and Masons' International Union of America, Cornell University, digitized November 30, 2011, https://books.google.com/books?id=e3QtAQAAMAAJ&dq=Clarence+Darrow,+Trade+Unions+in+Conjunction+with+Closed+Shop,+in+The+Bricklayer+and+the+Mason,+Official+Journal+of+the+Bricklayers+and+Masons+International+Union+of+America&source=gbs_navlinks_s.

29. Clive Wilmer, introduction to *News from Nowhere and Other Writings* by William Morris (New York: Penguin, 1994), ix–xliii.

30. Tracy Neumann, *Remaking the Rust Belt: The Postindustrial Transformation of North America* (Philadelphia: University of Pennsylvania Press, 2016), 86.

31. Ironically the case (*Dodge* et al., *v. Ford Motor Co.* et al.,) was brought against Henry Ford by early investors in the Ford Motor Company. See Kent Greenfield, "Corporate Law's Original Sin," *Washington Monthly*, January 4, 2015, https://washingtonmonthly.com/2015/01/04/sidebar-corporate-laws-original-sin/.

32. In response to their employees' organizing into unions, Starbucks insisted, "We are ALL Starbucks Partners—and we are better side-by-side" (see https://one.starbucks.com). They could, of course, just respect their workers' choice to join a union.

33. Sarah Jaffe, author of *Work Won't Love You Back*, quoted in "Happiness at Work: What Is That, Exactly?" *New York Times*, May 17, 2022.

34. A moral obligation to always treat people as ends has been referred to as Kant's "humanity principle." See, *Kant: Groundwork of the Metaphysics of Morals*, trans. Mary Gregor and Jens Timmerman, 2nd ed. (New York: Cambridge University Press, 2012).

35. Tacey Rychter, "For Flight Attendants A Summer of No Rest and Looming Menace," *New York Times*, September 4, 2021.

36. McLellan, "Economic and Philosophic Manuscripts," 99.

37. According to the Specialty Coffee Association, the "total number of farm-

workers involved in global coffee production numbers in the tens of millions." Coffee served in the United States is largely an imported product from numerous countries. The average "coffee picker" harvests between one hundred and two hundred pounds of coffee a day. Most workers earn less than the legal minimum wage, are subject to dangerous working conditions, and are subject to extensive labor rights violations. Many of the workers are children. (See "Farmworkers and Coffee: The Case for Inclusion," Specialty Coffee Association White Paper, California and the UK athttps://www.scanews.coffee/wp-content/uploads/2018/06/a -blueprint-for-farmworker-inclusion.pdf).

38. Adam Smith, *An Inquiry into the Nature and Causes of the Wealth of Nations*, 2007 online version, book 1, p. 13, https://www.ibiblio.org/ml/libri/s/SmithA _WealthNations_p.pdf.

39. The full and famous quote is, "It is not from the benevolence of the butcher, the brewer, or the baker, that we can expect our dinner, but from their regard to their own interest." Adam Smith, *An Inquiry*, 16.

40. Dave Jamieson, "Starbucks Union Notches Another Victory with Eighth Store," *Huffington Post*, March 25, 2022, https://www.huffpost.com/entry/starbucks -union-arizona_n_623e0fbbe4b0ccd4f51f21d8. At the time of this writing, the union representing store employees, Workers United, had filed petitions for union elections at 160 Starbucks locations.

41. *Hegel: The Phenomenology of Spirit: Translated with Introduction and Commentary*, ed. and trans. Michael Inwood (Oxford: Oxford University Press, 2018), 142.

42. David McLellan, "On James Mill," in *Karl Marx, Selected Writings*, 2nd ed. (Oxford: Oxford University Press), 130.

43. Inwood, *Hegel*, 142.

44. Hannah Arendt, *The Human Condition* (Chicago: University of Chicago Press, 1958), 7.

45. The phrase "miniatures of God" is used by Professor Ian Shapiro to describe philosopher John Locke's view of the way human beings are imbued by God with the power to create a material world. See Ian Shapiro, *The Real World of Democratic Theory* (Princeton: Princeton University Press, 2011), p. 48.

46. Robert Bruno, *Justified by Work: Identity and the Meaning of Faith in Chicago's Working-Class Churches* (Columbus: Ohio State University Press, 2008).

47. Psalm 82, Verses 1–8, New international Version, accessed February 15, 2023, https://www.biblegateway.com/passage/?search=Psalm%2082&version=NIV.

48. John Locke, "Of Property," in *Two Treatises on Government*, book 2, chap. 5, section 27, 1821, Bartleby.com Great Books Online, accessed February 15, 2023, https://www.bartleby.com/169/205.html.

49. "John Locke, "Of Property," in *Second Treatise of Government*, book 2, chap. 5, "Of Property," section 28, Bartleby.com Great Books Online, accessed February 15, 2023, https://www.bartleby.com/169/205.html.

50. Thomas Hobbes, *Leviathan: or, The Matter, Form and Power of a Common-*

Wealth Ecclesiastical and Civil, chapter 13, Bartleby.com Great Books Online, accessed February 15, 2023, at https://www.bartleby.com/34/5/13.html.

51. John Rawls, *A Theory of Justice* (Cambridge, Massachusetts: Belknap Press, 1977), 61.

52. From Karl Marx, *Communist Manifesto*, in *The Marx-Engels Reader*, ed. Robert C. Tucker (New York: W. W. Norton, 1972), 353.

Conclusion

1. Coral Murphy Marcos, "Nabisco Workers in 5 States Go on Strike in Standoff Over Contract," *New York Times*, August 25, 2021.

2. Stephen Franklin, "'We Are Emptying Out Their Shelves': Nabisco Workers' 5-Week Strike Won by Shutting Down Business as Usual," *In These Times*, September 20, 2021, https://inthesetimes.com/article/nabisco-workers-strike -union-labor-mondelez.

3. See Matthew, 25:35–45 and 5:1–12 (New International Version).

4. Alfred Lord Tennyson, "The Lotos-eaters," published in Tennyson's 1832 poetry collection, titled *Poems*, Poetry Foundation, accessed March 19, 2023, https://www.poetryfoundation.org/poems/45364/the-lotos-eaters.

5. Mike Konczal, *Freedom from the Market: America's Flight to Liberate Itself from the Grip of the Invisible Hand* (New York: New Press, 2022), 4.

6. Sherrod Brown, "Working Too Hard for Too Little: A Plan for Restoring the Value of Work in America," March 2017, https://www.brown.senate.gov/imo/ media/doc/Value%20of%20Work%20Speech_Sherrod%20Brown_03032017.pdf.

7. Brown, "Working Too Hard."

8. Ann Saphir, "U.S. Household Wealth Jumps to Record $136.9 Trillion, Fed Says," *Reuters*, June 10, 2021, https://www.reuters.com/world/us/us-household -wealth-rose-record-1369-trillion-q1-fed-says-2021-06-10/.

9. Ana Hernández Kent and Lowell R. Ricketts, "Has Wealth Inequality in America Changed over Time? Here Are Key Statistics," St. Louis Federal Reserve Bank, Center for Household Financial Stability, December 2, 2020, https://www .stlouisfed.org/open-vault/2020/december/has-wealth-inequality-changed-over -time-key-statistics.

10. Kent and Ricketts, "Has Wealth Inequality in America Changed?"

11. Kent and Ricketts, "Has Wealth Inequality in America Changed?"

12. Kate Morgan, "The Great Resignation: How Employers Drove Workers to Quit," *BBC*, July 1, 2021, https://www.bbc.com/worklife/article/20210629-the -great-resignation-how-employers-drove-workers-to-quit.

13. Ben Casselman, "The Number of U.S. Workers Quitting Their Jobs in September Was the Highest On Record," *New York Times*, November 12, 2021, https://www.nytimes.com/by/ben-casselman.

14. I was quoted in Natalie Pierre, "The 'Great Refusal' is Leading Illinois Residents to Quit their Jobs in Record Numbers," *State Journal Star Register*, November 8, 2021, https://www.sj-r.com/search/?q=Robert+Bruno.

15. Vivvek Chibber, *The Class Matrix: Social Theory after the Cultural Theory* (Cambridge, MA: Harvard University Press, 2022), 50.

16. Smith's quotes appear in Chibber's *Class Matrix* on page 51 and are drawn from Smith's *Wealth of Nations* (Chicago: University of Chicago Press, 1977), 98–99.

17. Nandita Bose, "U.S. Labor Secretary Supports Classifying Gig Workers as Employees," *Reuters*, April 29, 2021, https://www.reuters.com/world/us/exclusive -us-labor-secretary-says-most-gig-workers-should-be-classified-2021-04-29/.

18. Amazon Flex hires a person to use their own vehicle to deliver packages for Amazon but isn't on the firm's payroll. These drivers are treated as independent contractors and therefore not eligible for benefits required to be paid to employees. See, Amazon Flex website home page under "Adjust your work, not your life," accessed February 16, 2023, https://flex.amazon.com.

19. See Amazon Flex website https://flex.amazon.com; and Uber site, "About us" page, from the Mission Statement at https://www.uber.com/us/en/about/.

20. "US Staffing Industry Forecast: September 2022 Update," Staffing Industry Analysis at https://www2.staffingindustry.com/Editorial/Engineering-Staffing -Report/Sept.-22-2022/US-staffing-revenue-to-reach-record-212.8-billion-in -2022-SIA.

21. For example, the American Staffing Association reports that 36 percent of staffing employees are hired in industrial jobs, 24 percent in office—clerical and administrative posts, 21 percent in professional—managerial positions, 11 percent in engineering, information technology, and scientific occupations, and 8 percent in health care jobs. See "Fact Sheets & Analysis," Staffing Industry Statistics, accessed March 19, 2023, https://americanstaffing.net/research/fact -sheets-analysis-staffing-industry-trends/staffing-industry-statistics/.

22. Maia McDonald, Cristal Ramirez, and Sarah Conway, "Worker Advocates Say More Temp Worker Protections Are Needed," *City Bureau*, December 9, 2022, https://www.citybureau.org/newswire/2022/12/8/worker-advocates-say -more-temp-worker-protections-are-needed.

23. Karl Marx, *Comments on James Mill*, trans. Clemens Dutt for the *Collected Works* (1932), "Works of Marx and Engel," Marxists Internet Archive, https://www .marxists.org/archive/marx/works/1844/james-mill/index.htm.

24. "Illinois Future of Work Act," HB 645, Illinois General Assembly, Illinois Compiled Statutes (website), accessed March 19, 2023, https://www.ilga.gov/ legislation/ilcs/ilcs3.asp?ActID=4196&ChapterID=5&Print=True.

25. *Future of Work in Illinois*, May 2022, VII, Illinois Department of Commerce and Economic Development, Illinois Future of Work Task Force https:// dceo.illinois.gov/content/dam/soi/en/web/dceo/events/furture-of-work-force/ report_future-of-work-in-illinois-final.pdf?wcmmode=disabled.

26. *Future of Work in Illinois*, 9–10.

27. *Future of Work in Illinois*, VIII.

28. Dylan Bellisle, Alison Dickson, Peter Fugiel, Lonnie Golden, Larissa Petrucci, and Robert Bruno, *A Good Job, Not Just Any Job Defining and Measuring*

Employment Quality in Illinois, September 1, 2022, Project for Middle Class Renewal in the School of Labor and Employment Relations at the University of Illinois, Urbana-Champaign, https://lep.illinois.edu/wp-content/uploads/2022/09/A-Good-Job-Not-Just-Any-Job-9_1_22.pdf. In addition to the report, we also developed an innovative indicator of the quality of employment throughout the state and created an interactive dashboard (see https://employmentquality.illinois.edu). This interactive indicator is based on PMCR's analysis of original data collected from over 3,500 workers in Illinois in 2021.

29. "AFL-CIO Commission on The Future of Work and Unions," September 13, 2019, AFL-CIO, Report to the AFL-CIO General Board, https://aflcio.org/sites/default/files/2019-09/Report%20of%20the%20AFL-CIO%20Commission%20on%20the%20Future%20of%20Work%20and%20Unions_FINAL.pdf. I was a contributor to the Commission's work.

30. "Future of Work," McKinsey and Company, Featured Insights, accessed February 16, 2023, https://www.mckinsey.com/featured-insights/future-of-work.

31. Peter A. Creticos, "The Many Futures of Work: Possibilities and Perils," Conference Report, 2018, Institute for Work and the Economy, accessed February 16, 2023, https://static1.squarespace.com/static/5c97a6c6d7819e478b12c90e/t/5c9b8069e4966bfe70fdf397/1553694826326/Many+Futures+of+Work+Conference+Report.pdf.

32. Sarita Gupta, Stephen Lerner, and Joseph A. McCartin, "It's Not the 'Future of Work,' It's the Future of Workers That's in Doubt," *American Prospect*, August 31, 2018, https://prospect.org/labor/future-work-future-workers-doubt/.

33. Tobias Schulze-Cleven, Todd E. Vachon, eds., *Revaluing Work(ers) for Democracy and Sustainability*, Labor and Employment Relations Research Volume (Ithaca, NY: Cornell University Press, 2021).

34. Kai Erikson and Steven Peter Vallas, eds., *The Nature of Work: Sociological Perspectives* (Hartford, CT: Yale University Press, 1990), https://www.jstor.org/stable/j.ctt1xp3v27.4.

35. The ILO defines "decent work" as work that is "productive, delivers a fair income, provides security in the workplace and social protection for workers and their families, offers prospects for personal development and encourages social interaction, gives people the freedom to express their concerns and organize and participate in the decisions affecting their lives and guarantees equal opportunities and equal treatment for all." International Labour Organization. *Report of the Director-General: Decent Work.* Available at https://www.ilo.org/public/english/standards/relm/ilc/ilc87/rep-i.htm. Accessed August 12, 2022.

36. For example, "A State Agenda for America's Workers 18 Ways to Promote Good Jobs in the States," by the National Employment Law Project and EARN, Policy and Data Brief, December 2018, https://www.nelp.org/publication/state-agenda-americas-workers-18-ways-promote-good-jobs-states/; and Sharon Block and Benjamin Sachs's "Clean Slate for Worker Power: Building a Just Economy and Democracy, Harvard University, Labor and Worklife Program,"

accessed March 19, 2023, https://lwp.law.harvard.edu/publications/clean-slate
-worker-power-building-just-economy-and-democracy.

37. From "On James Mill" in *Karl Marx: Selected Writings*, ed. David McLellan, (Oxford: Oxford University Press, 2000), 128.

38. James Bernard Murphy, *The Moral Economy of Labor: Aristotelian Themes in Economic Theory* (New Haven: Yale University Press, 1993), 91.

39. Aristotle described his virtue ethics in the *Nicomachean Ethics*. See Aristotle, *Nicomachean Ethics*, trans. Robert C. Bartlett and Susan D. Collins (Chicago: University of Chicago Press, 2011).

40. Aristotle, *Nicomachean Ethics,* book 1, 8.

41. Jim Tankersley, "Railroad Unions and Companies Reach a Tentative Deal to Avoid a Strike," *New York Times*, September 15, 2022, https://www.nytimes.com/2022/09/15/business/rail-strike.html.

42. Karl Marx quoted in David McLellan, *Karl Marx: Selected Writings*, 2nd ed. (Oxford: Oxford University Press, 2000), 534–35.

43. Turns out many employers are not only thinking about a reduced workweek but adopting one and finding it very favorable. See Daiga Kamerāde, Senhu Wang, Brendan Burchell, Sarah Ursula Balderson, and Adam Coutts, "A shorter working week for everyone: How much paid work is needed for mental health and well-being?" *Social Science & Medicine*, no. 241 (November 2019): 1–9. Professor Brenda Burchell of Cambridge University noted that "People often talk about the five-day week [as] if it's something that was in the book of Genesis. That's very far from the truth." See, "The 4-day Week: Does it Actually Work?" *Financial Times*, December 3, 2022, https://www.ft.com/content/3ff0cc71-6cb1 -42bf-8271-bcc32dcfa63b.

44. Karl Marx, *Capital Volume One*, trans. Samuel Moore and Edward Aveling, chap.10, section 5, Moscow: Progress Publishers, 1867, online at Marxists Internet Archive, https://www.marxists.org/archive/marx/works/1867-c1/ch10 .htm, 181.

45. Marx, *Capital Volume One*, online version at https://www.marxists.org/ archive/marx/works/1867-c1/ch10.htm, 181.

46. Jodi Kantor and Arya Sundaram, "On The Clock And Tracked To The Minute," *New York Times*, August 15, 2022. Second quote is from North Carolina law professor, Ifeoma Ajunwa.

47. Michel Foucalt, *Discipline and Punish: The Birth of the Prison*, trans. Alan Sheridan (New York: Vintage Press, 1995).

48. William T. Greenwood, "Future Management Theory: A Comparative Evolution to a General Theory," *Academy of Management Journal* (1974): 503–13; Bruce Kaufman, *The Origins and Evolution of the Field of Industrial Relations in the United States* (Ithaca, NY: Cornell University Press, 1992); Vitor M. Marciano, "The Origins and Development of Human Resource Management," *Academy of Management, Academy of Management Proceedings* 1 (1995): 223–27; Badom Monbari Porbari and Girigiri Barinem Wisdom, "Theoretical Issues in Human

Resources Management: From Taylorism to Theory Z," *British Journal of Management and Marketing Studies* 4, no. 3 (2021):1–20.

49. Michel Foucault, "Two lectures," in *Critique and Power: Recasting the Foucault/Habermas Debate*, ed. Michael Kelly (Cambridge, MA: MIT Press), 17–46.

50. *Aristotle's Nicomachean Ethics*, trans. Robert C. Bartlett and Susan D. Collins, book 1, chap. 5, 1096a6, 7.

51. Locke explained, "As much land as a man tills, plants, improves, cultivates, and can use the product of, so much is his property." For instance, land owned and not feeding anyone is not properly the subject of personal ownership. John Locke, "Of Property," in *Second Treatise of Government*, section, 32, 13, https://english.hku.hk/staff/kjohnson/PDF/LockeJohnSECONDTREATISE1690.pdf.

52. Kate Bronfenbrenner. *No Holds Barred—The Intensification of Employer Opposition to Organizing* (Washington, DC: Economic Policy Institute, 2009).

53. US Bureau of Labor Statistics, *Union Members Summary*, January 22, 2021, https://www.bls.gov/news.release/union2.nr0.htm/.

54. Garret Keizer, "Labor's Last Stand," *Harper's Magazine*, September 2018, https://harpers.org/archive/2018/09/labors-last-stand-supreme-court-janus-decision-unions/.

55. *Janus v. American Federation of State, County, and Municipal Employees, 585 U.S. (2018)*, June 27, 2018, https://supreme.justia.com/cases/federal/us/585/16-1466/#tab-opinion-3921236.

56. Megan Brenan, "At 65%, Approval of Labor Unions in U.S. Remains High," *GALLUP*, September 3, 2020, https://news.gallup.com/poll/318980/approval-labor-unions-remains-high.aspx.

57. Gordon Lafer and Lola Loustaunau, "Fear at Work: An Inside Account of How Employers Threaten, Intimidate, and Harass Workers to Stop Them from Exercising Their Right to Collective Bargaining," *Economic Policy Institute*, July 23, 2020, https://files.epi.org/pdf/202305.pdf.

58. John Logan, "Employer Opposition in the US: Anti-Union Campaigning from the 1950s," in *Global Anti-Unionism Nature, Dynamics, Trajectories and Outcomes*, ed. Gregor Gall and Tony Dundon (London: Palgrave Macmillan, 2013).

59. Elizabeth Anderson, *Private Government: How Employers Rule Our Lives (and Why We Don't Talk about It)* (Princeton: Princeton University Press, 2017), 31.

60. Scott Hershovitz, *Nasty, Brutish, and Short: Adventures in Philosophy with My Kids* (New York: Penguin Press, 2022).

61. Steven K. Ashby, "Union Democracy in Today's Labor Movement," *Labor Studies Journal*, vol. 47, 2, 2021, 109–36.

62. Andrew Kolin, *Political Economy of Labor Repression in the United States* (New York: Lexington Books, 2017), 289.

63. *The State of Labor Market Competition*, U.S. Department of Treasury, Washington, DC, March 7, 2022, https://home.treasury.gov/system/files/136/State-of-Labor-Market-Competition-2022.pdf, 1–60.

64. Jay Shambaugh and Ryan Nunn, "Why Wages Aren't Growing in America," *Harvard Business Review*, October 24, 2017, https://hbr.org/2017/10/why-wages-arent-growing-in-america.

65. James Bernard Murphy, *The Moral Economy of labor: Aristotelian Themes in Economic Theory* (New Haven: Yale University Press,1993), 9.

66. On March 18, 1968, Martin Luther King, Jr. delivered his speech "All Labor Has Dignity" at Bishop Charles Mason Temple of the Church of God in Christ in Memphis, Tennessee. He was there in support of striking sanitation workers. The church was overflowing with workers and community supporters. Partial transcript of Martin Luther King Jr., "All Labor Has Dignity" Speech on the fiftieth anniversary of the March 18, 2018, speech, Beacon Broadside, A Project of Beacon Press. According to its website Beacon Broadside "is an online venue for essays, news items, and dispatches from respected writers, thinkers, and activists about our times." See "The 50th Anniversary of Martin Luther King, Jr.'s 'All Labor Has Dignity,'" Beacon Broadside (website), March 18, 2018, https://www.beaconbroadside.com/broadside/2018/03/the-50th-anniversary-of-martin-luther-king-jrs-all-labor-has-dignity.html.

67. Roxane Gay, "What to Expect at Work When you're Expecting," *New York Times*, November 7, 2021, https://www.nytimes.com/2021/11/05/business/what-to-think-at-work-when-youre-expecting.html?searchResultPosition=3.

68. Erin L. Kelly, "The Strange History of Employer-Sponsored Child Care: Interested Actors, Uncertainty, and the Transformation of Law in Organizational Fields," *American Journal of Sociology* 109, no. 3 (2013): 606–49.

69. Deborah Boucoyannis, "The Equalizing Hand: Why Adam Smith Thought the Market Should Produce Wealth Without Steep Inequality," *Perspectives on Politics* 11, no. 4 (December 2013): 1051–70, https://www.jstor.org/stable/43280930.

70. Oddo VM, Zhuang CC, Andrea SB, Eisenberg-Guyot J, Peckham T, Jacoby D, Hajat A, Changes in Precarious Employment in the United States: A Longitudinal Analysis," *Scandinavian Journal of Work Environmental Health* 47, no. 3 (2021): 171–80, doi:10.5271/sjweh.3939.

71. Deborah Boucoyannis, "Contrary to Popular and Academic Belief, Adam Smith Did Not Accept Inequality as a Necessary Trade-Off for a More Prosperous Economy," *London School of Economics* (blog), February 18, 2014, https://blogs.lse.ac.uk/politicsandpolicy/adam-smith-and-inequality/.

72. Adam Smith, *An Inquiry into the Nature and Causes of the Wealth of Nations*, book 2, Ibilio: The Public's Library and Digital Archive, 2007, https://www.ibiblio.org/ml/libri/s/SmithA_WealthNations_p.pdf, 200.

73. I offered these comments in a presentation to the Illinois Future of Work Task Force at a meeting titled "2021Creating Jobs that Sustain and Uplift," October 25, 2021. A video recording is available on the Illinois Department of Commerce and Economic Opportunity website, accessed March 19, 2023, https://dceo.illinois.gov/events/illinoisfutureofworktaskforce.html.

74. William Morris gave a lecture in Leicester, England titled "Art and Socialism" which was then published as *Art and Socialism*, 1884. The lecture is available on

the Marxist Archive website at https://www.marxists.org/archive/morris/works/1884/as/as.htm.

75. Ruth Yeoman, "Conceptualising Meaningful Work as a Fundamental Human Need," *Journal of Business Ethics* 125 (2014): 235–51.

76. Marx, *Capital*, vol. 1, 521.

77. REI Co-op at https://www.rei.com/about-rei.

78. Noam Schieber, "Workers at REI Store in Manhattan Seek to Form Retailer's Only Union," *New York Times*, January 24, 2022, https://www.nytimes.com/2022/01/23/business/economy/rei-union-manhattan-store.html.

79. Noam Scheiber, "REI Workers in New York Vote to Unionize," *New York Times*, March 2, 2022, https://www.nytimes.com/2022/03/02/business/rei-union-new-york.html.

80. "Resolution 5: A Nation of Immigrants," *AFL-CIO Convention*, Chicago, Illinois, December 3, 2001, https://aflcio.org/resolution/nation-immigrants.

81. David Uberti, "The Labor Beat Is Dead; Long Live the Labor Beat," *Columbia Journalism Review*, March 12, 2015, https://www.cjr.org/analysis/when_longtime_labor_reporter_steven.php.

82. "The PTA Disbands!" *The Simpsons*, season 6, episode 21, which featured a teacher strike manipulated by homer's teenage and unruly son Bart Simpson. See Wikipedia page at https://en.wikipedia.org/wiki/The_PTA_Disbands!, last edited December 15, 2022.

83. An example of a story I was quoted in was Steven Greenhouse, "'Striketober' Is Showing Workers' Rising Power—But Will it Lead to Lasting Change?" *The Guardian*, October 23, 2021, https://www.theguardian.com/us-news/2021/oct/23/striketober-unions-strikes-workers-lasting-change.

84. Emma Goldberg, "In a 'Workers Economy,' Who Really Holds the Cards?" *New York Times*, November 3, 2021, https://www.nytimes.com/2021/11/03/business/jobs-workers-economy.html.

85. Some of the more prominent of the non–mass media sources that some union workers read are *Jacobin*, *Dissent*, *Mother Jones*, the *Nation*, and *Labor Notes*.

86. Frederick T. Gates, *The Country School of Tomorrow* (New York: General Education Board, 1913).

87. *A Nation at Risk: The Imperative for Educational Reform*, A Report to the Nation and the Secretary of Education United States Department of Education by The National Commission on Excellence in Education, April 1983. Report available online at http://edreform.com/wp-content/uploads/2013/02/A_Nation_At_Risk_1983.pdf.

88. Alyson Klein, "Historic Summit Fueled Push for K-12 Standards," *Education Week*, September 23, 2014, https://www.edweek.org/teaching-learning/historic-summit-fueled-push-for-k-12-standards/2014/09/.

89. Juliana Menasce Horowitz and Nikki Graf, "Most U.S. Teens See Anxiety and Depression as a Major Problem Among Their Peers," *Pew Research Center*,

February 20, 2019, https://www.pewresearch.org/social-trends/2019/02/20/most
-u-s-teens-see-anxiety-and-depression-as-a-major-problem-among-their-peers/.

90. John Dewey, *Democracy and Education* (New York: McMillan, 1916). Text available online as part of the Electronic Classics Series, at Pennsylvania State University, 2001, https://nsee.memberclicks.net/assets/docs/KnowledgeCenter/BuildingExpEduc/BooksReports/10.%20democracy%20and%20education%20by%20dewey.pdf.

91. The Association for Supervision and Curriculum Development answered the question "What Is the Purpose of Education?" by adopting the belief statement recommended by its Committee on Platform of Beliefs in January 1957. An infographic of ASCD beliefs is available at https://files.ascd.org/staticfiles/ascd/pdf/journals/ed_update/eu201207_infographic.pdf. And the organization's full platform of beliefs is on their website, The Association for Supervision and Curriculum Development, accessed March 19, 2023, https://files.ascd.org/staticfiles/ascd/pdf/journals/ed_lead/el_195701_beliefs.pdf.

92. Arthur W. Foshay, "The Curriculum Matrix: Transcendence and Mathematics," *Journal of Curriculum and Supervision* 6, no. 4 (Summer 1991): 277–93, https://eric.ed.gov/?id=EJ428441.

93. Margaret Haley, "Why Teachers Should Organize," *Journal of Education* 60, no. 13 (1904).

94. "Larry Fink's 2022 Letter to CEOs: The Power of Capitalism," Blackrock (website), accessed March 19, 2023, https://www.blackrock.com/corporate/investor-relations/larry-fink-ceo-letter.

95. Jeffrey Bercuson, *A History of Political Thought: Property, Labor and Commerce from Plato to Piketty* (Toronto: University of Toronto Press, 2020), 18–19.

96. Karl Marx, *Theses on Feuerbach*, ed. C. J. Arthur (New York: International Publishers, 1970), 123.

97. Smith, *An Inquiry*, 200.

98. Smith, *An Inquiry*, 100.

99. Smith, *An Inquiry*, 199–200.

100. David McLellan, "On James Mill," *Karl Marx: Selected Writings*, Second Edition, Oxford: Oxford University Press, 132.

101. Michael Zweig, *America's Working Class Majority: America's Best Kept Secret* (Ithaca, NY: Cornell University Press, 2011).

102. Rakesh Kochhar, "The American Middle Class Is Stable in Size, But Losing Ground Financially to Upper-Income Families," Pew Research Center, September 6, 2018, https://www.pewresearch.org/fact-tank/2018/09/06/the-american-middle-class-is-stable-in-size-but-losing-ground-financially-to-upper-income-families/.

Index

ROBERT BRUNO is a professor of labor and employment relations at the University of Illinois Urbana-Champaign, where he also serves as Director of the Labor Education Program. He is the author of *Justified by Work: Identity and the Meaning of Faith in Chicago's Working-Class Churches*; *Steelworker Alley: How Class Works in Youngstown*; and *Reforming the Chicago Teamsters: The Story of Local 705*. He is the coauthor of *A Fight for the Soul of Public Education: The Chicago Teachers Strike*.

The University of Illinois Press
is a founding member of the
Association of University Presses.

———————————————

University of Illinois Press
1325 South Oak Street
Champaign, IL 61820-6903
www.press.uillinois.edu